⇒ THE ⇐
BOOK
GROUP
B O O K

THE BOOK GROUP BOOK

A
Thoughtful Guide
to
Forming and Enjoying
a
Stimulating Book
Discussion Group

Second Edition

ELLEN SLEZAK

Foreword by
MARGARET ATWOOD

CHICAGO REVIEW PRESS

Library of Congress Cataloging-in-Publication Data

The book group book : a thoughtful guide to
    forming and enjoying a stimulating book discussion
    group / [edited by] Ellen Slezak.—2nd ed.
      p.   cm.
  ISBN 1-55652-246-0 (pa)
  1. Group reading—United States. I. Slezak, Ellen.
LC6651.B66 1995   95-34849
374'.22—dc20   CIP

Second edition
Published by Chicago Review Press, Incorporated
814 North Franklin Street
Chicago, Illinois 60610
ISBN 1-55652-246-0
Printed in the United States of America

5 4 3 2 1

CONTENTS

Foreword

SEVERAL YEARS AGO, when I was planning to visit my old roommate of 1961–62, in North Carolina—a private visit—she said a strange thing to me. She said, "I'll have to give a tea. If I don't my book group will kill me."

"What is a book group?" I asked.

Well, where had I been? She explained: a book group is the people who will kill you if you have an author in your clutches and don't have the book group to tea.

(They came.)

But then I read *The Book Group Book*, and learned more. Book groups, it seems, are the best little old word of mouth in town. Book groups—which have undergone a surprising growth in numbers and variety over the last ten years—are an encouragement to authors, who keep being told that the book will soon be dead as a doornail. Book groups are to late twentieth-century America what salons were to eighteenth-century Paris, and what Improvement Societies were to the Victorians.

Of course, not everyone in Paris belonged to a salon and not every Victorian craved improvement; similarly, not everyone belongs to a book group. In book groups, like-minded

ix

souls gather; what they have in common seems to be that a) they can read, b) they *like* to read, and c) they like to talk about what they have read. It's the liking to talk about it that divides the nonbook group readers from the book group ones. Book groups are the graduate seminar, the encounter group, and the good old-fashioned village-pump gossip session, all rolled up into one.

What does this *talking about it* involve? When fiction is the subject, as it usually is, the talking about it usually consists of the group members trying to agree on what actually went on in the book, and whether they approve of what went on, and also whether they approve of the people who made it go on in this way, and what significance the author seems to have attached to what went on and also to the people who made it go on, and whether the significance provides a clue to our times, and whether they approve of *that*, and whether they enjoyed it, and whether they approve of one another's enjoyment. Literary criticism, in other words. Plot, character, and meaning, with maybe a few glances at structure and style.

Why this can take many pleasurable but sometimes contentious and nonunanimous hours has a great deal to do with the ambiguity and double-handedness of language itself, as pointed to by Mr. Dodgson when he claimed not to be able to interpret the Alice books: " . . . words mean more than we mean to express, when we use them, so a whole book ought to mean a great deal more than the writer meant." What V. S. Pritchett says at the beginning of his autobiography, *A Cab at the Door*, is true of most novelists: ". . . I came from a set of story tellers and moralists. . . . The story tellers were forever changing the tale and the moralists tampering with it in order to put it in an edifying light." The changing tale, the edifying light: these too are the concerns of the book group.

The old truisms about art—that it should hold a mirror up to Nature (notwithstanding the fact that mirror images are backwards illusions), and that it should both please and instruct—are neglected by writers at their peril. The peril is that the book group will have nothing to do with them. If the book group members aren't convinced on at least one level of verisimilitude, it's thumbs down for the book. If a book is pedantic and sermonizing, off with its head. And if a book is written only to please, as most genre fiction is, the book group's members may read it as individuals, but they won't choose to discuss it, because there won't be much to say. It's possible to discuss a billboard, true, but not for very long.

I suppose you could say that the real, hidden subject of a book group discussion is the book group members themselves. I think they are quite brave. They are ready to reveal, in semipublic, their own reactions, their own biases and doubts and convictions, and above all their own tastes; not everyone dares. The beauty of a book group for the members is that you don't get passed or failed for your opinions; whereas the beauty of it for an author is that it's a collective and very candid review that the author will never know anything about because it doesn't happen to appear in the newspapers.

Some book groups may dream of having their favorite author to tea, but they probably shouldn't bother. As (I think) *Elle* magazine put it, "Wanting to meet an author because you like his book is like wanting to meet a duck because you like paté." (The main event at the book group tea my old roommate threw was not anything I had to communicate, but the Lemon Squares, which were superb.) Most novelists lead outwardly dull lives, and are apt to drone on about their rheumatism or the price of car insurance; anything to avoid discussion of their trade secrets and inner lives. In any case, to a true book lover the author is merely the empty, shriveling husk that's left when the book has been squeezed out of her. Trust the tale and not the teller, I say: the book group has already got hold of the important part, which is the book itself.

Margaret Atwood

Introduction

AN OLD SNAPSHOT: my mom is sitting on the couch, the television is blaring, my sisters and I are fighting, and my mom turns another page in her book.

I have plenty of such pictures in my memory—you see, my mom reads all the time. Really, she carries a book with her wherever she goes, thinking she might stop for coffee and finish a chapter here, might be stuck in traffic and start another there. Did she bring a book into the delivery room? Would she deny it?

She goes to the library two or three times a week. When my sisters and I were kids, she brought us along. She never paid attention to the books I checked out—how else can I explain why I read all of Fletcher Knebel's political thrillers when I was twelve, understood maybe a tenth of *Lady Chatterley's Lover* when I was thirteen, and, to this day, enjoy rereading *Trixie Belden*. But clueless as she may have been to *what* I was reading, my mom is the reason I've always gone to books. I'm as sure of that as anything. A passion for reading may not be written into the DNA, but it must be a tendency that grows stronger when a child sits under a parent's reading light.

The essays that make up this new volume of *The Book Group Book* prove the point. In many of them, the writer tells of eavesdropping on her mother's book group and how curious she was about the women who sat in a circle and talked about a book—how it made her want to do the same thing. Their mothers should be proud, as those young readers have done just that. Maybe a desire to join a book group is less a tendency and more a legacy. I like that idea.

And if true, it bodes well for the eternal life of book groups and reading, for the grown-up contributors to this anthology can't help but influence the current crop of kids hanging out on the stairway, eavesdropping on the book group when it meets at their home.

The first edition of this book was published two years ago. Since then, book groups have exploded into the general public's consciousness. At least that's what I hear from people who have never been in a book group. But those who have for years gone about the business of reading and meeting to talk about their reading know better. Still, prime-time television has recently used book groups as fodder for laughs. In the past year, episodes of *Seinfeld*, *Ellen*, *SHE TV*, and *Saturday Night Live* have all tipped a comic hat to them. Maybe those nonbook group people have a point, and, clearly, I'm watching too much television.

The response to my call for essays this time around is the real proof of book groups' popularity, durability, and numbers. I received hundreds of essays. Reading them I learned about groups that were six months old and others that had been around for forty years. I was introduced to groups that read only the classics and others that are willing to give even *The Bridges of Madison County* a chance. From all these, I culled the forty or so essays you'll read here.

My choices are idiosyncratic, and, I hope, inclusive. I've tried to display all the different kinds of groups that are meeting monthly across the country. For instance, you'll read about groups that are composed of women, men, couples, African Americans, graduate students, criminal offenders, grandmothers, lesbians, feminists, gay men, library patrons, writers—you name it. It's clear that whoever you are, there's a group for you.

Because book groups come in so many shapes and sizes, I've given the essays further structure by grouping them together—somewhat. You'll find sections on sponsored or leadered groups, "special interest" groups, and general interest groups. And any of the groups in this book could fit into the first section, which I think of as "book groups as metaphor" but didn't title as such out of respect for Susan Sontag.

If you want to know more about a group described in an essay, check out Part VI, the alpha-ordered (by contributor) list section of the book. You may well find that the writer contributed a reading list also. Put the two together and you'll have a fully-developed picture of that group.

One note before I tell you more about the contributors. In a recent *New Yorker* essay, Jamaica Kincaid, writing about gardening books, recommends, "Ignore the introduction and the foreword . . . yes, staple the pages together, as I do to the introductions of all books I am going to read." I won't argue her advice about this introduction, but I do take issue with it regarding this book's foreword. Margaret Atwood is a book group favorite author—you'll see her name again and again and again in the essays and lists that make up this book—and you'll miss lots of laughs and her take on the work that book groups do if you skip her foreword to this book.

I won't go into detail and tell you about every essay, but I can't resist giving you a hint of what's inside.

Finally, a direct answer to the question of why men don't join book groups. Bob Lamm takes it on with thoughtful ease, quoting the price a man pays for adhering strictly to a "Guy Code" that does not encourage reading.

One fact of book groups that interests me is that they seductively force people to read things they don't want to, with sometimes surprising results. This is the case with

E. Shan Correa—her essay will probably convince more than one reader to give science fiction a try.

You'll also find some good tips and tools to make your group more satisfying. For instance, Ruth Kuehler offers a list of questions to help you critique a book—plenty of juice to jump-start a discussion. And consider the suggestion in Cindy Thelan and David Vick's essay. Their group gives each book a pre- and post-discussion rating, in and of itself a discussion starter.

In her essay, Diane Leslie writes of the profound influence fiction can have on its readers and illustrates her point with an anecdote about an Atwood novel that changed her life.

Jean Trounstine's and Robert Waxler's essays are further proof of how fiction can help us. The book groups they lead are comprised of criminal offenders who have been "sentenced to literature" instead of jail. When I read their essays, I choke up, and though I'm more than a bit of a sap, I think you will too. This is what reading is about—this is its power—this is proof of its potential for good.

But profitable? Read Joanne Simon and Lisa Soufal's essay for tips on starting a business-book reading group and putting more zip into your life nine-to-five.

A warning: you may be in a book group and not even know it. Read C. J. Arbor's piece and see if you agree with me that this writer protests too much.

After the essays, you'll find a book list section that's stuffed full of ideas to keep your group reading for years. You want more nonfiction? Go to David Wellenbrock's list. More feminist authors? Try Janet Tripp's suggestions. And don't miss John McFarland's book pairings—his group was foundering until they decided to choose two books for each meeting and bounce the discussion from one to another. And in yet one more illustration of book group openmindedness, Hedy Hustedde's Iowa group even read Rush Limbaugh's *The Way Things Ought to Be*, though one member chastised the group soundly for expecting her to do so.

*   *   *

I think about books and reading and their place in our lives a lot. In the early eighties, I worried that we'd all quit reading and flock to books on tape. Now I'm suspicious about CD-ROM. When I start to worry too much, I visit a book group, and it invariably cheers me up. Take the group I sat in on last October.

I was lucky enough to observe this group's book selection process for their January meeting. Eight members were present. Four wanted to read *Anna Karenina*. (*This is our chance to read a "big" book—we have two months*, they noted, since the group would be taking a December holiday break.) Four wanted to read *The Celestine Prophecy*. (*It's supposed to be good and it's short*, they argued, since the holidays were always hectic for them.) Unable to break the tie, the group called a long-distance member in Colorado (she reads the book and faxes written comments—they send her an audiotape of the meeting); she voted for *Celestine*. But the vote was too close or perhaps the lure of Anna, Vronsky, and Levin too strong even for the holiday shoppers. So they did what any self-respecting book group members would do: they all refused to budge and then decided to read *both* books for the January meeting. If only Congress were so reasonable.

So for anybody who's fretting about the demise of the printed book, or reading in general, I say as long as you have book groups willing to take on Tolstoy *and* any other writer simultaneously, what's to worry?

Newsletters, magazines, associations, and books devoted to book group members offer further proof that we probably won't be forced to give up the armchair and pillow in favor of the keyboard and pixels any time soon.

One of my favorite newsletters is *Select Fiction*, which bills itself as "A selective guide to well-received new fiction that did not hit *The New York Times* bestseller list—and possibly passed out of view too quickly to catch the eye of readers looking for good new novels and short stories, serious and otherwise." I love this publication because it does the legwork for me, pointing out small press gems and big publishers' midlist wonders alike. It's published five times a year, and you can find out more about it by contacting the editors at P.O. Box 1069, Sharon, CT 06069, (203) 364-0364.

BookLovers (P.O. Box 93485, Milwaukee, WI 53203-0485), a quarterly magazine that carries book group recommendations and reviews, author interviews, poetry reviews, and group profiles continues to thrive. And *Ex Libris* (33 Chandler St., Newton, MA 02158-1106, (617) 332-3152), a lively, bimonthly newsletter that contains reading lists, book group profiles, and more, has a special rate for book groups that want multiple copies.

This past year also saw the founding of the first organization devoted to book group members. The Association of Book Group Readers and Leaders (ABGRL, P.O. Box 885, Highland Park, IL 60035, (708) 266-0431) serves as an information clearinghouse. Membership brings a periodic newsletter and access to information about other groups.

Book group aids come in book form too. One of my favorites is Barbara Kerr Davis's *Read All Your Life: A Subject Guide to Fiction* (McFarland & Company, Inc., Jefferson, NC). This carefully written and researched book offers reading suggestions, short excerpts from novels, and discussion questions based on subject areas including self, family, society and politics, religion, and philosophy. Another book you may find useful is *BookNotes: The Booklover's Organizer* (Jackson Creek Press, Corvallis, OR). If you're like me, you write your reading wish list on scraps—napkins, newspapers, grocery store receipts. Marilyn McDonald created this tool so you can consolidate those scraps and lessen the risk of tossing them out with the old Kleenex in your winter coat pocket.

Of course, these are all just accoutrements. What your book group really needs to thrive is people with open minds (or even closed ones as long as they put up a good fight).

*   *   *

As it turns out, my mom and I don't talk much about books. We rarely read the same ones. She's into mysteries—I'm too paranoid. I like contemporary and classic fiction that helps me untangle the strings in my life—her strings are straight. We don't live in the same city, and neither one of us is a poster child for open communication and self-disclosure (we want the dirt on everybody else, but are reluctant to dish up our own). But when I visit her and we walk out to the car carrying books and then argue about who has to drive (it seems we're both in the middle of a good part), I don't see how conversation could make me feel closer to her.

Books will do that to you.

PART I

See, It's More Than Just a Book Group

People in book groups often tell me this. And the essays in this section show why, as they illustrate the bigger work that book groups and books do. Among other things, they connect people, showing us we're not alone in the troubles we face. This section opens and closes with essays by writers who point to the less obvious windfall that books and the groups that meet to discuss them can provide.

Communion

Robin M. Neidorf **Minneapolis, Minnesota**

BEFORE I KNEW what literature was, I knew book groups.

Throughout my childhood, my mother belonged to a book group, which met monthly at the house of one member or another. The book group intruded into the lives of my sister and me in small but memorable ways. At times Mom could not play with us or read to us because she had to finish her book for book group. At times our refrigerator was crowded with sliced fruit on trays and our pantry filled with cookies and pound cake that we could not touch; these were for book group.

We could have resented the book group, but the intrusions were relatively minor. My sister and I were generally content to play alone, and the group always left behind cake. If we thought about it at all, perhaps we dismissed the book group as unimportant adult stuff.

And then, on a lucky day in first grade when I happened to be home from school with some minor ailment, I witnessed the book group in our own living room.

I was not so sick that I couldn't get out of bed, and I was bored, so I crept down the stairs in my nightgown and hid behind the curve in the wall. From this vantage point, I could see that our living room was a circle of women on folding chairs, eating the forbidden goodies, drinking coffee out of Styrofoam cups (we were not yet saving the earth), and talking about books.

Did I hear which book they were discussing? I no longer remember. But the scene has stayed with me through the years in a way that few others from that period have. There was my mother, part of this group that was not my family. For the first time to my childish eyes, she was more than my mother. She was one of these women who met solely for the purpose of discussing books, and even in first grade, that seemed to me a high-minded, intellectual, admirable thing to do.

I did not know then, as I do now, that literature is a point of convergence between different readers' lives. Discussions of literature are, of course, intellectual exercises, but they can also serve as a bridge between the disparate lives of readers and thinkers. We see ourselves reflected in the works we read, we read passages out loud and say, "I thought I was the only one who felt that way," and we hear others say the same. Our experiences suddenly become more than what they are. Yet at the same time, they are strangely diminished to mere biographical moments; as our perspective shifts from the individual moment to the universal experience, life falls into an accidental pattern of choices and fates that could so easily have been otherwise.

A book group, however, goes deeper than an impromptu discussion of literature. A book group is a steady, ongoing process, whether the group lasts a month, a year, or a decade. A book group is not a classroom; there are no prerequisites or requirements. A book group is not therapy; there are no "adult children" there. An ongoing group has a group history, a context for discussion, and a variety of viewpoints, explicitly welcomed, which impromptu discussion, even between good friends, often lacks. A book group is a kind of communion.

*   *   *

I am now a member of a book group that has been meeting once a month for three years. While my mother's group, which met for several years and is now defunct, was made up of friends who selected together the themes and authors they wanted to cover, my group is made up of relative strangers (at least, we were three years ago) brought together by a common interest in the theme of the group.

The group is sponsored by the Bookshop of the Minnesota Women's Press in St. Paul, where the store motto is Book Groups Are Our Business. Groups are designed around a theme or an author, and up to twenty groups may be running simultaneously. Any given group may be composed primarily of people who already know each other from previous Bookshop groups, but each new group is a kind of chemistry experiment. Will it work this time or not? Will we find communion?

The name of my group is Meet a Woman Every Month: Biography, Autobiography, and Memoir. I chose it because, at the time, I was unhappy with the order and shape of my life. I had recently graduated from college. I felt like I had been fired from my lifelong job, and in a sense I had been. Suddenly, I could no longer define myself as "student." What was I? In my choice of book group, I sought out models of women's lives. I sought perspective on the process of composing a life.

What did I find? Simone de Beauvoir's intense intellectualism and equally intense devotion to Jean-Paul Sartre. Janet Frame's lyrical memoirs of growing up in New Zealand. Virginia Woolf's development as a writer, as well as her eventual breakdown and suicide. Jill Ker Conway's evocation of the droughts of her childhood in Australia.

As a group, we meet these women every month. We pick over the revelation of their lives. We argue over them, often running long past our scheduled hours.

With ten other women I would not otherwise have met, I have sat at a table too small for all of us, hungry because I've missed dinner, bladder painfully full because I cannot bear to miss a minute of the conversation, and completely engrossed in a debate about whether Anne Sexton was mentally ill, and what this issue does to our reading of her poetry and her life.

We have all come to book group from different places, with different priorities and distractions. Our discussions are not always firmly fixed on the book in question. Barb piques our envy with her stories of frequent trips to the Tetons and Lake Superior. Patty entertains us with tales of her teenage daughters. Our facilitator, Glenda, tells us about the difficulty of putting her mother's affairs in order after her mother's death, and also about the birth of her first grandchild who is, to the joy of the whole group, a girl. We all have pieces of our lives to share, discoveries we make and questions we pose to ourselves between meetings, month to month.

I have found my role models, my sense of perspective, my options. They are not, however, between paperback covers. They are sitting around a too-small table, arguing with me.

In the course of researching literary markets a few years ago, a few jobs ago, I discovered that women are twice as likely as men to be readers of literature. My own anecdotal evidence from participating in book groups, witnessing book groups, and talking to people about them suggests that women are not only more likely to read literature, they are also more likely to seek out the ways and means to discuss it. "More likely" does not even do the numbers justice. Book groups, forgive me the generalization, are made up of women.

When my mother met with her peers once a month throughout my childhood, they must have found the intellectual stimulation that eluded them in other aspects of their lives. When I joined the Biography, Autobiography, and Memoir group three years ago, I was doing the same thing. Is it coincidence that these groups, founded twenty years apart in different cities and by different people, are both all-female?

Or is there something hidden in the structure of book groups that attracts women and not men?

I wish I could say I knew why book groups do not attract men. I can't even say I know why they do attract women. I only know why they attract me.

I see a world in which girls have few role models of women who regularly talk to each other and enjoy one another's ideas and insights. Discussions between women are too frequently dismissed as gossip, kaffeeklatsch, girl talk, essentially unimportant chatter.

I know women who have been accused of being lesbians, as if that were a crime, simply because they take pleasure in the intellectual company of other women. I know women who preface all of their thoughtful remarks with the phrase, "I'm not a feminist, but . . ." I know women who are uncomfortable having an intelligent conversation with anyone at all. According to the constructs of gender that invade our upbringing, it is not "feminine" to think.

During high school, I had a friend who always made extremely insightful comments in our advanced placement English class. But she made them while scrunching her perm with manicured hands. It was a distracting gesture, affected just before we started our senior year, and one that contrasted with her knowledgeable statements about Sylvia Plath and Emily Dickinson. She would open her eyes wide, pout a little, scrunch her curls, and say exactly what was on her mind.

The gesture was ultimately very effective. I cannot bring to mind now a single intelligent thing she said about the literature we were reading and discussing in that class. But I remember the perm.

I think about my high-school friend when I go to book group. A member of my group once remarked what a relief it is to come to the Bookshop, to enjoy stimulating discussion without concern for anyone's hidden agenda, to leave her defenses at the door. But we have to pick them up again on the way out, collecting them the same way we collect our scarves and hats in the winter, vulnerable if we accidentally leave them behind.

When the chemistry experiment is successful and communion is achieved, group members have no need to couch their comments with an affected scrunch of the perm. And for many of us who have decided that the competitive coed classrooms of formal education had their time and place, which is now over and done, book groups are primarily *fun*. How many places can women be themselves, stimulate their minds, and relax?

In January 1993, my life took an unexpected turn. I started an independent graduate program in writing, and I was laid off from my job in the editorial department of a literary publisher. The graduate program I had been planning for, the layoff I had not.

Given the circumstances, I decided to scale back on my entertainment budget. The budget was already lean, and sadly, I cut out my book group.

It was the only decision that made sense, I told myself. I could use the enrollment fee for other things, like groceries and books for school. And I might not have time to read books for group, since I was working my way through a thirty-title semester book list for school.

The semester was a lonely one. I enjoyed my school work and my writing, but I had no regular contact with anyone but my partner. No coworkers, no companions to speak of, no book group. When I wasn't reading or writing for school, I tended to have involved discussions with my cat. It was embarrassing.

One afternoon late in the semester, I stopped in the Bookshop. Glenda was working at the front desk, and she told me the book group had asked about me. On impulse, I bought the book they were reading for the next month and said that I would attend the meeting. I hadn't been to a group in four or five months.

On book group night, the first Tuesday of the month, I arrived and was welcomed by my old companions and a few new people who had joined since my leave of absence began. We settled down to discuss Judy Chicago's *Through the Flower*. It was a heated discussion; half the group had loved the book, and half had hated it. I, normally quite vocal about my opinions, sat in near silence.

"What do you think, Robin?" Glenda finally asked.

"I think I've forgotten how to talk to people," I said lamely. It was true. I was woefully out of practice.

Book group lasts two hours, however, and by the end the old chemistry had taken over, fueled by equal parts laughter and thought exchange. By the end, it was as if I had never left. Driving home that night after leaving the Bookshop, I felt the buoyancy of connection, of counterpoint.

Of communion.

Reading Big

Wendy Underhill   **Boulder, Colorado**

HOW OFTEN DO you hear that television is rotting Americans' minds? Pretty often, right? And it's usually followed by the lament, "If only people were reading instead."

I buy both parts of that argument, basically. I even abide by them much of the time. Watching television is mildly decadent; reading is honorable.

But when I'm ensconced in a delightful novel, as I often am as a member of a book group, a long-buried Puritan in me whispers, "What's so honorable about lying in bed, snacking, and flipping pages?" It's as sure a way to ruin your eyes as enjoying the blue glow of The Box. And it's still a way to escape all the shoulds: housework, yard work, do-good work, paid work.

I remember enough of George Eliot's and Jane Austen's books to know that novels were the moral equivalent of television in the last century. (Serious people were expected to read sermons or other religious tracts.) Dickens, when he wrote, was aiming at the pulp market, not the highfalutin crowd. His writing made it the best of times; the conventional attitude toward his work made it the worst of times.

18

Best or worst, those times have changed. Now, it seems that to win goodness points you just have to read instead of watch.

Or perhaps not. All reading is not created equal. Steve Graham, who runs a delightful and independent bookstore in Boulder, Colorado, is a man who knows his reading (and a lot of other people's too). He says, "If you ask serious readers what they consider sinful in reading, it's eating bonbons and reading Harlequins."

Or westerns. My book group laughed at the thought of someone's father reading Louis L'Amour. But at the same meeting, we agreed to read *All the Pretty Horses* by Cormac McCarthy (a "literary" western). Our prejudices were showing. The unspoken rule is that we don't deign to read "genre" books: fantasy, romance, sci-fi, etc. It's a question of values, and we'll do the judging, thank you very much.

But where is pleasure on the value chart? I may not get it from bodice-rippers or westerns, but I do enjoy Dorothy Sayers's mysteries. There's no moral, educational, philosophical, or other -al about Sayers; she's just good fun, according to my definition. So how can I reject those who like murder the western way just because I prefer the "Ms. Scarlet in the billiard room with a candlestick" approach to death and mayhem?

Back to Graham for that answer. He says that "If you are OK about admitting that you read the occasional piece of pulp, fine. Everybody needs a rest."

Besides, a certain brand of indiscriminate reader keeps the book business afloat. These are the kind who read anything from VCR instruction booklets to church history, with an occasional collection of essays in between. (Graham's store gives a free book for every twelve you buy; normal readers work up to that over months, but these addicts get their freebie with each fix.)

Check out *Biblioholism: The Literary Addiction* by Tom Raabe for more details on this phenomenon. (The irony of printing a book to help the booklorn is probably not lost on the author or the buyers.)

True, this is a one-joke book, but it's a good one. Raabe is a guy who loses girlfriends, leases, and jobs because he loves books—buying them, seeing them, smelling them, and, occasionally, reading them. He's created a twelve-step bible to relief, not that it worked for him. The cover states that "for the last few years Raabe has worked as a freelance editor and writer in Denver, where he is now immobilized by his enormous book collection."

My own take on book buying is that it shows the difference between who we wish we were (what we buy) and who we really are (what we actually read). I, for instance, was proud the day I brought home David Barsamian's *Stenographers to Power: Media and Propaganda*. I hadn't ever quite listened to his radio interviews of the big boys of media criticism (sorry, he quotes no big girls), but I thought if I owned the book, I'd read this Important Stuff.

That was the same day I picked up *The Virtual Community: Homesteading the Electronic Frontier* by Howard Rheingold, another commendable book. Since then I've read two dozen novels, three health-related books, and a how-to manual on raising kids. But not *Stenographers* or *Virtual Community*.

Ah well, that's where book groups some in; they help us to think—and read—big.

When Book Club Becomes Community

Linda Francis, Dorothy Leland, Andrea Mason,
and friends   **Maynard, Massachusetts**

WHEN A GROUP of us sat down to talk about our book club and why it was important to us, we realized that after twelve years of meeting, we have evolved into something that has gone beyond just a group of women who meet on the fourth Friday of every month to discuss a book. Through a process of personal sharing that developed naturally from the book discussions, acquaintances have become friends, and we have witnessed and been a part of the growth of a community. Our book club created the structure, but the individual members, each contributing her own uniqueness to the group, have helped in that evolution. Once we were a book club that gave birth to a community. Now we are a community that meets in many settings, one of which is The Book Club.

Membership

Our total membership is large—perhaps some forty or fifty women at a time have their names on our mailing list—and our meetings often have upwards of thirty attendees.

Predominately a group of white women who live in small suburban towns about twenty-five miles west of Boston, we do have some members who travel "all the way out to the suburbs" from the city to join us regularly. There are just two criteria for membership: self-identification as a lesbian and a love of good books. We range in age from early thirties to mid-sixties; we are coupled and single; some members have never had children, while others are still raising children; some have grown children, and a few are grandmothers. We have a core group of long-term members, many of whom have been coming consistently to the group since its inception. And although we have never advertised our existence, new members find us, and have always been welcome.

Only a few members' homes have rooms large enough to accommodate us. We usually rotate our meetings among four or five different homes, located within a fifteen-mile radius of where most of the members live. Once a month, we begin arriving at 7:00 P.M. at the home where the discussion is being held. The discussion won't begin for another half hour, and we use this time to socialize, catch up with each other, and meet newcomers. Although we enjoy visiting with one another, we tend to begin our book discussion promptly at 7:30, knowing we'll have a chance to socialize more after we've had our final say and have chosen the book for the following month.

Discussions

How our discussions are facilitated is a good illustration of the development and changes in our group over its lifetime. One of the people who had started the group facilitated all of our discussions for the first two years. When this began to feel like a burden, she decided to share this role, inviting others to take it on. At first the group resisted the change, but now we have a core group of members who volunteer to lead on a regular basis. Most facilitators start off with a few questions to get us rolling and occasionally break in with a new question or observation to bring us back to the discussion when we stray too far from the topic. In the beginning years people jumped in whenever they had something to add. After reading Sonia Johnson's book, *Going Out of Our Minds*, about the need for women to take space and be heard, we had a period of time where discussions were more structured, and the meeting began by going around our circle and giving each woman a chance to say what she wanted to about the book. Lately, we are back to jumping in.

While each facilitator has her own style of leading, we all understand that everyone who wishes to speak must have an opportunity to do so. Newcomers are often amazed that, despite the size of the group, we usually maintain a focused discussion, and that people do have a chance to speak and be heard. While we have never had to create a rule about how we will carry out our discussions, we have developed a pattern of "appreciative listening."

At book club, everyone is entitled to her opinion, and others are entitled to disagree with it, sometimes quite vehemently. But no one is entitled to attack another for what she thinks, feels, or believes. The group's compassion and understanding allow this process to unfold successfully.

Book Selection

A ritual that we engage in on a monthly basis is selecting a book for the next month's meeting. In a sometimes chaotic atmosphere, members nominate titles, give a summary of the story's or book's main points and one person writes down the title and the author (always and only women authors whose books are available in paperback). If we're not sure whether the book is still in print, or available in paperback, we call a late-night bookstore in Boston and check.

To choose the book, we have two rounds of voting: in the first round each member gets three votes. Usually, during this round, one book will receive a very large number of votes, and to the uninitiated, this book appears to be a sure winner. But in our book club, *nothing* is certain, so part of the ritual during the first round of voting is for someone to warn playfully "It doesn't mean a thing" when it appears that a particular book will win in the second round. For the second round of voting, the top three titles are in a runoff, where each person has just one vote. The book with the most votes is the book we will read for the following month, and it's often true that the obvious winner from the first round doesn't win the second. The nominating and voting process can take as long as twenty minutes, and all the while, people are socializing, eating the snacks provided by our hosts, and asking "Can you tell me again what that one with the two women on the farm is about?"

Before the group begins to drift apart, we usually spend some time making community announcements about upcoming cultural events, women's dances, outdoor events, political rallies, or women's rights issues. Recently, because of an announcement at a book club meeting, a group of us joined together to support Emily's List, an organization that provides campaign funds to pro-choice Democratic women candidates. Newsletters are also handed out at this time, and we remind everyone to chip in a dollar or two to the hosts for the munchies they've provided. By now, it is somewhere between 9:30 P.M. and 10:00 P.M., but there is still some time for socializing before a typical meeting breaks up and people make their way home.

Special Events

The only time during the year that our book club routine varies is in December when we have a holiday potluck before the discussion. Our holiday meeting usually attracts some thirty-five to forty women, and we usually choose a book that is short and light.

In recent years, we play a game as an icebreaker during the socializing and dinner part of the evening. We place a sticker with the name of a famous woman—living, dead, or fictional—on the back of each member. She then must guess who she is by asking questions of new and old friends.

In addition to the guessing game, we also write a round-robin story, which we read at the end of the evening. In the early years of the group, we bought grab bag gifts for one another, and exchanged them after the book discussion. More recently, we have moved away from purchasing gifts to making gifts, and we take the money we would have spent on presents and make a donation, as a group, to a local shelter for homeless women—another example of how our book club has become more conscious of our status as a community.

Over the last four years, we have added a second ritual get-together, which is currently our only event without a literary theme: a New Year's Eve celebration to which everyone is invited. Nonmembers often join us for the celebration, and we have numbered as many as thirty for the evening's events. After eating at a local restaurant, we return to a member's home for our candle-lighting ceremony. Since we usually don't finish eating until almost midnight, we have empowered ourselves to hold off the coming of the New Year until our ritual is completed. We turn out the lights and each woman in the room holds a lighted candle. She then has an opportunity to give voice to her hopes for the coming year, after which she blows out her candle. When the room is completely dark, it is the beginning of the new year, the lights come on, there is hugging all around, and, of course, more eating and socializing.

Last year we reached a milestone in our openness as a lesbian community when several of us who were attending the Boston Pride Parade decided that we were ready to have a Book Club Float in the 1995 Parade. One of our members who runs a real estate business in the area has offered to sponsor the float, and another has volunteered to organize us to design and decorate it. It will be a kind of coming-of-age for our group, and many of us are very excited by the prospect.

Important Books and Significant Discussions

Initially, when faced with the task of conveying the flavor of our discussions for this essay, we wondered how it would be possible. After all, with so many of us, so many years, and so many books, where would we begin, how could we capture it all? We soon discovered that our book list held the key. By reviewing that list, each of us could remember salient moments when we learned something about ourselves, or each other; we recalled bits and snatches of discussions and characters—both real and fictional—whom we admired, who said what during a particular discussion, and how we felt or what we thought at the time. Over the course of twelve years, we have covered a wide number of topics: everything from looking for the perfect feminist hero to lesbian separatism; from women's reality to young girls' emotional development; from adventure in the world to exploring innermost thoughts and feelings.

Perhaps one of the most significant discussions we had early on in our life as a group was sparked by *In My Mother's House* by Kim Chernin. You would think it would be easy for a gathering of women to discuss mother-daughter relationships. It wasn't. Whenever we read a book where mother-daughter relationships were essential to the story, we would all acknowledge that this relationship existed, but that was where the discussion ended. We shied away from talking personally about our feelings as daughters and mothers, and our relationships in these roles. Chernin's book allowed us to open this door, and begin our exploration.

There was a great deal of discussion that evening about what makes a "good mother," which led to a discussion of how we experienced our own mothers. While some women found that the topic and the setting allowed them to openly discuss their relationships with their mothers and daughters, others expressed a strong desire to keep the discussion focused on the contents of the book, and not get into personal issues. It was an intense and emotionally charged discussion. Mother-daughter relationships remained a difficult issue in the book club for many years after that; it was almost a sore point.

Several years later Amy Tan's *The Joy Luck Club* led us into another discussion on this topic. This time, the facilitator gave us the option to focus our discussion on the book, or use the book as a jumping-off point for talking about these relationships in a personal way. The group chose the former and for more than two hours, we discussed the mother-daughter relationships in Tan's novel. We were just coming to closure on the discussion when one woman made a comment that she began to understand and feel closer to her mother when she herself became a mother. And a shift happened. Other women nodded and began to talk about what it meant to be a mother and a daughter.

Suddenly, our discussion moved from the text to a completely personal realm and went on for another two hours. We became more willing to blur the line between discussing the content of the books we read and the experiences and emotions we brought to the reading. As a result, we learned more about each other and were drawn closer together. It was an important turning point for us as a group.

During one period of time we spent several months exploring the writings of twentieth-century African American women. The vibrant language of novels such as *The Temple of My Familiar* and *The Color Purple* by Alice Walker gave us insights, and forced us to grapple with our own perceptions and the strong voices in these stories. We discussed how, as lesbians, we had much in common with the trials and struggles of these women, but also acknowledged that as white women, we could "pass" in a way that women of color could not. Maya Angelou's *I Know Why the Caged Bird Sings* helped us realize that as women we have a sense of poetry and song that can help us through the harshest realities. For many of us, the African American authors' writings led us on a personal voyage, giving us another level of safety for exploring our emotions.

With more and more books about lesbian and gay issues available in recent years, we have read a number of books that allowed us to explore our history and connection to lesbian and gay culture. And, because these books had such a strong connection to our lives, our discussions focused both on the test and on our personal experiences as lesbians. When we read Judy Grahn's *Another Mother Tongue*, we learned about how the history of words, beliefs, and activities (such as why high-school students think that wearing green on Thursdays means a person is gay) affected our coming out processes and what we believe about ourselves. An anthology called *The Persistent Desire* by Joan Nestle challenged us to face our internalized homophobia, as we explored issues of butches and femmes, and our stereotypes about women in these roles. *Stone Butch Blues*, a fictionalized account by Leslie Feinberg of her life as a woman who lived as a man, allowed us to talk about what sexual identity means to us individually, and how we live and fit into the larger society as women who love women.

The women we read about in these books had visibly and publicly made statements that said, "I am different and I need to be accepted for who I am." Reading about them helped us put our lives in perspective; we learned more about ourselves, and our own history, and we were thankful to these brave women for helping us get where we are today.

Novels such as those by Doris Grumbach (*The Ladies* and *Chamber Music*), as well as *The Memory Board* by Jane Rule and *Patience and Sarah* by Isabel Miller gave us role models, ideal living situations, and sensitive lesbian relationships to explore and discuss. And, lest we take ourselves too seriously, we have also read some lesbian novels for the sheer pleasure of reading about women like ourselves. Sometimes they were easy reads with little or no redeeming literary value, but they gave us a chance to laugh and have an evening of relaxing discussion.

Staying in Touch: Our Newsletter

As our community continues to grow, we have an increasing need to communicate outside our monthly meetings. During the past year, Linda had a revelation to start a book club newsletter. As she puts it:

> One Saturday morning, over coffee and cranberry muffins at a local coffee shop, I thought newsletter. We're such a diversified group and we are a community, so why not. The "why not" led to a few phone calls.
>
> A week later, two of us met at my house. I put six CDs on and we talked about newsletters until the last song stopped. Over pizza dinner, and with another member of the book club, we put together categories for the newsletter. We initially envisioned a place to share upcoming events, books we read, movie reviews, even an occasional recipe and op-ed piece.
>
> When we presented the idea of a newsletter at the next book club meeting, one member suggested that we include an interview of a member in each issue and that that member then be the interviewer for the next issue—a new feature was born. We collected five dollars from each member to cover copying and mailing costs. The first seven issues followed the original format and then the newsletter changed. Andrea and Kristina became "staff" people and committed to writing an article each month. Different members started sending in articles on topics as diverse as the Internet, role-playing, a houseboat trip on Lake Powell, gay pride, and the gay games in New York City. The planned categories diminished and the newsletter took on a hybrid personality—half "what's up" and half literary journal.

The newsletter comes out once a month and marked its second year of publication in October 1994. Recently we opened a newsletter bank account and purchased a stamp that reads "Next Month's Book, Title, Author," which we use to stamp on the back of the envelope, so that a member who misses the book club meeting knows the title of the new book as soon as the newsletter arrives.

This year in addition to features and essays, we've printed condolences; watched a romance grow from one of the "interview dates," asked people to support the purchase of a harvester to rip the water chestnuts out of a bird sanctuary pond and listed requests for submissions for articles and poetry to small journals. The round-robin interviews continue to be a favorite feature—each slightly different, but all fascinating and open portraits of members.

Recently we wished well to one member leaving our area for a ministry position in Canada. She left us twelve stamped and addressed envelopes and a note that read "Don't forget to send me my newsletters." She wrote and said she is starting a Canadian branch of the book club. We're still community.

A Community "Like Family"

When we announced at a recent book club meeting that some of us wanted our group to be included in *The Book Group Book*, everyone wholeheartedly endorsed the idea. Later, during the social hour, a member of the group approached one of us with a particularly touching request that we make sure we included how important the group had been to her over the years. "It's more than the discussions and the monthly meetings," she explained. "This group is like family. I've gotten so much support from the people here. It means so much to me."

She is not alone in those feelings; the book club means a great deal to all of us. The women writers we have met in our literary exploration during the last twelve years have exposed us to mother-and-daughter issues, brought our emotions to the surface, reminded us to be thankful for the butches, given us lesbian role models, and allowed us to be touched by the lives of more women than we will ever have a chance to meet in person. The books and the authors have inspired us, taught us, made us think, and helped us to change and grow. But perhaps most important, the forum we created to learn from these writers has brought together a varied and powerful group of lesbian women to create a community that can only grow stronger and more loving with each passing year.

A Book I Didn't Like

Diane Leslie   **Los Angeles, California**

AS A BOOK group consultant, I often tell book groups that it is possible for a work of fiction to have a profound and immediate influence on its reader. Even though I say it, I never thought it would happen to me.

Aside from speaking to book groups, I also host author readings at Dutton's Brentwood Bookstore in Los Angeles, and several years ago, when Margaret Atwood was doing a book tour for her novel *Cat's Eye*, the PEN organization decided to sponsor a party and a reading for her at our store. I was asked to be prepared to introduce Margaret Atwood just in case the president of PEN couldn't return from a London holiday in time to do so herself.

Preparation required me to read the book, of course, and I didn't like it one bit. *Cat's Eye* took up the plight of an adult artist named Elaine, a victim of child abuse. Oddly, the abuser, Cordelia, was another child, and she continued to have power over Elaine right on into and through adulthood.

I found myself extraordinarily irritated by Elaine—whose name, even now, I have trouble remembering—and since she narrates the book, this was a big problem. I couldn't understand or believe that Elaine, even as a child, wouldn't help herself—tell her parents, her brother, a teacher, fight back, run away, anything—to escape her monstrous friend. Wow, did I have contempt for Elaine, as well as for the author who created her.

Luckily the PEN president showed up for the reading, and I didn't have to lie my way through an evening with so terrific a writer, in her previous books at any rate, and intelligent, empathetic, and funny a person as Margaret Atwood. The evening was festive and successful—we sold 450 books. Best of all, for me, I assumed I wouldn't have to give *Cat's Eye* another thought.

However, a few weeks later one of our best customers, a most intelligent and discriminating reader, came into the store. "Have you read *Cat's Eye* yet?" she asked me breathily.

I could see stars of enthusiasm shimmering in her eyes, and I hated to be the voice of negativity. So, remembering she was a psychiatrist, I turned the tables on her. "Have you?" I asked.

"Oh yes," she said, "and if it weren't so beautifully written, so creatively organized, I would swear it was a case history."

Ice water seemed to flood my blood stream. She liked it? She thought it made psychological sense? Could I have missed something?

I ended up taking the damn book home and forced myself to read it again. This time I read with great fascination. It slowly penetrated my psyche why I had been so annoyed with the victim character of Elaine. For one thing, her parents were, in one important way, very much like mine. It took longer for me to accept the realization that I too had had an abusive childhood friend. And, no wonder I'd been avoiding, denying really, all thoughts on the subject—we were still friends! After thirty years, my very own Cordelia was still abusing me, and I was still silently taking it.

With *Cat's Eye* as my witness, I vowed to make a change. Now, I'm cowardly when it comes to confrontation, especially with this particular brilliant and aggressive woman, but I felt determined to conclude our sadomasochistic relationship come hell or high water.

To my amazement, in her brash, inimitable, ultimatumy way, my Cordelia made it easy on me. Although it was she who usually called me, every evening around bedtime since we had been ten years old, I stopped ever calling her. And I cut our conversations somewhat shorter. She still got in her quick digs about my children and my writing career, but before she could attack my logic, my knowledge, my pronunciation of a word, the way I cooked spaghetti, the car I drove, the color of my roof, my couch, my hair, the books I admired, or the husband I'd chosen, I said good-bye.

It was weeks before she noticed I hadn't been calling her. "Look," she said in her routine, aggressive manner, "it seems I'm doing all the work on this friendship, so tomorrow night you better call me." When I didn't, she called right up to say, "You were supposed to call tonight, remember?"

"I know," I replied.

"Well then," she said nastily, "I can only give you one more chance. You either call me within the next three days, or I'll consider this friendship terminated."

That was all it took. I had subjected myself to her abuse all those years, feeling rotten every time I talked to her, but rationalizing I was lucky she even cared. I hadn't even thought of her nasty remarks as abuse; somehow I believed I deserved her disdain.

Now I was free. And though it's been about four years since my liberation from my Cordelia, I haven't missed her at all. I consider myself incredibly lucky. A well-conceived novel and a chance remark saved me from a lifetime of low-grade torture.

The Book Club and My Grandmother's Crystal

Karen Ackland Santa Cruz, California

WE HAVE MET once a month for more than six years, having read the same book in the interim. It started when three of us who worked at the same software company decided that we wanted more than marketing plans and C programming in our lives and invited several others to form a reading group. We first met one Friday evening in spring 1988 to discuss Gabriel García Marquez's *Love in the Time of Cholera.* In retrospect, the romantic drifting end of that book has set the tone for our meetings. We are an unlikely group that found each other and we are holding on.

There is a twenty-year spread between our ages. We grew up all over the country—Maine, Iowa, Nevada, Illinois, and California. Our college degrees range from mathematics, English literature, and sociology to computer science. Our members include a gay man, a lesbian, a married couple who originally met when she was his high-school English teacher, and a single woman. If there is something that characterizes us, it is an unexpected tendency toward silliness.

The silliness began when we switched from meeting for dessert on Friday evenings to dinner on Saturdays and started matching the meals to the books. Cynthia and I took these theme dinners very seriously at first, going to the library to look up recipes in the Time/Life cookbooks behind the reference section. We had *Pollo con Piña à la Antigua* with Oscar Hijuelos's *The Mambo Kings Play Songs of Love* and Egyptian lamb stew, *yakhnit koosa*, with Naguib Mahfouz's *The Thief and the Dog*. We had "tea" in the park one Sunday afternoon and played croquet after reading *The Remains of the Day* by Kazuo Ishiguro. Barbara and Brian hosted the afternoon, bringing a table, linens, and complete tea service to the neighborhood park and showing up dressed in colonial whites. We even went camping in Big Sur where we ate barbecued salmon, drank a half case of good chardonnay, and talked about Harry Crews's *Body* on and off over the course of the weekend. I suggested that book, and still defend it as fun, although it may not have warranted a weekend of discussion. As we sat around the campfire, Jim, who is often irritated by the irregular punctuation of contemporary authors, dramatized a story from John Muir's travels in Alaska as an example of a "real" story.

It didn't take long until we started to choose books by the type of food we wanted to eat. In a group of opinionated people and adventuresome eaters it was often easier to pitch a cuisine than an unknown book or author. "We haven't had Indian," Barbara might say and so we read *Jasmine* by Bharati Mukherjee. "My sister cooks good Mexican food," Cindy said, and we invited ourselves to her house and read a collection of stories about Latin American women subtitled *The Magic and the Real*. Cindy isn't a cook, but she is a networker, and realizing that the editor of the collection, Celia de Zapata, taught at San Jose State, she invited her to join us and lead the discussion.

Our evenings have a pattern. They progress from the initial checking of who liked the book as we gather with a glass of wine around the hors d'oeuvres to a meandering conversation during dinner, winding up with the conclusion and selection of the next book over dessert and coffee. We keep our books within reach to prove a point, but, despite occasional efforts to mark and bring in a favorite passage, we are not a literary group and at times our sloppiness has irritated those with more academic backgrounds.

No one leads the discussion and we jump from subject to subject. We do not talk about tone or place or voice. We also do not talk about politics, the environment, or people at work. We talk about the book and in talking about the book, talk about ourselves. We know the discussion has ended when Greg asks, "Would you recommend this book to a friend?" We teased him about the question for a while, but now we wait for it, even asking it for him if he forgets, going around the room with everyone answering individually.

There are other traditions. Greg calls to say thank-you the day after the meeting. Barbara always sends a note. We bring out the good glasses and company dishes and make an effort with the table arrangements. Somewhere along the way I realized that these Saturday evenings were only slightly different from the monthly bridge potluck group that my parents have been part of for more than thirty years. The irony of this is not lost on me.

One of the pleasures of our book group has been talking on and on about a book, narrowing in on a topic over a period of time that would not be possible in a more directed meeting or class. Several of us combined the book club meeting of Michael Ondaatje's *The English Patient* with a visit to San Francisco to see the Teotihuacán show at the DeYoung Museum. We talked about the book for the hour-and-a-half drive to San Francisco, over dinner for several hours, and during the drive home. Jim didn't like the punctuation in that one either, but I challenge anyone ,not to like the book. Cormac McCarthy's *Blood Meridian* also provoked prolonged discussion. We called a special, second meeting since we didn't understand it the first time, but even after this we were still puzzled, though we continued to be seduced by the beauty of the writing and appalled by the violence.

Some have said that they like the group because it means that they read at least one book a month, but that's not my reason. I have always read a lot. What matters most to me about the group is its continuity. When we first started meeting, I didn't think we would become much of a group—we were too different. But the silliness and the good food kept us together and somewhere along the line I realized that we were a group. These people are my friends. We have thirty-four books in common.

We had gone on so long that I thought we would go on forever. We had survived members moving away, getting married, having babies, earning graduate degrees, and changing jobs. Yet last winter we stopped meeting and we haven't met now for more than seven months. We've talked about starting again. We've talked about why we stopped. Mainly, we got tired of talking about what we were going to do about Dan.

Dan is the boyfriend of a friend and he didn't fit in. He would walk into a room where the host or hostess had gone to a lot of work getting ready—we all have full-time jobs—and say, "I only come to these things for the free food." The type of man who feels he is needed to keep conversation going, Dan once laughed at the idea of a women-only book club, wondering what they could talk about. He wears his former poverty like a badge on his sleeve and dares you to take a swing at him. It was painful to watch him regularly demean his girlfriend, whom the rest of us like.

At first Dan didn't read the book, which didn't keep him from trying to dominate the conversation, but it made it easier to ignore him. Still it took energy to continue to direct the conversation back to the book after Dan had gone off on a tangent about local politics or the inequities of being a white male these days. The book club stopped being fun. It was not clear whose responsibility it was to solve the problem. But we didn't handle it well. We just stopped meeting.

We spent so much time talking about Dan outside the book club, taking polls of who disliked him, that we finally exhausted our energy for the group. An old friend recently told me, "I think a relationship has a compromise quota, and you can use that up in the first six months arguing about which house to buy." I think the book club had a tolerance quota and we used it up talking about Dan.

Five of us from the original group have decided to meet again next Saturday to discuss E. Annie Proulx's *The Shipping News*, but this time we're talking about rules or a trial period. I'm uncomfortable with the idea of a secret ballot to exclude someone—after all, our group celebrates differences—but I also dislike the idea of the book club just disappearing. And, of course, we always did have rules. The rules were to read the book, set a pretty table, and to listen when someone else was speaking. The rules had to do with manners.

Years ago, when I was coming to terms with the apparent dichotomy between my sixties values and my determination to have a nice place to live even though I moved around more than was healthy for either me or my belongings, I realized the importance of "nice things." I don't have crystal wine glasses because they are important—I have them because they were my grandmother's and she left them to me. But I use them because I like them. I came to see that not having things you can afford just because having them is nice, shows a lack of attention to detail and a failure to make choices in your life. Flaunting bad manners because it makes others uncomfortable is only bad manners. I will accept the responsibility of excluding others from the book club because, like crystal wine glasses, the group is a choice for good friends, good books, and good manners, and I intend to go on making that choice.

What We Talk about When We Talk about Books

Cindra Halm   **Minneapolis, Minnesota**

THE TAOISTS SAY we live in two worlds simultaneously. One, the "manifest" world, is corporeal and tangible, full of concrete objects, activities, jobs and events, full of our bodies moving and thinking, feeling and doing. The other, the "subtle" world, is unseen but felt, often unrealized but nonetheless present as influence, motivation, order, desire, change.

I've always liked this idea of parallel universes. I think of my father, the scientist, explaining how invisible energy converts itself to matter, then back to energy again in a perpetual cycle. Underneath the very visible green of spring's new leaves, the subtle and silent yellow of the sun works, photosynthesizing. Unseen electricity becomes the lighted lamp by which I read my books. And, underneath my books, and often my choice of books, quietly stands a familiar petite woman who never *told* me much about books at all: my mother.

I enjoy two books clubs. One could be called manifest— we are a group of six women in Minneapolis that convenes once a month on a Sunday evening to discuss literature. The privilege of host rotates, giving each person a semiannual opportunity to choose any book she desires—usually fiction—as well as the responsibility to provide a delicious treat. The host also provides information about the author and/or historical period, and guides the talk from the personal to the analytical; after six years in its current incarnation, we have grown to be good friends and we have a lot to catch up on every month. We have all been lifelong bibliophiles; many of us worked at an independent bookstore out of which the group developed. Now in my thirties, I feel grateful for the opportunity to draw on this wellspring of emotional and intellectual stimulation and support.

I also feel grateful for my mother's influence on my reading life. She and I comprise the second, the subtle book club. For years, the relationship tilted one way as my mother nurtured my desire and ability to read. I remember library visits as a regular and necessary habit. The pleasure of browsing in the stacks, catching snippets of language, adventure, and character, surpassed even the pleasure of reading itself, which pulled me like a magnet. So much possibility.

Possibility existed in our home as well, in those new and varied titles we borrowed by the bagful. My mother never censored my choices, nor did she separate her choices from those made by me and my sisters. As a teenager, I read hers too: *Flowers for Algernon* (I cried my head off); Robert Coles's *Children of Crisis* series (I was shocked and touched at the reality of poverty and helplessness); and *Interview with the Vampire* (Oh, my young hormones!).

Later, as a young adult who had moved out of state, I once told my mother about a novel I'd liked, and she told me about one *she'd* liked. The notion stuck. I now think of these recommendations to one another over the phone, over the years, as our book club, the one with no rules, no schedules, no lists. It operates simply on the desire to talk about books. Or does it?

What *do* we talk about when we talk about books? What subtle agendas, ulterior motives, or secret desires do we bring to the choices we make for our own reading or for someone else's? Could it be that my mother meant for me to find and read the books that she had brought back from the library for herself—to give me discovery, vocabulary, possibility? We reveal ourselves in our preferences or prejudices; we unfold a little of our histories, our assertions, our confusion. We want to share, in our recommendations, where we've been, where we are, or, most often I think, where we would like to be.

My mother saw for me and my generation greater opportunities than she felt she had had as a young woman in the fifties, and she wanted to encourage me. I know now that many of her choices for me (every birthday and holiday brought books) were motivated by the idea of capable, compassionate, and creative girl and woman characters. I received *Little Women* and *Anne of Green Gables*, and biographies of Harriet Tubman, Florence Nightingale, and Eleanor Roosevelt.

Several years ago, I gave my mother copies of two novels set in Minnesota, written by Minnesota writer Jon Hassler. I realized sometime later that, in addition to sharing strong narrative pull and quirky characters, I was sharing my pride and sense of belonging in a state that I'd come to call home. I was letting her know that I was OK. And when she recommended *The Cape Ann*, by Faith Sullivan, to me last year, I saw that she meant to show me some of the complex feelings, relationships, and decisions that women faced in the early part of the century. It elucidated a conversation about family dynamics we'd had earlier. Listen carefully when a book passes to or from your hand—when a title crosses your lips or ears—there's a full heart somewhere underneath, whispering. It may even be yours.

In my manifest book club, the one that forges ahead with its deadlines and required reading despite busy schedules, the birth of babies, work out of town, and illness, it's a thrill to choose literature that others will have to read and discuss. There's no voting, no consensus, no requirement that the person selecting know the book prior to selection. Just a willingness to put forth ... well, oneself.

I once chose a novel for the club because only days before, I had purchased it in a thrift shop solely on my attraction to its melodious title: *By Grand Central Station I Sat Down and Wept*. It turned out to be a poetic prose style classic first published in London in 1945, with a persona whose obsessive, intricate interior monologue reminded me of "The Yellow Wallpaper."

It was not an easy book to read; not everyone thought well of it. I'm not altogether sure I loved the book as much as the *idea* of the book. Through this choice, I was able to share with my group my fascination for, and (here's the personal part) my own desire to write poetry with sound-rich, repetition-dense, highly metaphorical, and heightened language. "This," I wanted to exclaim, "is a book I wish I'd written. This is what I love, what I would love to achieve." The night we discussed it, brimming with my secret agenda of baring a little of my soul, I probably praised the book's merits a little too highly!

What does it mean that one member, who frequently stays at home with small children, chooses novels whose characters reach epiphanies while on outings or journeys (*Anywhere But Here* by Mona Simpson, *A River Runs Through It* by Norman Maclean, *All the Pretty Horses* by Cormac McCarthy)? Or that another member, a traveler and lover of international style and cuisine, chooses English or European authors (Julian Barnes, Evelyn Waugh, Émile Zola)? Or that another, having finally settled in Minnesota, often returns to her southern roots through books (William Faulkner, Lewis Nordan, Dorothy Allison)? Of course, there are no easy or definitive answers, but there are patterns, associations, and connections to actual lives.

We live interior and exterior lives simultaneously. What happens when I read a book and I connect, pronounce it great, and tell others about it? Why are some books passed from hand to hand, from mouth to mouth as if some vital, abundant food? I like to think that in each of us, a subtle energy wants to take form in word-art, whether we write stories or read them, tell them, choose them, talk about them, touch them, give them away, or defend them. It's a working out, a wrestle to bring our unnamed selves into fruition, a giving, a receiving.

Like new leaves, we need both to absorb and release the sun. When you recommend a book, or read a recommended book, you allow light to rise to the surface of the common world. It is a bold thing, a surprising thing, a subversive thing to belong to a book club or two.

Watch out—you're telling more than you think.

PART II

Good Groups, Plain and Simple

Some book groups have an agenda—an oft-repeated reason for being and a book list that focuses tightly on a specific area of interest to the group. But plenty of groups have no special handle. They don't have an official leader. They don't read *only* anything. They'll try almost everything. They are as they appear to be—pretty special after all.

Too Busy to Read or Why You Won't Find Any White Whales around Here

Rodd Zolkos   **Chicago, Illinois**

OK, IN FAIRNESS to our book group, I begin this essay with a confession. The title is a lie. Oh, it was true once, some months ago when those words first took shape in that portion of my brain controlling the smartaleck functions. They emerged as I considered our group for this essay, time and again returning to what frequently seemed our mantra—keep it short.

Back then the White Whale seemed an impossible quest. To be sure, from time to time he'd venture near, coming almost within reach before sounding beneath the waves of fellow book group members' unenthusiastic responses and disappearing once again. How could they allow the leviathan to slip away, I wondered? Didn't they recognize how absolutely essential it was to overcome the monster, and in so doing triumph over our own nature (if that's the interpretation you prefer). Cursed whale! Wouldst thou never taste the barbed steel of our group's keen insights?

"Hah!" you say. If my passion for the Whale truly ran so hot, why not challenge him alone?

"Hound!" says I. "Would Ahab set out in a dinghy?" I think not. This manner of obsession demands company.

Besides, the challenge fit well with our group's effort to diversify its readings—a look at our list showed a woeful lack of nineteenth-century American whaling novels.

No, to my mind, the White Whale was a challenge best met as a group, and the only possible reason for our quaking at the sight of the great beast was the fear of its impressive bulk. And not simply a bulk measured by the number of pages, but the real heft given each page by a language thick with everything from pidgin English to the arcane lexicon of the American whaleman.

"It's too much," said some. "We have lives."

"But isn't book group a chance to improve those lives," I thought, "by allowing our minds to visit fantastic places and share all manner of magnificent experiences?" And what could possibly be more fantastic than cramming our minds together on the decks of a tiny, stinking, sailing craft bound on a three-year voyage with a crew whose goal was to wreak mayhem on the sea-going mammalian population only to become bit players in a ritual dance between a crazed captain bent on an unholy vengeance and the homicidal cetacean who'd prove his match?

Clearly, someday we must confront the Whale together.

When lo, perhaps our hearty book group crew finally caught the fever of my obsession. Without so much as a single doubloon nailed to a mast—or our group's latter day equivalent, the promise of free beer to any who made the journey—the group agreed to take on Melville's *Moby-Dick*.

Actually, I think the reason we finally took action lies in large part in a step our group made about a year ago. It followed an evaluation of where we were as a group and where we wanted to go, with much soul-searching over our future direction. And, indeed, whether there should even be a future.

Things had been getting a little ragged around the edges with our group. Meetings would change, months would slip by in which we wouldn't meet at all, and attendance was threatening to achieve that critical phone booth level. In assessing our status, some members wanted more structure, others more challenge. Ultimately, both were achieved, though the structure, I think, was key.

On a chart of organizations, our group would probably rank just a little north of anarchy. But over the years we've all kind of preferred it that way, picking one book and one meeting place at a time, with no leaders and no real rules (although reading the book is highly encouraged). And for a long time it worked, though as lives became busier and distractions became greater, it had grown obvious that a little bit of (trust me, I'm shuddering as I write this, just ask my loving spouse) "planning" was necessary.

Not too much, mind you. I think we stayed true to our scruffy minimalist roots even as we made two key planning decisions that seem to work well for us. First, we picked a regular evening each month which, with only the most extreme exceptions, is book group night—no questions, no arguments, no changes. Second, and probably more significantly, we took the radical step (for us) of choosing books and sites two months in advance.

Obviously, many book groups succeed quite nicely by planning their reading list a year at a time, and that's all well and good—for them. For whatever reason, I don't think anyone in our group would dare suggest we embrace planning in quite such extreme fashion. But, even at our group's most vibrant periods in the old, disorganized days, most everyone, possessed of a life, argued they didn't have time to read "long" books.

Now as I've alluded, my loving spouse, Kathy, herself a founding member of our group, has been known on rare occasions to take issue with what she considers my reluctance to "plan" more details of my life away from the workplace. The exception, she would allow in an irritated tone, being the odd tee time. Typically, I plead no contest, with but a plea for leniency based on days spent working in a highly structured, deadline-driven environment that prompts me to eschew planning to the extent possible in my social life.

That excuse doesn't cut it? You're right, your honor, and in fact I'll go so far as to allow that this little bit of extra planning by our book group is what made it possible for us to achieve something we couldn't in the past. Two months to work with gave members the time to tackle something like *Moby-Dick* and tend to their lives as well. Just as the *Pequod* would never set sail without its masters planning for the voyage by stocking it with casks of fresh water, barrels of salt pork, and plenty of extra canvas, so I can see where our chances of successfully navigating our group through more challenging books have been advanced by extending our planning an extra month down the road.

"Ah," you say, ready to guide sharpened steel to my analogy's hump, "planning ahead didn't save the *Pequod* or her crew when it took up with the White Whale." Hey, I read to the end. I know what happened. And, while our group had a far better time of it with the Whale than did the crew of that ill-fated Nantucket whaler, our encounter wasn't completely successful either. Not everyone showed up for *Moby-Dick*, though I think planning a decade ahead wouldn't have been enough to prompt the no-shows to sign on to this particular voyage of obsession.

And, I think none the less of them for it. After all, more than one recent conversation with some of my most well-read coworkers went something like this:

Well-read coworker: Read anything good lately?

Me: *Moby-Dick*.

Well-read coworker: The whole thing?

But at least with the advantage of the extra month, those who didn't make the journey were able to choose to miss the boat rather than have circumstances make the choice for them. And for the rest of us, it meant we could spend what all agreed was some quality time with old Moby, Ahab, Ishmael, and the rest of that wacky gang on board the *Pequod*.

And while nobody jumped up when the *Moby-Dick* discussion ended to suggest *Ulysses* for the meeting two months hence, I believe our new format will lead us to tackle some works we might previously have dismissed as too challenging for busy sorts like us.

For those of us who made the trip, it was truly a voyage of discovery. Those who hadn't read *Moby-Dick* before learned what all the fuss is about. We also learned a thing or two about whales. Most of all, though, we learned that massive works needn't be out of bounds for our group.

As for me, well, let's just say that if Kathy's eyeing the horizon for signs of my embracing planning, I'll spout this once. Planning works for our book group. It delivered us the White Whale.

For this group's reading list, see page 335.

Not Moby Books

Stephen A. Huth   **Oak Park, Illinois**

"HOW ABOUT MOBY Books," was Patti's suggestion for a name, roundly ignored just as had been all the other suggestions, from Harvey Street Book Club to Books Are Us to No Name Book Club.

"But I thought we needed a name to get the discount from Barbara's Bookstore," I said.

Bob looked up from the date book he always carried, "No, not anymore. They'll reserve books for us now without a name."

"I think we get a kick out of not having a name," Jim offered, and he got two objections, two sneers, and one "So, what's wrong with that?"

After fifteen years of talking together, we steadfastly remain without a name, often without a plan for how to discuss a book, but with several necessary unwritten rules. We've tried to establish firmer rules over the years. What we have discovered is that a minimal set of standards ensures that we get together and the rest of it works itself out.

The members of the group are an increasingly odd subset of American culture, at least if you believe what you read (for example, the first edition of this book). We are married couples who come to book club as couples. All but one of the couples has children, and our children were a primary reason why we first met.

Until reading the first edition of the *Book Group Book*, I had not realized our group was such an oddity: married men and women together, enjoying books and each other's conversations. Maybe we could be the fodder of an anthropological study. No, only one or two would agree to such an exercise, the rest would refuse, and the sample would be even more skewed.

Who Are We, Then?

Over the course of our fifteen years, just twenty individuals have been members.

Originally, the book club included Sara and Dave, Don and Nadine, John and Harriet, Bob and Jody, and Patti and me. The original members all lived within a block of each other, and all except Bob and Jody had small children. At first we brought our babies along. That ended quickly, but being just a few doors away from our firstborn nevertheless was comforting in those first years. With the advent of bedroom monitors, parents could even listen to their babies sleeping (or crying) while they were at book club.

Dave was a computer analyst for retail stores; Sara was a former teacher. After two years, they moved, although Dave always will be remembered for choosing *Small Is Beautiful*, a book disliked by all except Dave.

A few years later, John and Harriet also left the book club. John was the owner of a local kitchen supply distributorship. Harriet was an arts instructor at a local art university. The group still mentions the time John served chocolate that had been stored in his basement—next to the kitty litter.

The other original members are still kicking around.

Jody is a high-school teacher of German and occasionally history. Bob is a clinical psychologist who works at a university counseling center and has a part-time private practice.

Don teaches in a Chicago public school for kids who have not graduated from eighth grade, but are not yet sixteen. Nadine works part-time at the local library and has started back to school for a masters degree in library science. They have two sons, fifteen and fourteen.

Patti is a clinical psychologist; she has been in private practice for more than ten years, and she supervises graduate students in clinical psychology. I am the managing editor for a small publishing firm in Chicago. We have two daughters, fifteen and seven.

Changes to the Group

Over the years two other couples came and went.

Mark, who is an architect, and Gail, who is a physical therapist, briefly joined but found too many schedule conflicts.

The couple who bought Dave and Sara's house also inherited a group membership. Lynn and Dave (a different Dave) had four children. Lynn eventually went back to school and was ordained as a minister, which was why they moved and left our group. Dave was the executive director of a civil rights commission.

And three couples came and stayed.

Lee writes freelance, most often in the medical field. Brad is a benefits director for a financial services firm. Lee and Brad have two daughters, eight and four.

Susan also writes freelance. Jim is a lawyer who recently started his own general practice firm. Susan and Jim have one daughter, seven years old.

Lilian is a psychiatrist in private practice. Richard is a lawyer for a downtown Chicago bank. Lilian and Richard have one son, nineteen years old.

Not until Patti and I moved about five blocks north a few years ago did the group lose its one-block status. We still are close: Don and Nadine and Lee and Brad live on the same block; Susan and Jim, Jody and Bob, and Patti and I live on the same block; Richard and Lilian live just five blocks away.

Standard Operating Procedure

How we run the book club was established early on and, like several recent popular novels we have read, revolves at least partially around food. Several procedures have remained virtually unchanged for fifteen years (maybe we are more rigid than we would like to believe).

The book club rotates at couples' homes, and the hosts choose the book. Allowing one member to choose the book we read each time is part of what many of us like. The consequence is that we often read books we otherwise might not have even known of. I would not have read Salman Rushdie's *Midnight's Children* or Robert Caro's *Paths to Power*, two of my favorite books during the last fifteen years, unless a book club member had chosen them.

We meet on Saturday evenings, and usually simple munchies and beer and wine are served. Sometimes, the food will fit the book: we have served papadams with Indian books, whiskey with southern novels, and sardines for Clyde Edgerton's *In Memory of Junior*.

Because we are neighbors, much of our first half hour is spent in gossip. Oak Park is a tight-knit community, and quite likely everyone will know something about each new piece of town rumor.

Eventually, we get to the book at hand—and we often are surprised how easy the discussion goes with some books, how deadening with others. I am sure other book clubs also learn early on that a good book and a good book club book are two different creations.

As mentioned earlier, three book club members do some type of writing as a profession, but most members are not oriented toward the written word academically or professionally. Our discussion reflects this and tends not to meander into the realm of technique. We do concern ourselves with the whys and the wherefores of our books, and our discussions often veer into implications the book might have for our own lives or the world around us.

Our discussions include many interruptions, occasional raised voices, good-natured and frequent disagreements, and a great deal of laughter. Our book list provides a random sample of reactions to some of the books we've read.

If we sustain a conversation strictly about the chosen book for more than ninety minutes, we consider the book at least to have achieved status as a good book club book. Then we move to dessert and coffee. This is another time to catch up on personal and community news, to try out some wonderful sweet creations, and to plan the next book time.

Over the years, we have had a few parties in conjunction with our club, none more memorable than one in December when we decided to read aloud Charles Dickens's *A Christmas Carol*.

We still argue about exactly what happened. A few of us tried to begin the reading, but we managed no more than a few pages before jokes about our speaking abilities, general interruptions, and complete disregard of the reading finally caused us to quit. We still chide each other about who was to blame (as author here, I get to say that I was one of those who made no jokes, did not interrupt, and was completely attentive). Well, we did talk about the book some, never considered the event as an impediment to the book club, and continued the party. As a telling consequence, we have not tried another oral reading.

We have remained small—six couples our working maximum. We can take indirect credit for the formation of one other book club because of this limit. A couple asked about joining, we said we were full, and they simply started their own group—also mostly couples (maybe our group is not that odd after all).

I think our book club has remained stable over the years primarily because of its social nature and because the monthly meetings give each of us an excuse to read yet another book. Sure, we are annoyed when members do not read a book, come to book club, or don't join in the discussion. Sure, we get upset when only a few folks show up after a dessert has taken four hours to make. But over the years, I have come to esteem our get-togethers both for their insights into the books we read and their contribution to the stability of our lives.

We are all busy, and the monthly meetings are often difficult to arrange. And that is part of what makes the coming together so valuable—we bother to find a time to see each other, to schedule our group into our lives. Even if we don't have a name, each month we place a value on our effort.

For this group's reading list, see page 286.

Literary Lunch Bunch

Betty Kuhl   **Baker City, Oregon**

OUR TOWN, BAKER City, Oregon, population 9,500, is in the eastern part of the state. We are 300 miles from Portland and 120 miles from Boise, Idaho, so except that we are on I-84, we are somewhat isolated. We make our livings ranching, lumbering, and working in federal offices, mostly the United States Forest Service and the Bureau of Land Management. Tourism is becoming more important with the renovation of our town's historic buildings and the sesquicentennial celebration of the Oregon Trail, which runs through our county.

Twenty years ago the American Association of University Women (AAUW) sponsored two book groups in our area. One met evenings for working women who preferred contemporary fiction. After a few years this group disbanded. Our group met with sack lunches at noon at the home of a special AAUW member, Leona Fleetwood. She had been a full-scholarship student at Washington University in St. Louis and had come west to teach school at some of the early gold-mining towns in our area. She later served as Baker City librarian for many years. She was confined to her home, and we were all happy to meet there because she was a fountain of knowledge about many things, especially literature. She had even introduced children's literature to many of our offspring through the puppet shows she professionally produced at the library each Saturday morning.

Our group chose an author each month and we would each try to read at least one book by him or her and usually two or three. Most books were borrowed from the library, as there was no bookstore in the county at that time. Later, Leona and I and two other women opened a bookstore that still flourishes. Our library is wonderful though, and for years we had the honor of having the largest circulation of books per capita in the state. Some reasoned this was because of our long, cold winters; there was nothing to do but read.

We eventually opened the book group to others who weren't AAUW members, but we kept the membership at around eight. Only fourteen different women have belonged to the group, and we are now fairly constant with five old faithfuls, all in our early seventies. Others left town, Leona died, two lost their hearing, and three lost interest as we advanced toward more heavy reading.

After Leona died, we met in the library meeting room for several years. Interest waned and attendance was sporadic because we lacked the stimulus of Leona's leadership. We started meeting in each other's homes. The hostess calls a few days in advance to remind us. It is unusual that anyone is missing, and we are always on time. Sometimes I feel we should take in a few more members, but right now we are such a congenial group, I hesitate to rock the boat. We certainly serve as a support group to one another, and we adjust our meeting dates to accommodate vacations, doctor appointments, and acts of God.

The hostess prepares coffee, tea, and a sweet treat, but we each bring a sack lunch. When I owned the bookstore and had to return to work at one, we usually all disbanded together at that time. Now that my daughter and her husband own the store, we often linger until two and find the extra time provides more in-depth discussions and still allows lots of time to catch up on families, trips, and local current events.

Although we are compatible and good friends, chances are we will not see one another until our next meeting. We have a special intimate bond through our love of books and seem to prefer this exclusive association rather than expanding our relationship to other areas.

Contrary to one Baker City newcomer's statement that she was sure one could not find a single copy of *The New Yorker* in Baker County, three of our book group members subscribe to it and often bring something from the current issue into the discussion.

One of our most remembered books was *The Aquarian Conspiracy* by Marilyn Ferguson. It was an inspiration to us all. Only half jokingly, we all expressed the belief that we had been living according to these theories and that is how and why we had come together in a book group. We have all been active in our community, supporting worthwhile endeavors and serving on numerous boards and committees. We have each lived here at least twenty years.

We have read a good share of the prominent women authors, both contemporary and classic. We have covered most of the western writers, especially admiring Wallace Stegner and Vardis Fisher. We read poetry at least once a year—that is my favorite meeting. Because of all the material we receive at the bookstore, we are able to enjoy the *Bloomsbury Review* each quarter plus publishers' advance reviews.

We have expanded our horizons in our reading and have found new dimensions of exploring great works of literature. I am sure all of us would give up other pleasures long before we would abandon the Literary Lunch Bunch.

Back Bay Book Group

Mary M. Blair   **Boston, Massachusetts**

WE BEGAN IN March 1993 as a special-interest group of the Neighborhood Association of the Back Bay in Boston. The NABB represents the political, legal, and social concerns of its members. Ours was the fourth daytime group to form in recent years. There is always a waiting list of readers. It is now the policy that, once established, the day and evening groups are no longer affiliated with NABB.

The Group

We are twelve women who meet on the second Thursday of each month at 10:30 A.M. Ranging in ages from fifty to seventy-plus, we are married, single, widowed, and divorced. A variety of talents and professions brings both harmony and discord to our meetings. We include two authors, a psychologist, two artists, a paralegal, a retired secretary, an accountant, and a real estate agent. Almost all of us do volunteer work at places ranging from the Boston Symphony Orchestra to local homeless shelters. A number of us have taught school at some point in our lives. Some have graduate degrees; one is working on her doctorate.

Meetings are held in members' apartments; none of us live in a single-family home. We are all within walking distance as the Back Bay is a fairly concentrated area of the city. The first thirty minutes are spent reacquainting ourselves and catching up on each other's families and accomplishments. This chitchat did not take very long at first, but now that we know each other better and have more of our lives to share, we must look to our leader to rein us in and get to the book. During the next hour we defend, criticize, denounce, or praise the chosen book. Conflicting opinions are tolerated in a (usually) friendly manner. No blood has yet been drawn; but tempers do rise from time to time.

In the last few minutes, as we are gathering coats and using the powder room, the next important issue arises: where to have lunch. We didn't begin by including lunch in our plans, but we are reluctant to say good-bye. We walk to a nearby restaurant, often still discussing the book, and end our day together about two o'clock. During this time many of us have made plans to see a movie, play, ballet, or to get together in some way before the next meeting.

The Books

Every three months we take the time to choose our next three books. Members nominate and defend their choices. The only requirement is that the book be available in paperback. At the outset we decided to concentrate on fiction. With one exception, the nonfiction we have read did not provide much food for discussion.

Rather timidly, we began *A River Runs Through It*. The film was showing locally. This did not much appeal to us, but it was a beginning and made us see that we needed "meatier" material. "Too much fly-fishing for us city girls," said one member.

A Thousand Acres provided fuel for a deep and often painful session. "I hated that bastard!" was the opening statement. We all agreed on Jane Smiley's wonderful character development and went on to the subject of memory repression. Our psychologist member was a great help in this area. "Do you really remember the pain of childbirth?" she asked, defending the reality of memory repression.

You Just Don't Understand was one of our least favorite choices. We agreed that men and women *do* communicate differently, and we didn't feel the book said much more than that. We were pointed back to fiction.

Both *The Bean Trees* and *Animal Dreams* were favorites. One member remarked that she "admired the free spirit of the author," and she "hated to have these books end." We all felt that, and the most recent Barbara Kingsolver novel will surely be on our list soon.

"A family's and a nation's trauma," were appreciated in *The House of the Spirits*. Members who had read Isabel Allende's other works felt this was her best. The women in her story were especially admired.

In summer we needed some lighter reading, so we decided on *The Bridges of Madison County*. Our discussion put this on the "best-cellar" list. Some of us were embarrassed to have read such a trifling, but we had some good laughs at Robert James Waller's expense.

The Remains of the Day was more to our liking. Many members also saw the film. Here was a character like none other we had met and we all hoped that the hint of a love story would develop into more. The narrow scope and emotional prison of this man's life was beautifully crafted by the author.

Yet another film led us to *The Age of Innocence*. The stifling rules of behavior, where one must abide by the dictates of one's society regardless of individual choice or desire, were unknown to us. It was difficult to empathize with the opulence of old New York society contrasted with the lack of personal freedom.

A love-hate relationship developed with the discussion of *The Palace Walk* and the second book of this trilogy, *Palace of Desire*. Some members thought they were the best books we had read thus far and others thought some characters so unlikable that it was difficult to get beyond them and see the book as a whole. Our discussion led to one of family dynamics and dominant versus submissive members of a related group of people. Our anger at the treatment of the women in this story was an underlying theme. The third book will be read in the future.

High on the list of disliked books was *The Gastronomical Me*, another nonfiction choice. "Boring," was a common remark, as well as, "I felt like I never wanted to eat again." We couldn't even argue about this one and so, despite our feelings about the book, we went to lunch.

The one nonfiction book we admired was *The Road from Coorain*. The descriptions of the Australian outback, the difficult life of the author and her splendid achievements were an inspiration. Jill Ker Conway is a neighbor and will be invited soon to join us to talk about her life and work.

The war-damaged individuals and their personal mysteries in *The English Patient* left us emotionally exhausted. The author related their war horrors brilliantly and we sympathized with them as they healed their physical and psychic wounds. There was so much intrigue and so much said obliquely that many of us decided that this would go into our reread piles. "It doesn't digest with just one reading," said one member.

The difficulties of living in a foreign country was the theme for our discussion of *Stones for Ibarra*. Several members have lived in other parts of the world and they related their problems and frustrations, especially in regard to being women in male-ordered societies. The book itself received mixed reviews. "I just couldn't get into it," said one member. Others thought it was wonderful.

The Awakening was considered quite mild by most of the group. The subject of an unfaithful wife is no longer a taboo issue and we felt the story reached its only logical conclusion. "Dated literature," was the general comment.

A summer home on the ocean in Kennebunkport, Maine, was the perfect setting for *A Yellow Raft in Blue Water*. This was an all-day meeting with lunch provided by our hostess. This, our first field trip, was a great success. Everyone agreed that the book was a wonderful portrayal of three Native American women and how they came to be adults, each in her own generation.

Only four members were present for our discussion of *Mariette in Ecstasy*, as it was July. This was our most stimulating discussion to date. We wondered what had actually happened in the book. Was it a mystical religious experience, self-hypnosis, or a physical manifestation of delusion? We were perplexed, and it was frustrating not to have a definitive answer. We admired the fact that this book was written by a man and that he could so clearly describe the characters of these nuns, each with her unique, but not necessarily nice, personality.

"This is so real!" was the comment on the next book, *The Weight of Winter*. An added bonus for us were the descriptions of snow, as we read it during the hottest, most humid summer Boston had ever had. This third book about the families in a town in northern Maine became one of our favorites. The characters, who varied in attractiveness, were believable, funny, and tragic. Those of us who had lived in small towns identified them as people from our pasts.

The Future

When our group was first formed, membership was open to all members of the NABB. It just happened that there were no men who were interested in joining at that time. When members were asked recently if a man or men would now be welcome in our group, the majority voted no. Most members felt that the freedom of our discussions would not necessarily be limited, but would be steered into different directions. We are happy as we are with our little "sorority," though we would invite a man as a guest speaker or visiting author.

Our group is more firmly rooted with each meeting. We have become good friends and look forward to many years of reading and discussing what brought us together in the first place: books.

Thirty Years of Treasures: Books and Friends

Carolyn Sosnoski   **Old Lyme, Connecticut**

ON A SUMMER evening in the seventies, I took my two young daughters and a friend of theirs to a meeting of the Book Group at Sandy's home. The children played upstairs in the "mother-in-law" quarters that were unoccupied at the time. Downstairs we began our discussion of *One Flew Over the Cuckoo's Nest* by Ken Kesey.

During the discussion one of our members excused herself to use the ladies' room. Suddenly, we heard shrieks of laughter. The woman emerged from the bathroom, in hysterics, and Sandy began to laugh, too. Then the three girls came pounding down the stairs, clamoring to know what was happening.

Sandy led them to the bathroom and showed them a hand mirror on the counter, with a noted taped to it that read "Use it if you dare." She explained to the girls how Big Nurse in the book we were discussing had used a hand mirror to check how well the patients had cleaned the toilet bowls. The note Sandy had taped to the underside of the rim of the bowl read, "I never thought you'd stoop so low" (in reverse printing, of course, so it came out right in the mirror).

Our book group has been going strong for almost thirty years. Paula, our acknowledged leader, and I met in fall 1964 through Paula's husband, John, when I had been a member of a great books discussion group at a nearby high school and John had taught that September in the Adult Education Program. Paula and I were each expecting first babies, which turned out to be daughters born within a couple of weeks of each other in November.

During the early months of 1965, Paula and I visited back and forth for lunch or coffee. We compared notes on the babies, and also on what we had been reading. In June 1965, we each cornered a friend or two and gathered at Paula's home one evening to discuss two short stories, Faulkner's "That Evening Sun," and Jackson's "The Lottery." Much of our early reading was classical or "semiclassical." We read works by Shakespeare, Shaw, Ibsen, Flaubert, Dostoevsky, Hemingway, Stendhal, and Camus. We were so excited about the book group in those early days that we wanted to meet every two weeks, but we soon realized that wasn't possible. We settled on once a month.

We each take a turn hosting the group in our home. A couple of members live quite a distance, and since it is not practical to travel to their homes, they bring refreshments to our Christmas meeting, which is usually held at Sandy's.

We generally have planning sessions about every six months. We are fairly informal about the process of choosing books. The person who suggests a book, which must be agreed upon by all members, becomes the leader of the discussion of that book.

The leader finds background material on the author and guides the group in analyzing the theme, style, and characters. She usually tries to find literary reviews to share with the group. Our oldest member, who is in her eighties, just loves reviews.

Sometimes our reading revolves around a theme. About four years ago, we used a newspaper column by Ellen Goodman as a guide for our summer reading. We read Mary

Gordon's *The Other Side*, Sue Miller's *Family Pictures*, and Wallace Stegner's *Crossing to Safety*. Occasionally, our local libraries offer a series of discussions based on a theme such as family relationships. Some of us have participated in these discussions and have brought ideas back to our own book group.

For many years the August meeting of the book group was special. Paula's sister Joan, a professor of French and dean of freshman students at a local, private, liberal arts college, would lead the discussion. She'd suggest something ahead of time, often a play, and tell us which translation to get. Sometimes we were able to find the selection in our libraries, or she would put a number of copies on hold at the college bookstore.

When Joan was our leader, the discussion was more like a class. She had so many details and anecdotes to share. She had been to France many times and had seen performances of most of the plays done there in French. She had also taught the plays and stories to her college students, so she could anticipate the questions that we asked about the themes, characters, playwrights, and settings.

Joan died two years ago. Her funeral at the college chapel was a celebration of her life. She had touched the lives of many. In our book group, we miss her immensely.

The December meeting is at Sandy's; she has usually decorated for the holidays, and the refreshments are appropriate for a holiday gathering. We read poetry at this meeting. For a number of years, Sandy chose the poems and had copies for everyone and distributed them ahead of time. Recently, group members have picked a favorite poem or two and have brought copies for everyone else. It is always a festive and enjoyable time.

Mary is known as the member who calls the author to ask for an interpretation of the ending of the book. Many years ago we read a book called *Holdfast Gaines* by a local author. The conclusion was ambiguous, so Mary called the author.

Ever since, when we can't agree on the meaning of something we are discussing, we suggest that Mary call the author.

When we read Rosalyn Carter's *Lady from Plains*, Mary wrote to Mrs. Carter and told her of our group's interest in her book, inviting her to our meeting. Mrs. Carter graciously declined, but wished us well, in a letter that we read at the meeting. Mary also is famous for dressing up as the gangster character Abbadabba Berman from E. L. Doctorow's novel *Billy Bathgate* when we discussed that book.

Our most recent meeting was held at the church that one of our members attends. Ann, a social worker, presented a video program on dealing with stress. It was a relaxing and helpful evening. We learned to see the absurdity in a difficult situation, to take ourselves more lightly, and to find some action to take. The video was based on a book by C. W. Metcalf and Roma Felible titled, *Lighten Up, Survival Skills for People under Pressure*.

We have had three or four new members come into our group recently, bringing our numbers to twelve at the last meeting (with one member missing). Though it takes the group a while to assimilate these new members, they add greatly to it. From the start, they participated actively and added new ideas and dimensions to our discussions.

I've asked several group members why they think our group has managed to exist for so many years. No one is sure, but there are a few theories. Our original members were all at home with young children. And though we enjoyed the privilege of being full-time mothers and homemakers, we also enjoyed reading and craved more intellectual stimulation. Also, many of us were transplanted from our home cities or states. We were looking for new acquaintances and friends with the common interest of reading.

No doubt another reason for our longevity is that Paula is a strong but diplomatic leader who is liked and respected by all members of the group. She was an English major in college and has always been a voracious reader and is articulate in expressing her ideas. She also encourages others to express their opinions and makes sure everyone has a chance to speak. She has been a good role model for all of us and has encouraged us when we take our turn leading the discussion.

During the early years of the group, there were members who were looking for a purely social outlet. They lost the books, often didn't read them, or didn't do their "homework." They soon realized that this was not the group for them and dropped out of their own accord.

We have been supportive of each other in happy and sad events in our lives. We attended one member's retirement dinner a few years ago. Many of us attended the funeral for another member's husband a few months ago. We try to show that we care about each other, especially when we are experiencing illness or other trouble in our lives. Humor is undoubtedly another factor in our longevity. We laugh a lot and try not to take ourselves too seriously.

We have taken time to celebrate our years together. On our tenth anniversary, we had a special cake, and we have a photo of ourselves looking thin and tan and young. On our twenty-fifth anniversary, we had a potluck dinner at one of our member's homes. We invited past members to join us at that time, and many of them came and celebrated with us. I'll have to tell you about the thirtieth-anniversary celebration in another edition.

For this group's reading list, see page 315.

The Chapter
Four Society

Cindy Thelen and
David Vick   **Western Springs, Illinois**

IT'S INTERESTING TO sense people's reactions when you
mention that you belong to a book club. By their tone of
voice or expressions, you know they are imagining a stuffy
group of pseudo-intellectuals discussing a dry piece of classic
literature. Or they're flashing back to their English lit class in
high school and wondering why any sane person would will-
ingly re-create that experience as an adult.

Well, anyone attending one of our group meetings would
very quickly have all of those stereotypes and images shattered. Our meetings are characterized by lively conversations
(sometimes two or three going on simultaneously and almost
always quite loud), food and drink (the more, the better), and
laughter (lots and lots of it).

We started with a small group of friends gathered around
a kitchen table four years ago. Our goals were simple—to
read all of those books that, due to our busy schedules, we
never seem to get around to—and, what's more, to discuss
them with others who were reading them at the same time.
Today the group has grown to twelve members (off and on)
and still includes the original founding members. Most of the

group lives in the Chicago area, but we communicate via mail, telephone, and taped messages with a member who has relocated to Colorado.

We began the group with one premise—the only "rule" would be that we all read whatever book is chosen, whether or not it's a book we think we're going to like. This premise still serves as our guiding foundation. It broadens our reading horizons and helps us to discover new authors, genres, and subject matters that we may not have considered in the past. As we have discovered along the way, some of these choices (though certainly not all) turn out to be treasures.

This rule also helped us choose our name. In the first year, one of our selections was Stephen Hawking's *A Brief History of Time.* (Yes, we were *really* looking to expand our horizons with that choice.) Since this book covers subjects ranging from black holes in the universe to quantum physics, it can become complex, especially for nonscientists. Each member, charged with the responsibility of completing the book, diligently attempted to grasp the concepts described by the author. We read and reread chapters, trying to understand. The shortest chapter in the book—chapter four—was the most confusing to us. To some, this was the point at which they gave up their quest for an in-depth understanding of physics. When we conceded that chapter four had beat our book group, we rewarded the victory by taking its name.

The strength of the Chapter Four Society lies in the diversity of its members. The Society is made up of women (two-thirds) and men (one-third), single and married, with children and without, with differing levels of formal education, and various occupations and religious and political views. Most of the members are originally from the Chicago area, but several have been transplanted from other locations, including three who were born abroad.

The relationships among the members vary; the founding members have been good friends for a number of years. New members are recruited from coworkers, friends, acquaintances, and relatives. We have tried to limit the number of active members to about a dozen, so that we have a manageable number for a meaningful discussion. Some particularly enthusiastic members started by reading the books before they were officially invited to join the group.

The requirements for joining the Chapter Four Society are few, but important. You have to be able to follow (and participate in) at least two or three conversations at once, you have to laugh, and you have to respect the book selections of other members.

The logistics of our group are fairly straightforward. We rotate the honor of selecting the book each month. Originally, this rotation schedule was based on when a member joined, with new members moving to the end of the list. Currently, we set a selection schedule for the year at the January meeting. This way we know when each member will choose for that year, but each book is not announced until the end of the previous month's meeting. January's book is usually decided by a group vote (or "voot grope," as it has come to be known after a meeting at which a particularly potent sangria was served). We never limit ourselves to a certain type of book—anything goes. We simply have decided to respect the decision and recommendation of the person making the selection.

Our meetings are held on the third or fourth Friday evening of each month, eleven times a year (we usually skip the end of December due to the holiday). The member selecting the book hosts the party. This changing location eliminates the possibility of the group being a burden for anyone and adds a bit of fun. The host decides the evening's fare, which can range from chips and pretzels to a full meal. Theme food, such as carrot cake for *Watership Down* or Milky Ways and Starbursts for *A Brief History of Time*, is sometimes served. Typically, we have several appetizers, drinks, more drinks, dessert, and coffee. Most hosts have gotten the message that good food and, more important, a variety of beverages are the key. Our group has even become beer connoisseurs, with stern glances given to the host serving only domestic lite.

The evening begins with "social time"—somewhat unnecessary as this group is characterized by being social at all hours. When we get around to discussing the book (and so far we always do ... eventually), we begin with a pre-discussion rating where each member assigns the book a rating of one to four. Loosely defined, one is poor, two is fair, three is good, and four is excellent. We've had numerous conversations about the rating system—how each person interprets it, whether it has any value, whether we need both pre- and post-discussion ratings, whether we can give fractional or zero ratings. In any case, it works for us as a good starting place for discussion.

The format and structure of the discussion are up to the hosting member. Some hosts choose to provide biographical information about the author or historical information about the time period; others describe the reason for their selection or provide current media information on the subject. Sometimes we just launch right into the discussion. The Society is flexible and creative as to the style of the discussion. There is a conscious attempt to allow each member to express his or her opinion. But sometimes emotions reach a fever pitch, with side discussions and shouts erupting from all points in the room. Our out-of-town member is then left with a tape recording that could be mistaken for the trading floor at the Chicago Board of Trade.

The topics discussed are as varied as the subject matters of the books and the members themselves. For some people, the characterization in books is very important. Could they identify with any of the characters? Did they care about what happened to them? For others, the setting may be important. Did the author paint a picture of the locations? Were physical scenes described so that you felt like you were there? Others focus on how the book made them feel. Did it have an impact on their lives? Did it make them think or feel differently about anything? Could they identify with a particular moral/ethical dilemma? Sometimes, our discussions have zeroed in on the author's style, including everything from point of view to word choice. Some members prepare discussion materials prior to their arrival. We've seen everything from pop quizzes to genetic charts of the characters. We've even had discussions about the artwork on the cover and the size and format of the book. (Did you know that *Einstein's Dreams* fits perfectly into an overcoat pocket and even has a built-in bookmark?)

After it appears that all opinions have been exhausted (anywhere from thirty minutes to three hours later), each member gives a post-discussion rating. We record these ratings in the Society's archives as a history of the group's opinion of the book. This is definitely not an exact science (how does one compare Sidney Sheldon to Shakespeare?), but it does preserve the group members' feelings at the time the book was read and discussed. The idea of the pre- and post-ratings is to measure how a member has gained (or lost) appreciation for a book after discussing it with others. Recently, along with the post-discussion rating, we also have begun to ask each member to assign a word or phrase that best describes his or her feelings about the book.

After our discussion, we usually continue to socialize as we eat more dessert. Sometimes, we veer off into other activities (depending upon how tired and/or silly we are). One night we decided to write a novel (we have written the first few paragraphs and have outlined more); another night one of our members gave us an art lesson; on another occasion we watched the video of the movie version of our current book. Sometimes the host just can't get rid of us!

At each meeting, everyone contributes two dollars to the Society's treasury. These payments accumulate and at the end of the year we vote on a charitable organization to which we'll donate the money. Past recipients have included a local hospital, which purchased books for its children's ward, and an inner-city music school, which purchased music books. Our goal is to share our love of reading with those who may not be able to afford it.

As with most groups, the Society has suffered its share of growing pains. We have gone through periods when attendance has been low and too few members have completed the book to have a meaningful discussion. For us, the keys to surviving these troubled times have been persistence and a "spark." A spark can be the introduction of new members to replace those who, due to busy schedules and flagging interest, can no longer make a commitment to the group. New members add a whole new dimension to the group dynamics, and often offer opinions which may not have been previously expressed. Also, current members feel a renewed sense of dedication when it's the first discussion for a new member.

Another area that the group is constantly working through is the members' differing needs for structure and control. We have had many debates about the structure of the group itself, including, but not limited to, topics such as: discussion guidelines, agendas, rating systems, what should be included in our archives, who keeps the archives, whether we need archives, how books are chosen, when books are chosen, how new members are chosen, do we need a set of bylaws, who prepares the next newsletter, do we need a newsletter, etc.

Often, we have basically agreed to disagree. That is, we are all aware that each person has different needs in these areas. Some members would prefer to operate completely informally, with absolutely no structure; others like the idea of having bylaws, agendas, minutes, officers, and specific discussion outlines. Since this is an example of the very diversity we claim to value, we have agreed to leave it up to each member to do whatever he or she wants when hosting the meeting. This way, each member can have his or her needs fulfilled at some point during the year, and we can all look forward to variety in the format, as well as the content of each discussion.

Our list of books is, well, eclectic. It includes classics, modern fiction, and some nonfiction. We have experimented with different genres, such as short stories and plays. Some of the best discussions have been on books that have engendered widely differing opinions, such as *The Painted Bird* (ratings ranged the full gamut, from zero to four on this one) and *Frankenstein* (pro-creature v. pro-doctor). The topics suggested by some of the books discussed have included good v. evil, the nature/existence of a supreme being, equal rights, sex, power, domination, survival, racism, stereotypes, alcoholism, addiction, metaphysics, and the meaning of life. I guess it's easy to see why some discussions get a little heated!

Our advice to those of you looking to start or join a book club is simple. You need to keep only three things in mind: respect, diversity, and laughter. If the members truly respect one another, they will listen with an open mind to divergent opinions and read new and different books; it will be a true learning experience for everyone. If members are diverse—whether in gender, age, occupation, religion, ethnic background, life experiences—you will all benefit. And laughter is definitely the key.

Belonging to a book club can be one of life's most enjoyable experiences. Our members truly care about one another and have a good time because they feel free to be themselves. I'm sure these are the reasons our group has thrived for four years.

The Chapter Four Society is already planning a fifth anniversary party at a mountain retreat. As we continue to grow and learn, we know that our diversity and commitment will take us through our fifth year and into the next century.

Four Women Reading

Edie Jaye Cohen, Shelley Rose, Rita Wuebbeler,
and Lane Rappaport   **Atlanta, Georgia**

OUR READING GROUP, which is small, is as Lane Rappaport describes below, like a "well-made patchwork quilt." Like panels in a quilt, each of the four women in our group seems similar on the surface. However, a closer look shows our subtleties; each woman is unique, her voice strong and distinct. Each voice is represented in the following four essays that reveal how snugly the years have stitched us together.

Edie Jaye Cohen: The book group is the longest committed relationship I have been in as an adult. Four women comprise our group: two straight, two lesbians. Two of us are Jewish. Two of us are native southerners, and one is German. All of us are well traveled. Our ages span a mere decade, with three of us clustered in our mid-thirties. We are feminists all, and our desire to read books by or about women brought us together.

What has happened over the years, however, is that while the books remain our reason for meeting, we have become the story. Over simple meals or elaborate hors d'oeuvres, in one living room or another, through every season, ours are the stories we tell first, and I believe ours are the stories we come to hear. During a conversation one day, Rita commented that we had all been witnesses to a lot in each other's lives, and I was struck by that truth.

Over the years, the book group has alternately been for me a source of joy and ambivalence, and at times I have wanted to withdraw, not always finding there the sustenance I sought. I never have withdrawn or spoken of it, and now as I think of Rita's words and the three women with whom I share this experience, I know why: from one book group meeting to the next, we have chronicled our journey together from youth into maturity.

At some point years ago, we began bringing each other a bookmark from our travels. Before beginning any new book, I sort through my bookmarks and pick the one I believe will complement the story I am about to read. The connection is unclear, yet a relationship develops. The relationship consists of a story, a listener, and a means of marking place. The relationship I have to these three women is much the same. We are the story, and like a bookmark in a book, the book group marks our place in the passage of our lives together.

Shelley Rose: Our book group first got together in January 1988. I had just read Sonia Johnson's book *Going Out of Our Minds,* and I was so moved, confused, inspired, and activated that I needed to talk to others about the book. I invited (nagged) three friends to read the book and invited them over to discuss it.

We sat in front of a fire on the living-room floor with munchies and wine and had a wonderful, several-hour-long discussion. Topics from the book led us in numerous directions and our conversation branched off onto one road after another.

We all left that evening feeling so warm, close, and stimulated. We knew before the evening ended that we had to do it again. We set the next date and decided to each bring prose or poetry to read aloud and share with the group.

Almost seven years later, we are still at it. Meeting every four to six weeks, we easily reach consensus on a book to read. Book group feels as much like a support group as a reading group now. It is special time set aside to be with this group of women. Occasionally someone may not finish a book; sometimes we barely discuss the book. But, I always look forward to the time set aside for book group. If nothing else, it provides me with the reason I need to ensure that I read at least one book a month.

Rita Wuebbeler: Having left my native country of Germany eight years ago to live and work in the United States, I often long for the feeling of having family. The book group is part of my "new" American family that gives me support and nurturing. This occurs not only in the mental sense, but in the physical one as well, since one of our book group rituals is sharing a small meal together at the beginning of each meeting.

More important than the physical nurturing is the mental support and inspiration we give to each other. During the course of our existence, two of us have opened our own businesses (one selling bookmarks), one has found an editing job that she enjoys, and the fourth one is directing a regional arts advocacy organization that all of us support. One of us has bought a house, one has sold one, two have moved to new apartments and/or houses. We have taken trips together, held book group meetings at the beach and in the mountains. We have shared friends in far away countries ("Why don't you stay with my old friend in England on your next trip?"), and have been witnesses to each other's breakups and new loves.

The book group has made us a deeply bonded quartet that loves to read and share books, ideas, stories, and bookmarks, which we bring to each other from our journeys. And each bookmark represents a piece of the colorful tapestry of our lives woven into each other.

Lane Rappaport: Our small reading group can be described as a well-made patchwork quilt. We represent a hodgepodge of backgrounds and patterns that bring a richness to our discussions. Incorporating a true sharing of information, ideas, activities, and valued friendship, our group is unique. We are an interesting, supportive, energetic, cerebral, vibrant, vocal, and individualistic group of women, and we enjoy our time together very much.

This year marks our seventh year together. In our fast-track society, this seems an anomaly. Because of our stability, a definite community spirit exists. We perform various activities to enhance that community spirit and select books that help us understand more about the world and its people. For example, we made a weekend vacation from the idea of meeting in another city. We packed our bags and traveled to Florida. Besides enjoying the sunshine, the sea, and the beach, we thrived on the camaraderie of sisterhood.

Our book choice that month was *West with the Night* by Beryl Markham. Markham wrote autobiographically about her experiences in Africa and her solo flight across the Atlantic Ocean, from east to west (the first completed flight). It was an inspiring book filled with adventure and suspense. In a way, her book was symbolic for our reading group since we made an adventure that weekend. Perhaps soon we will truly make a patchwork quilt including squares of our book list titles.

Beach Book Group

Kathleen Hug   **Hermosa Beach, California**

I DECIDED TO start a book group after a friend in Chicago sent me *The Bean Trees* by Barbara Kingsolver, which her book group had read and enjoyed. I didn't have the first clue how a book group was conducted, but I liked the idea of being stretched and challenged by other's reading choices and opinions.

I recruited a friend to help spread the word, and we had our first meeting in October 1993. One member had attended a few meetings of a library book group. Other than that, none of us had ever been in a book group.

To get started, we each wrote down one title we wanted to read, and then agreed to select one title per month and to meet at a different member's home each month. We stressed that we wanted to read literature, but the only hard-and-fast rule at that point was no self-help books, since most of us had read our share of those. I was disappointed, but undaunted, when four out of the ten attendees at that first meeting chose *The Bridges of Madison County*—not the stretch or challenge I had in mind.

At the next few meetings, we continued to discuss how to structure the group. Only about half of us were finishing the books, and some of us didn't even buy them, instead coming to meetings just for the fellowship and social contact. We noticed that two or three members consistently came prepared and contributed, while another two or three consistently did not. Some members were unwilling to read a book a month, some were not interested in reading challenging material, and after a while, attendance dropped to four regulars.

When the one member who had book group experience and the greatest insight and most well-formed opinions about what we were reading moved to the East Coast, it became clear the group was not evolving the way the founders had hoped.

That Christmas, my Chicago friend sent me the original *Book Group Book*, and it became instrumental in forming clear guidelines for our group. We read excerpts from the book at meetings, and each month a different member would take it home. Infused with enthusiasm, we gathered the group to discuss the ideas we had gleaned, and decided we needed a lot more structure.

We elected a secretary to keep minutes. We gave the group a name. We restructured the book selection process so that each member would suggest two titles and provide information about the author and a brief synopsis of each book. Then the group, informed voters, chose one of the titles. This improved the quality of the selections. We decided that the person whose title we were reading would be the moderator of the discussion of that book, and that she should do some research on the author, obtain reviews and information about the book if possible, and lead the discussion. We decided that instead of reading a book in December, we would have a holiday party and exchange some of our favorite books.

Our most important and most difficult to enforce decision was to stress the importance of having all present fully prepared. We wouldn't actually throw anyone out for failing to finish a book, but we made it taboo. We wanted to discourage use of the group for social fulfillment only. We wanted to provide a forum of women who love to read and to share ideas. If the group was destined to shrink because of these guidelines, so be it.

The results have been encouraging. Attendance continues to wax and wane, but most members come prepared to participate. The addition of reviews and biographical information about the authors stimulates the discussion and the desire to read other works by the authors. We have enjoyed comparing our opinions to those of the reviewers.

Our book group serves many purposes. Primarily, it is a place where women from varied backgrounds can discuss ideas about books. However, it's also a place for fellowship, networking, and support. Although our interests are varied, we all share a love of books and a commitment to the growth and evolution of our book group.

By the way, we never did read *The Bridges of Madison County*.

Once Begun,
We Are Mighty

Carol Huber　　　　　　　　**Morton, Washington**

MY BOOK GROUP has saved my life. We meet once a month to discuss a book we have agreed to read. Sometimes we don't all read it; sometimes we don't read it all; and some of us, I suspect, don't read it until it has been discussed by the group.

We live in and around Morton, Washington, where the hottest spot in town is Spiffy's Fine Dining and Car Wash, and even they close at six. The whole town pretty much closes at six, although we have a new gas station with a machine that dispenses soft ice cream, even in the winter. Winter ice cream is just one of the things that's hard to find here. The letter T was missing from the post office front for more than a year—officially proclaiming us "Moron." The nearest movie theater is an hour west, but we can rent *How to Stalk an Elk* at Mike's Cable. We compensate.

Morton is in a little valley between Mt. St. Helens and Mt. Rainier. Surrounded by volcanoes we go on eating bacon and eggs—it's not cholesterol that clogs our veins.

We are all women in our book group, though Bert, the husband of one of our members, usually reads the book and sometimes hangs around for the discussion. Reading is women's work in this part of the woods. Most of us are schoolteachers, two are wives of schoolteachers, one is a social worker, and one a half-blind novelist. She reads Talking Books and the rest of us get ours from the library in Randle. Morton doesn't have a library. There was talk of getting one. "What for?" people asked, "Who would use it?" There are 1,200 people in Morton; those who insist on reading drive to Randle.

Barb (Bert's wife) calls the librarian with our book list and those who have library cards get a copy in the mail. Those who don't, search out paperbacks or make the drive to Powell's, a five-floor bookstore in Portland. Obviously they are serving most of the Northwest. The novelist calls Talking Books and they send tapes.

These methods are not wholly satisfying, even when implemented by our annual field trip to Powell's. Once, no talking book existed. Another time Barb went to Randle to order *The Bean Trees* by Barbara Kingsolver. But *The Bean Trees* had sixty-five holds! Barb had to come up with another book quickly. (She is very efficient.) Now it so happened that at the previous meeting a member had asked if anyone had read a book called *The Beans of Egypt, Maine*. "Beans," Barb thought, "Beans." We read *The Beans of Egypt, Maine*.

We read one book a month. We try not to choose really thick books two months in a row—it's hard for the teachers to get their reading done. Still, the books on our list are frequently thick. Once a year we read a nonfiction work and a classic novel. Those who knew we were going to be in the first *Book Group Book* were worried that our group wouldn't hold up and we'd look like a bunch of hicks. Choosing is difficult even without sixty-five holds. Although only one person wanted to read *Tess of the d'Urbervilles*, she forced it on the group. She was the only one who read it and claims she loves Hardy. The rest of us grew silent. Well, it was summer, and in summer, we're feisty. We have decided behind her back that she will not be allowed to choose any more books.

We have also decided to avoid books being made into movies. This rule was passed after we read *Prince of Tides*, *Fried Green Tomatoes*, and *Cold Sassy Tree*. We were upset to discover mid-read that Paris Trout was available on video.

Everything about the book-choosing business is testy. No one wants to commit herself to being wholly for or against a book. One loves it; one loathes it. What do you do? Liatris is a speed-reader and brings dozens of titles to the table. We can't read them all.

Having our group profiled in *The Book Group Book* has had an almost profound effect on us. I had a phone call from a Morton woman who claims she's never heard of me. This, apparently, means I cannot be living in Morton. All the group members bought copies and while Janet still disputes my first edition claim that she was in the bathroom reading the last chapter, one of the Lindas (we have two—it was her bathroom) vows she is going to finish every book this year.

We take turns leading the discussion and being the host. Our meetings go like this: about four of us are on time. Any four. These four usually know who is coming and who is not. Then we wait for Kathy. While we wait, we try not to talk about the book. Sometimes we spend this time deciding where we will meet next month. Our best-attended meeting is the picnic that heralds the end of the school year. This year the novelist brought Nola, a poet friend from Pennsylvania. (We don't read poetry. We consider it from time to time and lapse into silence. We did not tell this to Nola.) The group was such a hit she has invited us to come to her house for a meeting and we are saving up. "Stay in Morton," Nola says. "You can't get women like that just anywhere."

When Kathy arrives, Barb steers us quickly into the discussion. Barb is our leader, though we give her no credit. The discussion must be established firmly for at this point there is the danger that the teachers will take off on some school stuff and the rest of us will not be able to stop them. They are much better since one of us asked pointedly one night if we were going to talk about the book at all.

There is a slow start. Nobody wants to commit herself. Here lies danger. This is where it becomes likely that someone who has not finished the book will say that she found the work difficult to "get into." Anyone who hasn't finished repeats the comment and the book is condemned. This is what happened to *Tess*.

But when someone jumps in with a comment, we are off. Even those who didn't finish are eager to share observations and delights. Everyone finds something different and bits are read aloud. We almost had to carry the discussion of *The River Why* over for a second month for those who got bogged down in the first forty pages. Once begun we are mighty. The novelist says the book could be shorter by a third. Linda 1 remembers every twist of plot and Liatris is captured by the voice. The talk is delicious. It is not just because we love books. We know that whatever our families and careers provide, this is our cultural hub. I once heard a musician say she couldn't take it in the woods. I guess you don't form a group to read sheet music. We are all together, except for those who have gone to a soccer game or school board meeting.

After the success of that meeting, we've had a slow summer. Liatris went to France, and Barb is visiting the Dutch cousins. Bev was on a mountain top in Idaho, watching for fires. Marie made beet relish from her garden. Linda 1 was out with the horses. There are compensations.

In winter we are speedy. School and morning will come early. There may be black ice on the road. We will start on time and break for home as soon as we are slaked. But we go on. New members will be brought along by old. We are friends in the truest sense, as dependent on each other as the Donner party. Where we live our book group is life support.

PART III

Groups with a Twist

Some book groups are unabashedly special interest. They may read only nonfiction, or only fiction by gay men, or they may restrict membership to feminist women. Some have less formal agendas and probably wouldn't identify themselves as "special" in any way. But when you read about and visit as many book groups as I have, you begin to see that some groups really have stretched in an attempt to meet members' needs. These special-interest groups are flexible, not restrictive. You're a writer? Fine, join a book group—it will accommodate you. You say you hate book groups? Don't look now, but your group is so ad hoc, you don't even know it exists.

Throw the Book at Them

Jean R. Trounstine **Tewksbury, Massachusetts**

THERESA CAME UP to me after the first class and took off her baseball cap. "Thanks," she said, somewhat sheepishly, digging her foot into the floor, her eyes fleeing my face. "I liked the stories." We were an odd couple; me, a college professor carrying briefcase and books, and she, unemployed, a former addict and alcoholic, recently sentenced to literature and probation instead of prison. We stood together for that moment, not in a courtroom but in the president's office at a community college where I taught. Theresa had just completed her first seminar in Changing Lives through Literature, but she wasn't ready to go.

"What did you like about the stories?" I asked her, equally unsure of my footing, trying to read her desire to lag behind the others who had already left the classroom.

Snapping her hat back on her head, she looked up and smiled. "Those women. I'm surprised that I liked them because they're like me."

I continued to think long and hard about Theresa's comment as I drove home that evening, considering the six women I had just met. One lived nearby, but five had come twenty miles by van from a neighboring city in Massachusetts to

Middlesex Community College in Lowell. Women without much formal education, without transportation or support, they had been arrested over and over, been in and out of jail. They came armed only with hope. They had a desire to try once and for all to find a way out of crime through a deceptively simple program that I had the nerve to think might actually do what it advertised: change their lives.

I was no stranger to this population. I had worked in prisons in Massachusetts for the past seven years, creating a drama program that had taught me the power of the arts and humanities to transform lives. I had seen women, illiterate and insecure, become alive on stage. One key had been to help them create characters that used parts of themselves. Another was providing challenging literature that they felt was beyond their grasp. To make what was impossible, possible—that was my goal.

But here I was, trying another program, one I was beginning, in many ways like Theresa, for the first time. I had seen up close how our prisons are burdened by expense and repeat offenders. I had seen how many criminals are warehoused rather than trained or educated, how good programs are few and far between. I yearned to find out if I could make a difference with these women, women on probation. I had been impressed with the success rate of the men's program, started a year before. I wanted to create a program for women, to try to affect their lives before they got to prison.

As I drove home that first night, I thought about the women (whose names have been changed here to protect their privacy). Besides Theresa, there was Addie, a waitress who had dropped out of school in ninth grade and had no support from the father of her child. Devora, a woman with AIDS, whose record spanned several pages, had earned her GED behind bars. Jesse was twenty, a young mother with three children, unemployed, and living in a local shelter. Nina, a Latina woman with nine brothers and eight sisters, had never held a job or completed high school. Bonnie was a forty-three-year-old single mother and former prostitute with a history of childhood sexual abuse. Two of the women had bounced back to the streets before the first session ever began.

They all had done some prison time and had knocked around the criminal justice system, having served sentences for crimes such as possession of drugs, prostitution, assault and battery, shoplifting, and theft. But these women were different from their male counterparts. They had no support from worried wives and no encouragement to find jobs. Their drinking and drugging had often brought them abusive boyfriends who threatened their lives and parents who kicked them out of the house. Most had managed their pregnancies and young children alone. They all had lives of failed commitments, longings, and unfulfilled dreams. They all had ceased to believe in themselves.

Just like the mother in Tillie Olsen's short story, "I Stand Here Ironing," I thought, a bit smugly, proud of my choice, as I rounded the corner onto my tree-lined street. We had begun the seminar with this story because I knew the offenders would identify with both the mother and daughter characters. Most of women's literature does not take us into struggles on the high seas or paint pictures of fighting the elements, but rather shows us life in a smaller sphere where women triumph or at least survive against all odds.

The women had listened intently to find out about the characters while I read aloud. Afterward, we talked about whom they sympathized with. Like these offenders, Tillie Olsen's narrator struggles to make ends meet. She is deserted by her husband and has to make choices that are heartbreaking: putting her child, Emily, in an institution; going to work and leaving Emily with the lady in the downstairs apartment; bringing her home sick to a house full of other children. The daughter eventually finds fulfillment on stage but does poorly in school. Theresa had said, "The mother tries so hard to understand where she went wrong. But it's too late for Emily." I had assured her it was not.

*   *   *

Two weeks later, we all returned to the oblong table in the president's office, an academic environment that challenged them and a room that encouraged the women to feel special. They had been told to read Anne Tyler's *Dinner at the Homesick Restaurant*, to take notes and to think about the characters. They were not to be tested or quizzed; they would not have writing exercises.

What they brought to the table was their ability to understand, "to pick out what was most important," as Addie said, and to be able to listen to the insights of others. This time, Judge Joseph Dever, the judge who had sentenced most of them, and Val Harris, their probation officer, sat with them, as equals, ready to participate in the discussion. I chose Tyler's book because it emphasizes relationships and because I hoped it would enable the women to see that all families have problems.

Bonnie arrived late, her son having been in an accident. She talked about how hard it was to read the book, while working two jobs, going to school, and raising her children. Not surprisingly, she had mixed reactions about the mother, Pearl Tull, a cold but feisty lady who raises three kids in an unsympathetic world.

"That's my family," exclaimed Jesse, who looked to be a typical college student and, in spite of her homeless status, loved to read. She had dropped out of school in the eleventh grade after having a baby, and saw this program as a lifeline. "I understand my mother more after reading this book. Just like Pearl, you couldn't love her but you couldn't hate her. Every so often, she'd yell and scream, but you couldn't blame her, raising three kids all by herself." Somehow we all knew she was talking about her own strength, as well as her mother's. She had seen herself by understanding Pearl.

Nina, dark haired with solemn eyes, sat quietly, looking furtively around the room. She shrugged her shoulders when she finally admitted that she did not read the whole book. She "couldn't get into it," she confessed. "I had too many problems this week." I knew that Nina was in therapy and dealing with an abusive uncle who had terrorized her from childhood. Nina was confused, and reading about this family had frightened her. I asked her to write a book report to clarify her thinking after she finished it, but when we filed out of the room that evening, she ran quickly to the elevator, clutching her cigarettes.

I drove home that night, anxious and alone. Teaching this course was different from my regular college classes. I saw the women every two weeks. And in between they had to live their lives without drugs and alcohol, attending other programs required of their probation, and dealing with more stress, it seemed to me, than the average student. I wanted the books to touch them, teach them, and give them courage. I wanted them to feel the power of language and find that literature offers redemption, a way out; but their lives were dark. I feared that twelve weeks might leave them, like Nina, running for the elevator.

"Where is the hope in this book?" I asked the evening we were discussing Toni Morrison's *The Bluest Eye*. Nina, who had not turned in her book report, sat twirling her dark hair around a pencil. She looked up, "There is no hope. It's awful what happens to Pecola." Pecola, the sad African American girl who wants desperately to have blue eyes so she will fit into the white world, is raped by her father.

Bonnie agreed, saying she hated reading the book. Her repeated battles with alcoholism and drugs had landed her in prison. "A better place than home," she cringed, where she, like Pecola, had dealt with incest. But Theresa, an African American, heatedly began to argue with them, pointing out how Claudia, the narrator, survives to tell the story of her growing-up, with wisdom and insight into her community. She pointed out how Pecola is lost but not all children are. Bonnie then admitted she had hated reading the book because it hurt. All of a sudden Nina looked up and smiled at Bonnie, and in that brief exchange, they both realized that they were not alone. I wondered if that were as important as the lessons they learned from the characters.

"I think Claudia is the hope," said Theresa, defending a book she had read twice because she understood the world Morrison describes. We then discussed how we could all identify with Claudia, the survivor, the one who lives to tell the story. Nina, still struggling with her own memories of being abused, seemed unsure. I left the class, afraid we would lose her.

But it is not just the texts that are empowering for these women. A healing happens in the discussions, as they seek to understand together how characters get through their struggles. The class allows them to hear each other's perspectives, to share their ideas, and to see that their opinions are valued. Thus, by class three, the women had formed a bond, nodding at each other's comments, taking cigarette breaks together, laughing, and telling stories.

And so, Nina came back, to delight in Sandra Cisneros's *House on Mango Street*, the poetic tale of a Mexican American girl who grows up in a poor Chicano neighborhood in Chicago and dreams about having a home. Nina saw herself in Esperanza, whose name means "hope" in Spanish. She talked about her favorite part, the time when Louie stole a yellow Cadillac and flew down the street, followed by cops, with Esperanza waving at him. She talked animatedly about Esperanza's ability to survive with so little. Addie, divorced and wanting to get out of her waitress job, saw courage in Esperanza, who wants to move out of the ghetto. Nina proudly announced that Esperanza realized she must come back and help her people.

By this time, the probation officer told me she looked at the seminar as her bimonthly reading group. The class held an unexpected intimacy for all of us, including Judge Dever, a gentle man, who countered many of the women's negative experiences with men. We had originally imagined a female judge, thinking that some subjects would be better discussed with only women present. From the beginning, it was clear that we were primarily a group of women interested in women's issues. Men could participate in, but could not dominate the discussion.

Judge Dever became a role model in the class, not an authority figure: he listened, paid attention to what the women said, vigorously shared his ideas, and validated their insights. He felt our discussions were as interesting as those he had been in with other judges. I too was feeling free of constraints: no papers to correct, no tests, no grades. I had the luxury of listening and of enjoying many different perspectives. Changing Lives was changing me as well.

The women were growing in ways I hadn't anticipated. Theresa said she felt proud of her heritage after reading Toni Morrison and wanted to read all the rest of her books; she also enrolled in a local community college for the next semester. Jesse too decided on college, aiming to be a nurse. The other women reported feeling better about themselves; they were staying out of trouble and completing something they never imagined they could. The impossible was becoming possible.

With Barbara Kingsolver's *Animal Dreams*, the women almost fell into the room and began discussing the book as if it revealed the lives of their favorite friends. Jesse and Devora loved dissecting the male-female relationships as shown through the main character, Codi, and her Native American lover, Loyd. "I wish I had a man like Loyd," said Devora, whose boyfriend beat her, "but Loyd with one l, is he for real?"

The women laughed a lot that evening because the book allowed them to fantasize and act like kids sharing secrets. They talked about Loyd's strength and sensitivity. Nina decided he was a "wimp," but Devora kept wondering if she could ever find someone as kind as he. Jesse, facing the cold and winter at the shelter, wanted to focus on Codi, "a privileged woman," she said, "because she has a home." We all saw the character in a new way after that.

Jesse went on to compare Codi to Esther, the main character in Sylvia Plath's *The Bell Jar*, which we had read two weeks before, who also seemed to Jesse to have so much. "I never understood why she went crazy," she said of Esther, who is a promising young journalist, but who has not faced her father's death. The women started talking about the characters they had met, almost as if they were in the room. I didn't want our discussions to stop and wished sometimes that I could hop in the van and ride back with them to their homes.

Twelve weeks after we began, I entered a packed courtroom. Judge Dever, now in his robes, was in the lead. It was a regular district court day for the hundred or so people who milled around the first session, but for us, it was graduation day for Changing Lives through Literature.

The graduates sat in the front row with their families and friends. They were dressed up and ready to receive a positive judgment in a room where they had once been tried for their crimes. "All rise," the courtroom hushed and we walked up to the judge's bench.

Judge Dever began by saluting the women's achievements in the name of the law. I followed, telling the interested onlookers about the difficulty of the books we had read and about the nature of the course. Then, Val Harris gave the onlookers an overview of the women's plans for their futures. Judge Dever led us down into the courtroom, where one by one, we presented the women with framed certificates and roses. After the ceremony, Jesse asked the Judge to pose for pictures with her and her three daughters.

Changing Lives through Literature may not be for everyone. This program must be voluntary. In fact, some men and women have chosen to go to prison rather than be "sentenced to literature," as I often tell my community college students. Some offenders, perhaps as many as 65 percent, are illiterate, and these people can't be candidates for the program.

However, more than 100 men and 21 women with a combined record of more than 750 convictions have completed the course. "Only six have been convicted of new crimes and nine face pending charges," the *Boston Globe* reported of eighty men in August 1993, citing that men convicted of similar crimes had a far greater recidivist rate. Although the women's program is still too new for any statistics to be meaningful, we have had only a few rearrests and are encouraged that the program seems to be keeping people out of prison. Costing less than $500 per student, the program is far more cost-effective than prison at $30,000 a year per bed.

The women who choose this program are not necessarily avid readers, nor are they aware of the power of literature. They are, however, willing to look at their lives through the characters they meet. In discovering very dark places, they also find joy, new choices, new thoughts, and hope.

"This is just the beginning for me," said Theresa the day of graduation. And, as we walked out of the courtroom, I noticed she was carrying her books.

A Journey
down the River

Robert Waxler N. Dartmouth, Massachusetts

ON THAT FIRST night, Jeff came with his father, a man in his early fifties, I guessed, short and stocky, with a permanent limp and a cane. His stepmother stayed out in the parking lot, seated for over two hours in the front of the paneled truck, smoking, waiting for the two men to return from the humanities building with the news.

Much later, I would be told that Jeff's old man had spent several years in Walpole, the toughest prison in the state. He had come up to the university that night to make sure that his son made it into the classroom, an uncertain place, known to them only as a vague location on a college campus where a judge had sent eight criminal offenders to participate with me, an English professor, in discussions about literature. For these eight male offenders with 148 convictions among them, this kind of seminar, I assumed, beat going to jail.

Jeff quit school after eighth grade. He became a drug dealer, making, according to his own reports, more money than most college graduates. Now, twenty-two years old, with a young daughter and a dedicated girlfriend, he wanted a change, not only a change from the revolving door of drugs and violence, but a fundamental change of life, a change from the dead beat of late twentieth-century culture. Jeff would tell me later that I looked anxious that first night, a little frightened. I told him that he was wrong about that; he was the one with the sweaty palms. He was Pygmalion, and I was the professor. Or was it really the other way around?

I had always believed that good literature had a healing power. It could change lives. At its best, it made people self-reflective, thoughtful. And, yes, during the twelve weeks that these men gathered together to talk about stories concerned with male identity, violence, and confronting authority, literature did prove that it could make a difference. The initial anxiety that we all felt that first night gave way to a kind of magic. We found ourselves sitting around a table, listening to each other, amazed by the variety of perspectives. "How do I stack up against your college students?" Jeff wanted to know. In fact, they were all teaching me more than I could tell them.

One night we were discussing *Deliverance*, a novel by James Dickey about four suburban men who decide to take a white-water canoe trip through the backwoods of rural Georgia. These men on the water get much more than they bargained for. The journey down the raging river draws these middle-aged suburbanites into a confrontation with their own primal selves, finally killing one of them and permanently changing all of them.

In the novel, Lewis is the macho man in the group, the apparent leader, filled with confidence and possessing a hard and well-disciplined body. As we talk about Lewis that night though, we begin to see flaws in the man. His bravado inspires action, yet he seems overconfident. He strikes out without thinking and so never learns from his mistakes. His friends depend on him because they cannot depend on themselves. If they have become too comfortable and soft through suburban living, Lewis has become too egotistical and self-centered. In the end, it is not Lewis, but his buddy Ed who demonstrates genuine courage by delivering the men from the primal rage of the river.

"As I was reading the novel," said John, one of the offenders around the table that night, "I was trying to picture myself in the characters' places." John had finally identified, not with Lewis, but with Ed. Ed tended to lay back and wasn't the leader type, John claimed. "But when he had to, he took over. That's how I am. I procrastinate, but I can do what has to be done."

In a sense, both John and Ed must have recognized themselves through their experience, through that journey down the river. They became empowered, found their strength, understood they could make choices. And as I look back now on that first series of literary seminars for male offenders conducted nearly three years ago on the campus at UMass Dartmouth, I imagine that we all went through similar experiences in those twelve weeks in that seminar room. We were drawn together through language, articulating the shape of our selves through the limitations of characters discovered in stories. Around that long wooden table, we were all somehow set free.

I will be starting the ninth series of discussions soon, but that first one is the one I'll never forget. I compare the others with that one when I can, but often in memory the others simply blur into the original. I know though that all these men love adventure stories, plots with action that hold their interest. But once we get into the rhythm of discussion, it is not the plot but the characters that possess us. It is as if each character mirrors an aspect of our own lives.

Sea Wolf by Jack London remains one of our favorites, a story of a rugged sea captain, Wolf Larsen, a great American hero, once met never to be forgotten. Larsen is a man of gigantic passion and rage, a monomaniac committed to the belief that might makes right. He is convinced that power defines all relationships. In the story, Larsen is contrasted with Humphrey Van Weeden, a wealthy young man who at first cannot stand on his own two legs and who, unlike Larsen, believes in immortality and the value of the human spirit.

Van Weeden is a literary critic who remains passive and incapable of taking care of himself until he is thrown into a life-threatening confrontation with Larsen. Then, like Ed in *Deliverance*, he seems to gain the energy and aggressive power of self that allows him to emerge finally as a more complete man than his rival Larsen. In the story, Larsen dies; Van Weeden is delivered. "I used to be like Wolf Larsen," one of the men in the group claimed one time. "I thought I could manipulate everyone. I was stupid then."

These men are often filled with rage and over the years they have externalized that rage, often turning it against others. For them, the passive and dependent Van Weeden is a wimp who must remind them of some of the female school teachers who taught them literature and language in the classrooms that helped mark their failures. I like to believe that in the seminar room that image associated with language and literature changes for them just as Van Weeden changes and gains his manhood as *Sea Wolf* moves forward to its completion. The rage of these male offenders is shaped into the energy of words and that shaping power becomes its own ritual, a ritual validated for them by the other male participants around that long wooden table. We are all engaged during those moments in an initiation into a new world defined by language and literature.

If literature helps change their lives by making these men comfortable with language and themselves, the judge in this program also makes a difference. These criminal offenders have for too long felt isolated, as if they were caught in an enormous present moment, unable to extricate themselves from it. They have been marginalized and pushed aside by the mainstream. In essence they have been silenced. Language becomes a social force in these discussions, an enabling power that binds them together and allows them to recognize that they are capable of humanizing the world that surrounds them. They learn that they can create a future for themselves.

But these men have also felt the dull round of the criminal justice system, the punishing authority of a judge in dark robes. If literature is to change them by allowing them to connect with its magic, then the criminal justice system must also change in their eyes. Literature helps these men to see that there are many perspectives on an event, many interpretations of a story. It allows them to understand that as men they can legitimately pursue the meaning and complexity of literature and language. So too, through the rituals of this program they learn that judges can be more than the dark robes of authority.

It was after a tennis match that I first suggested to my friend Bob Kane, a district court judge, that we try this literature program. I had always believed that literature should play a central role in public policy issues and so I challenged Bob with an idea. "Take eight tough guys coming before your bench who you are ready to send to jail and send them instead up to the university for a series of discussions about literature," I suggested. "If you're willing to do that, I'm willing to design the seminar and lead the discussions."

And so it began. No doubt it took considerable courage on the part of the judge, a feared prosecutor in an earlier phase of his life, to agree to such an apparently soft idea, but once we got going we realized that the judge himself was not only an important administrator in the process, but a central participant in the drama of changing the lives of all those seated around that seminar table. He too claims that it's been one of the best experiences of his life.

As a professor of literature, I could engage in discussions with these men as part of my expected role, but this judge, Bob Kane, proved unusual in this context. For the criminal offenders, a judge traditionally represented the enemy, a symbol of the criminal justice system that punished them. Ordinarily, the image of the judge confirmed their alienation from the mainstream of society. He was an authority figure who menaced them, and who refused to validate their humanity. He was the dark robe that simply passed judgment on their criminal behavior, often with only a few perfunctory words.

Judge Kane rewrote that story for these men. Not only did he give them another chance by recognizing their promise, but he often sat at the table with us, contributing his insights and interpretations of the literature. He became a voice equal to the other voices around that seminar room. For the criminal offenders, the judge became a man among other men, still a representative of the authority of the criminal justice system, but now also a representative with a human heart ready to certify and validate these other men as part of a group that included him. In open court, as part of a final graduation ceremony, these men received praise and certification of their work from the judge. As a result, the story of the relationship between these men and the criminal justice system changed.

The men in this program are smart. They have often survived brutal family histories, drug and alcohol addiction, and their own pent-up rage. They range in age from nineteen to forty-five. Some are married; some are not. Some have children of their own—a future that they want to contact, even help to nurture. Language and literature can help deter violence and crime and at the same time add important dimensions to a sense of manhood. These men know that now.

As Jeff once put it, walking into a college classroom where his opinions are valued by a college professor and a judge was a challenge superior to the one he found on the streets. I am convinced that through their reading and discussion of literature, these men are all bringing hope away from that long wooden table in our seminar room.

Serious Reading

David Wellenbrock **Stockton, California**

A MAJOR PLEASURE of reading serious nonfiction books is discussing the ideas in those books. In college, this discussion is not limited to the classroom. Instead, a common fund of knowledge is built and the sources of this knowledge often find their way into conversation and discussion all over campus. But after college and outside a university setting, this common fund tends to dissipate and seems sometimes not to exist at all. The result is that many of us read fewer and fewer serious nonfiction books. About fifteen years ago, I found a few people who agreed with me that the added fillip and pleasure derived from the fairly hard work of reading such books was missing from our lives.

Initially, we tried to remedy this with a reading group, consisting of three and then four couples. That group originally intended to read about half fiction and half nonfiction. But the mix of personalities was unsuccessful and the group imploded after two years.

Almost immediately, in October 1982, we set up another reading group. This group had some different guidelines and a new composition. The group is faithful to those guidelines and is thriving, twelve years and more than eighty books later.

Thinking about it, we see four main reasons for our success: quality membership, a challenging reading list, stable organization, and a regular order of proceeding.

What We Look for in Members

Membership is critical. There is a need for some diversity of perspective, but it cannot be so great that every discussion reduces itself to first principles. There is also a need to maintain a reasonable size—a sufficient number so that various viewpoints are expressed, but not so many that the participants have little opportunity to talk. We started with six members and immediately increased to eight. For a number of years we worked very hard to make sure every member could make every meeting. We now have eleven members and assume that two to four members will miss each meeting. This leaves us in fine shape, as we have found that eight participants is a very good number for a discussion.

We were fortunate at the time of formation to have four of us who had known each other for about twenty years (three classmates and a professor). This started us off with a large common fund of knowledge and a core membership of very compatible people.

We've had some turnover through the years, but we've been careful about making additions. We try to keep professions and perspectives in balance. Specifically, we are careful not to invite too many lawyers or people associated with Raymond College, University of the Pacific. Members have included lawyers, college professors, bureaucrats, students, business people, a farmer, a journalist, a doctor, a dentist, and a state legislator. The group has a social aspect also, and we try to nurture it by selecting compatible, nice people.

We have, on occasion, invited people for a specific meeting. For example, we were joined by an eastern European immigrant for a discussion of Vaclev Havel. For the discussion of *The Enigma of Japanese Power*, we invited a college professor who had taught history in Japan for a number of years during the postwar period and who was returning for the pending school year. Group membership was not offered to these guests, but everyone seemed to enjoy and benefit from the variation.

When selecting members, particularly if the nominee is known to only one person, we generally invite the person for a single session and, if the group reaction is favorable, suggest full membership a few days later. We have had a number of one-meeting members. But we keep the situation from being uncomfortable by extending invitations only for one session.

Losing members is a more serious problem. When members move out of the area, there is no issue. Even a member who rarely shows up isn't much of a problem. In such a case, we keep the person informed of the next meetings for a while, but if they miss several meetings in a row, we ask if they want to continue. If they do, we let them know that if they miss two successive meetings, they will be dropped. In such a case, we simply don't inform them of the next session. A bigger problem occurs when a member is not working out, or becomes disruptive. In this case, the group must do something.

The major sources of disruption are a lack of intellectual honesty, continual negativity in discussion, and failure to maintain the scope and course of the discussion. Presumably, a member or two must talk to the disruptive force, explain the problem, and agree on a course of action. The person may have to be dropped from the group.

This summary of what's disruptive in turn gives some insight into what we're looking for in potential members. The primary qualities are that members be nice, well informed, intellectually honest, and self-confident. "Niceness" is under-valued in America at this time, but there's a lot to be said for civility, manners, and consideration; the group is an impor-tant social, as well as intellectual, element in our lives. We value people who are sufficiently informed and bright so that they can make positive contributions to the meetings and discussions. We also want people who will follow the evidence and logic. And it is important that members don't take the discussions personally—to attack a strongly held idea is not the same as attacking the person who holds it, but by the same token, in attacking an idea or intellectual position, members must be sure not to attack the person holding that idea or position.

Reading Challenging Nonfiction

Our reading list, while selected by consensus, consists of nonfiction. (We have not been absolutists and have actually selected a couple of novels. However, the primary motivation for one selection was that one member denied having read a novel for about forty years. It seems unlikely that another novel will be selected in the near term, unless it is virtually speculative thinking, such as Carl Sagan's *Contact*.) As evidenced by our reading list, social sciences, public policy, and philosophy have formed the core of our readings. Occasionally we have selected a topic rather than a particular work.

Members make recommendations in various manners. Among these have been: bringing in a book and letting everyone take a look at it; bringing in a book review; nominating and describing the book verbally. Fortunately, our members don't have agendas and the selection process has not posed any significant problems. The number of recommendations waxes and wanes and we try to keep a bit of a backlog for lean times. (Often the backlog serves as a springboard for other nominations.)

Often a very new book is nominated. We generally try to wait at least six months before having a go at such a book. On a practical level, the book will probably be out in paperback and more readily available at the library. What's more, the media hype will be off the book.

In selecting a book, it is not necessary that everyone falls in love with it. Indeed, some of our best discussions have been about books with which everyone, or nearly everyone, had serious disagreements. For example, *Anarchy, State, and Utopia* by Robert Nozick came under heavy criticism, but on the way home one member commented that the discussion was so good, it should have been tape recorded.

Our reading has not been subject specific, but we do tend to return to themes. These themes are long-term interests of the membership, even though we have never attempted to delineate what they are. They have evolved as the membership has changed, as the temper of the times and intellectual thought has changed, and as we have increased our common fund of knowledge.

Part of the value of a reading group is the element of randomness and breadth it gives to its members' own reading. It provides sufficient impetus to read books one might otherwise slough off. It provides reading suggestions that one simply would not come across, if left to one's own resources. Other people's preferences push us out of our intellectual nests. Our method of book selection has served us well; it is a benefit that is appreciated more and more as time goes on.

Stability, without Ironclad Organizing Principles

Our group has little organization. A self-appointed secretary has maintained records of what was read and where we have met and when. In the early years, that person was responsible for any rescheduling that was required, but that role has been eliminated. Now if anyone wants to reschedule, that person has to do the arranging. Rescheduling has almost been eliminated because, as mentioned above, we have increased our membership and accepted the fact that people will occasionally be absent.

The group has been very careful about making changes. The formula we have developed has been successful over many years. Undoubtedly, much of the success has to do with the membership. But it is believed that our conservative approach to changing the group has been important. When changes are made, it is generally by consensus and they are made over the course of a few meetings, rather than at a single setting. For example, we have never added more than two members in any one year so that the group culture could be maintained. When we did add two members at the same time, they were couples.

We do not appoint a discussion leader for any meeting. Typically, the discussion begins spontaneously. Many of our members have taught so someone is always ready to fill the initial void with a question, often directed at the book's nominator. Discussions have no format and they are generally wide ranging. The less interesting the book, the wider the field of discussion seems.

A Regular Order of Proceeding

While we don't have ironclad rules for discussion, an order of proceeding has evolved and is now well established. We meet at 7:30 P.M. and as soon as most of the expected members arrive, we address the housekeeping issues.

The first question is when will we next meet. We generally try to meet every six or eight weeks. If we meet more frequently, the reading becomes a chore rather than a pleasure. In addition, this permits enough time to obtain the book, which has been a problem at times. If we meet less frequently, interest fades. Obviously, there are deviations, particularly around Christmas.

The next question is where will we next meet. Meetings are rotated from home to home, though not in any strict order. We go to Eric's only once each year as he lives in San

Francisco, and that is generally on a Friday evening. The host provides coffee and pastries.

The most intriguing question is what will we next read. This can take some time to answer, but the process is interesting in itself. Some books have been nominated intermittently before finally being accepted or dropped. The most successful nominations are when the book is brought in, rather than merely described or presented through a review.

Generally, by this time, everyone has arrived and the discussion begins. The meetings run between two and three hours. There is no preset termination time.

We would be glad to answer inquiries about our group and why it has worked so well for so many years.

For this group's reading list, see page 332.

A Good Little Idea at Work

Joanne Simon and
Lisa Soufal   **Appleton, Wisconsin**

IT'S A FRIDAY afternoon in December on a blustery Wisconsin day, and about thirty local company members have braved the weather to gather at a nearby hotel for lunch. As everyone fills a plate and ambles into the room, they are given a random seating assignment. Then, after exchanging a few pleasantries, they get down to their real business for being there. A high-powered corporate meeting? Not exactly. They're talking about this month's book.

"Oh, a book club," you might yawn. "At work? How stuffy." But our group of corporate book worms is far from dull. In fact, as a new participant who had dutifully read the book and was prepared for a polite roundtable discussion, I was surprised to find myself laughing out loud and enjoying the free and easy exchange of ideas. Not only do we discuss the hottest new books from the business shelves, we also take the gold mine of new information leaping off the pages in those books and apply it to our own jobs. At AAL Capital Management Corporation in Appleton, Wisconsin, the founders of this club have reinvented one of the most time-honored ways of discussing new ideas and used it to inject new energy into the corporate culture. They've created their very own Book of the Month Club—at work.

AAL Capital Management Corporation is a NASD securities broker-dealer and a subsidiary of Aid Association for Lutherans, one of the nation's leading fraternal benefit societies. From its inception in 1987, AAL Capital Management Corporation has grown from seven employees to 103 employees and has attained more than two billion dollars in assets under management. It is the third largest mutual fund company in Wisconsin, and it ranks among the top 100 fund management companies in the country. Success leaves clues, and at least some of those clues might have been found in a bestseller or two from the business book section.

At this particular meeting in December, we are talking about *The Ten Commandments of Business and How to Break Them* by Bill Fromm. We found a lot of good ideas in this book, even if some of them made us laugh. For instance, Fromm suggests that hugging your coworkers and customers might not be a bad idea. As we discussed this prospect, most of us were uneasy with it, and, as you can imagine, this became a standing joke for months to come.

But the fact that we can joke together is a testament to the woman whose idea it was to start the Book of the Month Club in the first place. The president, Rochelle Lamm Wallach, has a long dossier of successes, and she believes wholeheartedly in encouraging "personal ownership" in the company. This value has rubbed off on company employees, which is particularly evident at the Book of the Month Club meeting where all trust that their opinions will be taken seriously. They will be heard. We are encouraged to talk freely and openly in small groups and to the group at large, to argue our points, and to listen to what others have to say.

In addition to talking about the book itself, the book club is seen as a forum for bending the president's ear without fear of talking too much or stepping on toes. In fact, Lamm Wallach encourages that sort of thing. Mostly she listens, sometimes she talks, but she always appreciates the input.

"From time to time I hear from people that they were up late at night pacing the floors about a company issue," Lamm Wallach recently said to the group. "Next time you're up pacing, call me!" she commands. "Chances are, if you're up, I'm up doing the same thing." Everyone laughs, but they know she's serious.

On May 19, 1993, the company held its first book club luncheon. It was organized in an effort to capture some of the great business ideas already discovered and published in books, and so far it is working. Books are chosen through suggestions from the group. Each month a new book with a business-related topic is introduced to the company and made available to anyone who wants to participate.

Everyone in the company is invited to the meeting—from the newest entry-level clerks on up through the ranks of the senior officers. The group is truly a collage of the company—managers, customer service representatives, vice presidents, secretaries, accountants, lawyers, and marketers. Our president hosts the luncheon for the month's participants, where they discuss the morsels of truth and knowledge found in the books, and then talk about how they can apply them to AAL Capital Management Corporation.

Books are chosen through suggestions from book club participants, company members and bookstore advice. We also survey participants from time to time to find out how the group can be improved, from the timing of the meetings, the type of books we read, to what we eat for lunch and how "heart healthy" our meals should be. Many of the books are on display in the company vending area to generate interest in the book club.

Reading a book might seem rather elementary compared to the high-powered seminars and workshops offered today, but we've discovered that real gems are often found in something simple. Above all, it brings people together.

Shirley Hearden, a retirement plan specialist who has been with the company since its beginning, thinks the book club is a great melting pot of employees. "Especially as we grow larger, this gives us a chance to interact with people we wouldn't have a chance to otherwise," she said. "I enjoy hearing other points of view on things, and everybody seems to pick out something a little different to share with the group. Plus it rewards me for reading the books!" Hearden happened to win the grand-prize weekend getaway for two to the Pfister Hotel in Milwaukee and tickets to a show, awarded for faithfully reading all of the books last year.

Bookworms who have unblemished reading records for the year are all eligible to receive a prize. This year, nine people were in the running, and it was a very exciting moment at the book club luncheon when their names were dropped in a hat and winners were drawn at random. In addition to the grand prize, the second-prize winner won an evening for two at a performing arts center with dinner at a restaurant of his or her choice, and the third prize was season tickets to a local theater company. Much to their delight, the other six diligent bookworms each received a fifty dollar gift certificate to a bookstore, a useful and worthy consolation gift for this group.

The prizes and luncheons are fun, but one of the most truly rewarding reasons to start a book club at work is to see how ideas and resources found in books can translate into real, tangible results in the workplace. Sometimes, when our group feels strongly that a new idea could help solve an issue in the company, separate committees spin off from the group to hammer it out and create a workable policy. Even the smallest change in policy or procedure can have powerful results.

For example, after reading the book, *Customers for Life*, by Carl Sewell, the group was inspired to talk about giving higher levels of "empowerment" to all employees, which they narrowed down to mean "energizing people to improve quality, productivity, and employee satisfaction." They discovered that feeling empowered to make decisions and solve problems critical to the company's success was of great importance to them. The president agreed that the issue was a big one that needed to be addressed in more detail. A group of three employees met to do more research, and reported their findings to the book club.

During that process, a very important chain reaction occurred. Those three people went back to their departments and talked about empowerment with their superiors and to other employees in department meetings. Giving employees the resources to make decisions on their own became even more integrated into management goals, and soon managers all over the company were taking a closer look at their departments to see how empowerment could fit in. In big ways and small ways, managers started paving the way for employees to use their own good judgment and take the initiative to solve a customer's problem. Empowerment is now a flourishing component of the company's philosophy.

The volunteer facilitator of the book club often comes up with creative and imaginative ideas to enhance the discussion. When we read *ZAPP! The Lightening of Empowerment*, by Bill Byham, our current facilitator, Lisa Soufal, created buttons for the group featuring a martian holding a zap gun and saying, "I've been ZAPPED!" She also made a beanie hat with lightening bolts on the sides. During the meeting, each person who came up with a great idea wore the ZAPP hat until somebody else came up with an idea, at which time the hat was transferred to the sound of a ZAPP from a toy zap gun. We had so much fun we decided that this book should be mandatory reading for the officers of the company, and so they each received a copy and also discussed the book.

While experiencing such palpable results might whet one's appetite to start a book club at work, at our company that's not the sole reason employees like to get involved. Many of those attending the book club feel that even if all of the talk never manifests in immediate changes in their jobs, it affects their work just the same.

The books and discussion provoke a deeper look at their attitudes and remind them that their contributions, whatever they may be, play an important role in the company's success.

After the meeting, it's only natural that when employees return to their desks, they bring with them a new sense of purpose and a few more reasons to be committed to their organization and to their careers.

For this group's reading list, see page 314.

Writer's Group 101: The Evolution of a Book Group

John M. Roderick **West Hartford, Connecticut**

IT STARTED OUT as small as small-world stories get. I was browsing along the book displays at the annual convention of the American Society of Journalists and Authors in New York City when a remotely familiar voice asked, "Is that really you?" I looked up and there was the bright, smiling face of Patricia, one of my star "older" students in a course in feature writing of some ten years ago. We laughed at our simultaneous "What-are-you-doing-heres?" and joined each other for the conference lunch.

I learned that Patricia had continued with her avid interest in writing and had developed that talent into a successful one-woman company where she produced scripts, brochures, and a host of related writing projects for clients in industry and the business world. She learned that her old journalism instructor still had a penchant for the more creative side and had just completed his first novel and was wondering what to do with it now. Patricia gasped in amazement. "I did, too!"

At the ASJA convention luncheon, to a massive crowd filling the banquet hall of the Hyatt Regency, then Mayor of New York Edward Koch, was presenting a keynote speech on his book that recently hit the bestseller list. He was explaining how he always wanted to write and why he chose to write about his experiences as mayor. As he absorbed the communal admiration from this group of fellow writers, Patricia and I exchanged glances and said almost simultaneously, "We could be up there."

There was no boasting in it: just the realization that successful writing starts with the desire to write; develops with the discipline to write; improves with the willingness to revise; evolves with the courage to send work to editors; and succeeds when all of the above combine in some kind of serendipity and a publisher says "yes." From that moment on, I think both Patricia and I had resolved that our closet novel writing efforts were going to become more public.

Our public sharing would begin in a modest way: we agreed to send each other a draft of our completed novels. A month later we met again over lunch and talked nonstop for three hours about the strengths and weaknesses we saw in each other's work. We moved to discussing other writer's books. She said it reminded her of when she was in my class ten years before. It reminded me of the same thing only this time I was learning as much about my own efforts in this writing pursuit as Patricia was about hers. Our mutual excitement about how our scratchings on paper moved another person to laughter or tears fueled the same fire that must be smoldering to spend so much time at this activity we call writing in the first place.

We decided then and there that this experience of sharing words in such critical detail was too valuable to lapse into a typical it-was-nice-bumping-into-you departure. Patricia knew two other writers, a publisher of a small weekly newspaper and a budding psychologist with a penchant for capturing the unusual in the ordinary events of our lives. Thrown together by the energy and enthusiasm of Patricia, our writer's group of four evolved.

We began meeting once a month at Patricia's house. We had agreed that each of us would bring whatever we were working on and share it with the group by reading it aloud. I'm not sure why but we never reached a consensus that an added element would be gained if we also brought copies for the others to read. We agreed that hearing the writer read his or her own work gave a dimension that might otherwise be lost in our interpretation of their words. I suspect, however, that, in my case anyway, the pressure of the deadline of these monthly meetings had just as much to do with my resistance to making copies for everyone ahead of time. There was no "ahead of time." Often it was just knowing that I would be meeting with these three other writers and that *they* would be bringing something to the table that motivated me to produce.

In fact, that was the first benefit of the group that manifested. It made us all imminently aware that our writing was not for ourselves only; it was for an audience and we owed that audience something. Knowing that the reader over my shoulder (or in this case, the listener) was there, changed the process of my writing or, at least, part of the intent. I had always wanted to be true to the vision I was trying to capture in words, but now I became vividly aware that I wanted others to like that vision also.

Soon we discovered that many of the problems that we were encountering as writers had a common ring to them. What does point of view really mean? How is it established? Does it matter if it shifts? We wondered how other writers solved these problems. Before long we were bringing other peoples' work to our gatherings—published works of those who had found a solution.

We began reading each other's discoveries. Sometimes they were successful novels whose practitioners discovered techniques that worked (Elmore Leonard's practice of getting inside the head of a multiplicity of players or Judy Blume's immediacy of first person). Sometimes they were articles, like those in *The Writer* or *Writer's Digest*, that explored technique. Nonfiction as well as fiction found in magazines helped us formulate our ideas and served as models to emulate in our own writing. Our fledgling writer's group was becoming a book group without us ever intending it to happen.

The personal effort that I brought to the proceedings was a thorough revision of that novel I had shared with Patricia, chapter by chapter, month after month. There was enough continuity of the story and story line for my audience's insights to grow more and more valuable as we all got deeper into the tale. We took notes throughout our readings. Each, in turn, talked to the writer about what he or she specifically liked or did not like. The critiques were offered in a manner of mutual respect and kindness, even when our evaluations were harsh. We grew to trust this harshness, and the revisions that resulted were always improvements, sometimes dramatic ones. We embellished with examples we discovered elsewhere ("remember when Joyce Carol Oates wrote . . ." or "imagine if John Irving were writing that scene: how would it change?").

We often found things to laugh about during our exchanges—an essential ingredient to balance the sometimes negative reactions. We usually started each session by filling each other in about the rest of our lives during the month since our last get-together. A lot can happen in a month. Patricia was in a serious boating accident in one interim. Judy's divorce became final. The other Judy's newspaper folded. I was hospitalized. But whatever events shook our lives, we continued to write and to read and to share these efforts with each other.

Support groups have grown important in our society where a hectic pace often mitigates against making real connections. And support for writing, with its whimsical nature and sometimes resistant spirit, is no exception. We each grew as writers from the experience. Contributing significantly to that growth were the examples we drew from other writers who became a part of our discussion and our mutual reading background.

Under the guidance of this writer's-reader's group, I completed that first novel and have begun the pursuit for an agent. Patricia is well on her way toward finishing her novel. Judy the editor came up with numerous editorials that found their way to her readership. And Judy the psychologist discovered the voice that allowed her to share her ideas with a larger reading audience.

We all benefited through sharing what we were reading, the books and articles that said something to us. Our writing improved, to be sure. We gained insights into the process and how we related to that process. Through the immediate reaction of this audience we had grown to trust so fervently, we came to appreciate the potential power of our own words as well. We became motivated to continue with an activity that, at times, repays us with little more than frustration and rejection. But we persist. We know that if we can move this small group with our words, we can move the world as well. What's more, it goes without saying, we became friends.

Woven between the dozens of stories and scripts and chapters shared were the events of our lives that made us more than just writers and readers; we were people who wrote and read. That recognition of what we had in common helped us to appreciate our individual uniqueness as well. Writer's Group 101: it became as vital as the words we wanted to share.

Nubian Pathways to Community

F. R. Lewis   **Albany, New York**

NUBIAN PATHWAYS IS a bookstore that grew from a study group, six men who met in each other's homes and did not find in Albany—once the inner-city neighborhood's only independent bookstore gave up the fight—books that addressed issues affecting their community, their families, their friends, and themselves. Most of the books they sought came from small, black-owned publishing houses that distributed mainly, if not entirely, to larger metropolitan areas.

Now that Nubian Pathways is in business, books are on the shelves and the store's coowner Nathaniel Bracey—a member of that founding study group—can produce multiple copies of any title within a week. The three book groups currently meeting in his store plan two books ahead, however, and grant at least a month for books to come in.

"I let them know what's out there and they pick what they want to study," Bracey says. "The nonfiction groups read history, social and political science, psychology, books on crime, health, family. They perform a kind of collective research. The literature group reads black bestsellers."

There is a symbiosis between business building and community building: a kind of business as fellowship. Nubian

Pathways is the first, and only, black bookstore in New York State's capital city, located up the avenue from a music store and next to a black-owned beauty shop. Bracey describes the store and the reading groups as part of a surge of interest by blacks in their heritage, a reaction, in a way, to the civil rights movement.

"What we're doing—whether reading fiction or scholarship—is learning how to make our lengthy history on this planet part of our current lives. That's been the challenge to blacks in the eighties and now in the nineties."

Something basic to community, something almost ritual in nature and seemingly descended from the time people explored the mysteries of their lives by firelight happens during book group sessions, as six to ten men and/or women discuss the books they've chosen, a circle of talkers together working toward understanding the problems that plague and the joys that enrich their times and lives, sharing discoveries and understandings.

During two hours Sunday afternoon and Monday and Tuesday nights at the close of the business day, in the rear of the store, each group occupies a sofa, office-type wooden desk chairs, and metal folding chairs. The rug touched by the soles of each shoe might be handmade, and participants meet in a setting of coral painted walls, ceremonial masks, dark-skinned faces that look out from book jackets, African wood carvings, dashikis, woven grass bags—not too much of any one thing—and the candelabrum of Kwanzaa, an African American holiday that celebrates a code of behavior, as well as individual and group accomplishment. The groups are part of the store's atmosphere, customers are in and out the front door to browse shelves and to inquire how they might become part of this community of readers.

Nubian Pathways opened on Central Avenue in July 1993. By September, a woman named Peyton Harrison had gathered other women to make a group called the African-American Literature Club and approached Bracey and his partner, C. Neal Currie, to talk about meeting space. The women find their connections through fiction: bestsellers by black writers, books in which old and new, ongoing legend and ongoing life often combine to help nurture the spirit of community. Among topics generated during the discussion of Gloria Naylor's *Mama Day*, for example, were angels in the New Age, violence on television, and the meaning of family; the session concluded with an astrology reading by one of the participants.

"Even in our fiction group the study is serious. The discussion is not only of the work as literature, but also in terms of what the story means now. And a bestselling novel or short story collection by a black writer wasn't necessarily published last week."

Bracey and Currie added a sign-up/interest list to the brochures displayed on the front countertop. Before long, a Monday night nonfiction group got underway. Then there were men and women who came in and said, "I have an idea," and "I want to know," and "I want to meet." Some of these eager individuals ended up in groups that met on Friday nights and Saturday afternoons. The newest group, the Tuesday night nonfiction, got underway in September 1994. Typically, Bracey attends the first few meetings, helping members learn to be part of a study group.

"People are new to each other and may be new to the process," says Bracey, "so it's important for the owner to help each group establish a rhythm and then to let them know you're available as a resource."

Not every group has been successful.

"A successful group has a core: members of a successful group commit to attend every meeting," says Bracey. "We insist on it: that prospective members promise to attend every meeting. The other thing a group needs to be successful is to complete its assignments."

By completing assignments, Bracey means more than reading each book, more than contributing to each discussion, more than being prepared when one's turn comes to act as facilitator. (The groups have no formal leader; Bracey is an occasional guest.)

"Their assignment is to bond as a group," Bracey says. "That takes not only chemistry, but lots of hard work. Each member can have his or her say, they can even argue, but they need to respect each other."

The Friday and Saturday groups did not complete their assignments.

The owners of Nubian Pathways expect new groups will form, however. Once a book group has met several times, has established the identity that comes from "bonding," it tends to be less welcoming to new members.

"And there are other things to keep in mind," Bracey says. "Suspending the groups for the summer is a good idea. We did that this year—ended in June, picked September dates and books—and come September, everyone was eager to be underway."

For members of the fiction group, the writer of the novel or short story collection they read for each monthly meeting "tells our stories and we become a part of the tradition of passing those stories along." For the nonfiction group, one topic can absorb several meetings as members consider books that range from popular to scholarly.

Historically, the types of groups sheltered by Nubian Pathways have arisen naturally, spontaneously, randomly. A few people discovered shared interest in a subject, began to meet, study, explore. In a manner of speaking, Nubian Pathways stimulates and encourages formal reproduction of this phenomenon. The bookstore provides a center, group members agree, brings people together, helps foster community, makes the books, the writers, the topics, the heritage important by paying attention to them.

The bookstore and its reading groups serve a social function as well. One woman coming to Albany from a neighboring state sought companionship in an activity she already loved. A man from Guyana learns more about his adopted country.

"And what you learn by talking about the books you've read tends to stay with you," book group participants agree.

Bracey's business partner and fellow study group member, Currie, has been known to describe Nubian Pathways through its book groups as functioning as a "modern barber shop, people coming together to discuss serious issues in a social setting." Like Bracey, he feels the enterprise builds a sense of community, he calls it, "community of shared interest," and a collective responsibility for what happens in and to that community.

Out of all this activity, a new group has been spawned. Friends of Nubian Pathways is described by Bracey as an "extended family." Nubian Pathways and its Friends have joined student groups at the University of Albany to present public programs by notable black writers and scholars in a downtown setting. Altogether, the commercial enterprise, its book groups, and its Friends are part of a movement that promotes community, as well as the reading of books.

Let Your Goals Determine Your Guidelines

John W. Hasbrouck   **Chicago, Illinois**

I'VE HEARD IT said that "reading alone is like drinking alone," but for some reason I just couldn't bring myself to agree. I've always loved to read alone. How could it be a vice? Then I began to understand. It's not that one shouldn't read alone, but that reading and discussing a book with others is simply better. Being in book discussion groups has made me a better reader, speaker, and listener.

In early 1993, I formed two book discussion groups in Chicago. One was a great books discussion group concerned with liberal education for adults, formed through the Great Books Foundation. The other was a special-interest group concerned with exploring a specific genre of imaginative literature. This group was formed through an independent library and archival institution.

The distinct goals of the two groups make for an interesting study in contrast. The different formats appropriate to them as determined by their respective goals tended to illuminate one another. While I had my hands full leading two groups, I found that my experience in each helped me view the other with a fresh perspective.

I became interested in great books through the work of philosopher and educator Mortimer J. Adler. Dr. Adler cofounded the Great Books Foundation in 1947, and he has championed great books discussion since the twenties. Great books discussion exists for adults who want to improve their understanding of fundamental ideas, and their skills in the liberal arts of reading, speaking, and listening.

An important moment leading to the formation of the group occurred when I discovered Dr. Adler's unpublished manuscript, "Manual for Discussion Leaders: Preliminary Draft for Use in Great Books Community Groups." From it I learned the nuts and bolts of great books discussion. Of course, I could learn only so much without actually leading a group, but I did learn a basic concept of liberal education: people should learn to think and to think well for themselves.

I also learned to distinguish three levels of questioning: analytic, or what does the author say; interpretive, or what does the author mean; and, evaluative, or what of it. Analytical questions are matters of fact and have a single right answer; interpretive questions can have several right, though contradictory, answers; and evaluative questions are answered by judgments formed by opinion.

It so happens that opinions are not all created equal, but are more or less well founded. It's through discussion that differences of opinion are resolved.

Reading about how to lead a group was one thing; actually forming a group and putting these ideas into practice was another story. I approached various friends, neighbors, and coworkers I thought might be interested in joining. In my enthusiasm, I even confronted strangers in used bookstores and on public transportation who were reading great books, inviting them to join the group. Soon we had enough people to get started.

Our first discussion, on the Declaration of Independence, took place in the Wicker Park Fieldhouse, a city-owned building. Nearly everyone was late, and I thought maybe the group wasn't going to get off the ground. But soon people began wandering in and the Wicker Park Great Books Group was launched. The stark, empty room, featuring pale yellow brick walls, linoleum floors, and metal folding chairs, actually helped discussion—there were no distractions. But eventually, the group's craving for cappuccino prompted a move to a neighborhood café, which has since become our stomping ground.

The Declaration of Independence was ideal for a first discussion, since its fundamental tenets are open to wide interpretation. Phrases like "self-evident truths," "unalienable rights," and "all men are created equal," with which we had all been familiar since childhood, suddenly struck us with their full weight. Dissecting these concepts, we began to read this document as we never had before.

Interpretive and evaluative questions were provided by the Foundation, as were discussion guidelines. At the end of the meeting, many questions were left unanswered, but everybody was excited. I'd heard that it would be a good idea to end the first meeting when discussion was at a high point, telling everybody that this is only a taste of what's to come. The ploy worked.

One advantage to starting a group through the Great Books Foundation is that it provides several series of readings collected in inexpensive paperbacks along with prepared questions. This eliminates the need to spend time creating a reading list. The Foundation puts a lot of thought into the choice of readings, the order of their presentation, and the questions. As I will explain later, my other group had to devise its own system to choose books for discussion.

Another plus is that the readings are generally short and people are able to read them carefully without feeling overloaded. Many are self-contained excerpts from larger works. The Foundation recommends that participants read selections at least twice, but I've met people who read them four or five times before coming in. These people can really contribute to discussion.

Most people feel that the recommended guidelines help discussion, but rules do get broken, and sometimes the meeting becomes a free-for-all (which can be great). The key isn't so much to follow the rules to the letter, but simply to keep the guidelines in mind and refer to them when needed.

One rule in great books discussion is that comments should be supported by the text. This means everybody has to be alert while reading and commenting. It's an exercise in thinking. We avoid outside sources like biography, historical material, and literary criticism. This material can be fascinating, but the goal here is not to learn about an author or culture. Ideas are what's important. The goal is to communicate well and better understand fundamental ideas. Historical facts and the opinions of others don't change the meaning or soundness of ideas expressed in the text. It's up to participants to find these ideas and deal with them. In great books discussion, bringing in outside sources is letting someone else do the thinking for you.

One of the first lessons I learned was when apparent disagreement arose concerning a question about the selection. I say "apparent" because, quite often, it was just that. Participants may have actually agreed, but had expressed their positions from different viewpoints, resulting in a misunderstanding. Other times, participants had not clearly established the issue at hand, and were in fact dealing with different issues altogether. In these situations, real disagreement (or agreement, for that matter) is impossible. This is a lesson in communication: speaking and listening—skills we had come together to improve.

The issue of "partial agreement" is related to this. Sometimes participants insist that others either agree totally with them or be told that their views are completely wrong. Partial agreement is when people make a sincere effort to discover common ground. It may have to start on the most basic level. Had they read the same book? Yes. So at once, there is some agreement, however small. Are they dealing with the same question? Yes. Progress is made slowly.

Eventually, it can be determined precisely where their views diverge. Then real discussion takes place—rhetoric happens. People are more or less persuaded that a given interpretation or evaluation is valid.

Even in works of nonfiction, ideas may not always be explicitly stated. It becomes the group's job to discover and evaluate the author's positions. In imaginative works, ideas will often be implicit and open to differing interpretations. Again, it's up to participants to analyze the work to find out what is being said, interpret it so as to determine what it means and, ultimately, to evaluate its relative worth.

Dealing with short excerpts from philosophical writers can require a lot of patience. The text may seem obscure. These discussions may never get past the analytical stage. Still, however far we do get, there is always that sense of having made progress, having somehow deepened our understanding. For example, only four or five people came to the discussion of Karl Marx's *Alienated Labor*, and none of us felt we had a grasp on the reading. It seemed to be over everybody's head. We decided to focus on two paragraphs to see if we could figure things out. This turned out to be one of the best discussions ever. By the end, we had learned more about Marx's ideas and his method than any of us had learned by reading alone. To me, this was proof positive of the value of close reading in a group.

I've found my experience in a great books discussion group to be rewarding socially, as well as intellectually. Sitting down with a group of adults who have come together with a genuine desire to learn and immediately entering into friendly meaningful conversation about important issues and ideas, sometimes with people I've only just met, is a great thing to do.

My other book group, the Gerber/Hart Gay Men's Fiction Discussion Group, was formed through the Gerber/Hart Gay and Lesbian Library and Archives, located on Chicago's North Side. The group is devoted to advancing gay cultural literacy through the exchange of ideas surrounding important books with gay themes. Like other areas of special interest, it's at once narrow and broad—narrow in that it's more or less distinct from other areas of inquiry, and broad in the diversity of subject matter available.

When I approached Gerber/Hart's board of directors with the idea of starting a men's discussion group, they were enthusiastic. A women's discussion group had been meeting for several years and the board was immediately interested in having someone coordinate a men's group. It was decided that the group would meet monthly and a notice was placed in several local gay newspapers. All that was left to do was to create a reading list.

Selecting books for discussion was something I didn't have to worry about in the Wicker Park group. The Great Books Foundation creates its reading lists from the three-thousand-year tradition of the West, a tradition that has been called "the civilization of the dialogue." These books, being centuries old, can be judged with an objectivity unavailable to groups reading contemporary works. Nonetheless, an appropriate reading list can be created in a special-interest group if the group's goals are well defined.

I created the group's initial reading list after searching out the "canonical" works within the field. After reading through several historical works and the recommended reading lists of some well-known authors, I arrived at a list of acknowledged classics for the first six meetings.

The group, though small in the beginning, was a success from the start. We first discussed *The City and the Pillar* by Gore Vidal. People were very opinionated about the book's value, written when Vidal was twenty-one. An interesting aspect of this selection was that Vidal actually rewrote the book with a different ending fifteen years after it appeared, republishing it with an afterword detailing his thoughts surrounding it.

The goal of any group determines the format of the meetings. Since the purpose of this group is not to improve skills in the liberal arts, but rather to become a more informed person with a better understanding of a particular culture, the guidelines for discussion are different from those of the great books group.

For example, while the book remains the focus, outside sources such as biography, history, and criticism are welcomed and even encouraged. Any material that sheds light on the book or its author can increase one's understanding of the book's meaning and place within the culture. Gore Vidal's afterword to the rewrite of *The City and the Pillar* is a perfect example of this.

Aesthetic judgments play a large part in Gerber/Hart discussions. Interestingly, while discussing books considered to be classics, our group found that a "classic" may not necessarily be a great work of art. This, however, was rarely disappointing or surprising. That a not-so-great book produced by someone from a particular cultural milieu has become a classic can be attributed to many factors. What's important is that the even if a book didn't provide a great literary experience, its discussion can provide a better understanding of the culture from which the book came. Naturally, the reverse can also be true. A great novel may be all but unknown to the audience who could most appreciate it.

As the group became more established, we decided that the selection process should be democratic. We came up with an easy, fair, effective system to accomplish this. At the last meeting of every six-month period, members suggest books they'd like to discuss. Members are asked to consider their suggestions from several angles. Does the book have historical value? Does it deal with a range of ideas that will stimulate discussion? Is it long? Controversial? Brand-new? Popular? Difficult? Available? Boring?

A comprehensive list of suggestions is created and copies are passed out. Everybody then marks six books he's interested in discussing. The discussion leader then determines the six books that received the most votes, asking for a show of hands in the case of a tie. The group then quickly and somewhat arbitrarily decides in what order the books will be discussed. The process generally takes about thirty minutes, and is quite reliable in helping select good books that people want to read.

The Gerber/Hart group established itself quickly and within six months a core group of members attended and still attend nearly every discussion. For some reason, this was quite different from the Wicker Park group, which took much longer to establish. Just before I started the Wicker Park group, an experienced great books discussion leader told me the group should be pretty much established "in about three years." I thought he was joking. Now I know better. Things came together sooner than my friend predicted, but it still took longer than I originally thought it would. While it didn't happen overnight, it was worth the effort.

A special-interest group such as the Gerber/Hart Gay Men's Fiction Discussion Group is a great opportunity to bring together people with common interests who come from varied backgrounds. New friendships occur naturally. Outings, dinners, and other diversions are easy to plan with a roomful of acquaintances. In 1994, several members of the Gerber/Hart group went to see the Chicago production of *Angels in America*, Tony Kushner's Pulitzer Prize–winning play, which the group had discussed. Of course, we discussed the play after the performance and compared the experience of reading it to seeing it performed.

Whether you're in a great books group with people who have nothing in common but a desire to learn, or a group where people share a common interest, book discussion groups are at once fun, interesting, exasperating, and entertaining. They won't replace solitary reading, but they will expand your world.

A Chorus for
Four Voices

Becky Hemperly, Sandra Deden, Gloria LaBrecque,
Erika Abrahamsson **Medford, Massachusetts**

BOOK GROUPS COME in many forms, from large, theme-oriented ones to less formal, meet and eat varieties. Our book group is a chorus, composed of four distinct voices that create harmonies and counterpoints for each other. Each member has her time as a soloist. Everyone gets a chance to sing melody. The group began as a duet, grew to a trio, then to a quartet. The piece goes like this.

Becky: I started a book group to avoid arrest. I needed to keep myself from clutching a half-groggy subway commuter by the lapels and demanding his views on skewed marriage surveys and the she-devil image of women in the movies. I had to prevent myself from calling up every talk radio show in town. I wanted to avoid pummeling my friends and coworkers with a database full of facts and figures about the repression of women in American society (those enraging, engaging facts you always wished you had on hand).

I was reading Susan Faludi's *Backlash: The Undeclared War against American Women.* This book should come with a warning label: DO NOT READ THIS ALONE! This is a book to be discussed, harped on, disputed, embraced. It proves that you don't need a CD-ROM drive to experience interactive media. One of my problems was that no one else I knew had read *Backlash*. And to make things worse, I was facing the first September in twenty-four years during which I was not in school. Gone were the built-in, book-chewing, idea-thrashing sessions that had become as comfortable as my old college sweatshirt.

So I did the only natural thing—I called Sandy, a graduate school friend, grabbed her by the lapels, and began flogging her with details from Faludi's book. After thirty minutes, she consented and a book group was born.

Initially, Sandy and I were a bit reluctant to call ourselves a book group, but all the components were there: we met regularly, usually for two hours every two weeks. We enjoyed reading, discussing, and handling books. We had intelligent, meaningful conversations about writing style, the role of editing, character development, the use of writing devices, and more. We learned more about each other and our views of the world. And of course, we ate.

In our book group, consensus was easy to come by, and we quickly decided to focus on reading creative nonfiction. Why? First, we were both former English majors who felt that the curricula we'd been weaned on was high fat and fiction heavy. Second, as nonfiction writers ourselves, we hoped that studying various types of creative nonfiction would provide insights for our own works. We took turns choosing which books to read, a practice we still follow.

Sandy: Becky and I were sitting in a café drinking coffee, having an intense conversation about *Backlash*. This conversation was intertwined with our mutual complaint that there should be a group around for us to join as readers and writers of literary nonfiction. At some point, our "should" became "why not?" and we had our book group.

This spontaneity isn't to say that the idea came out of nowhere. The idea of belonging to a group had been with me since I decided to become a writer. I was jealous of famous groups of writers such as Gertrude Stein's gang in Paris in the twenties and the Boston area poets in the fifties including Robert Lowell, Elizabeth Bishop, Sylvia Plath, Maxine Kumin, and Anne Sexton. I wanted to be part of such a group the way the Scarecrow from *The Wizard of Oz* wanted a brain. If I only had a writers' group, then I'd be a real writer.

I met a poet, who recommended that I join a group led by her friend. I was ecstatic: I was on my way to Emerald City. My euphoria soon shriveled when I called the group leader and discovered the session would cost three hundred dollars for ten weeks. I was pretty sure that Hemingway didn't pay Gertrude Stein to sit in her living room.

Instead I decided to enter a graduate writing program and in a class called Writing the Nonfiction Book, I met Becky and discovered that genre of writing called creative nonfiction, originally dubbed the "New Journalism" in the fifties.

My longing to be connected to reading and writing nonfiction was fulfilled when Becky and I began discussing *Backlash*. For me the book group has become a special time when modern life—the TV, radio, telephone—cannot intrude. In our living rooms, backyards, and neighborhood cafés, I can spend time simply and richly, enjoying conversations about the books at hand. And like the Scarecrow who realizes that he had a brain all along, I have come to realize I am a writer. And that to gather with people who are intelligent and care deeply about words and writing is all I ever needed to support my habit.

Another more practical benefit of the group has been to slow down my reading speed. I have a tendency to devour books whole, reading them quickly to find out what happens next, only to forget most of what I've read as soon as I finish. The group helps me to slow down, savor and delight in the words, phrases, and subtleties. Discussing important points with others also cements the book in my mind and leads to discoveries I would have missed at my usual breakneck pace.

Becky: Although we did make an effort to savor each book, Sandy and I still managed to read a fair number of works. After our beginning with *Backlash*, we moved to *The Soul of a*

New Machine by Tracy Kidder. We had both heard so much about this book from friends and professors, we felt we had to give it a try. While not a flint to spark debate, *Soul* showed how a book can go from being a groundbreaking exposé to a history book and still maintain its initial integrity and hold its readers.

We followed by reading *Wouldn't Take Nothing for My Journey Now* by Maya Angelou, which I couldn't help thinking of as Wouldn't Pay Nothing for This Book Again. Given how much Sandy and I had enjoyed Angelou's previous works, we could only explain this padded yet slim and thinly-written volume as the publisher's attempt to capitalize on the author's increased name recognition following President Clinton's inauguration. Nevertheless, the book provoked animated discussions about the importance of editors, both the writer's internal editor and the editors of large publishing houses.

After our experience with the Angelou book, we decided to choose a book that we knew a bit more about. *New York in the 50s* by Dan Wakefield filled that criterion. Both Sandy and I had worked with Wakefield as a teacher and advisor during our graduate school years. In this case, the book took on added interest because we knew the author and yet glimpsed other aspects of our mentor that we hadn't seen before.

Sandy: Dan described his own literary scene in Greenwich Village in the fifties, when he and his peers actually used novels to help them understand their lives. They would quote these books to each other, and could even recall passages today.

Becky: And while my living room was far from the White Horse Tavern, we like to think that the flavor of the discussions were much the same.

Sandy: Soon after finishing Dan's book, our fledgling book group began to grow. We don't actively recruit members, but we don't discourage people who inquire about the group. For many people the focus on nonfiction is not a good fit, but Gloria, a friend from high school, indulged our passion and perhaps found an outlet for her own connection with words.

Gloria: Why did I join the group? Well, although I've been a somewhat avid reader of all types of literary genre, I found that reading can be quite isolating. When I lived in Connecticut near my friends and family, I thought it rather natural to discuss the latest Grisham novel with anyone who had read it, or even to talk about what was written in the newspaper with my mom. Since I moved to Rhode Island by myself, I have realized that having no one to talk to about reading is like watching a TV sitcom alone—it's not much fun laughing by yourself. So when Sandy kept talking about her "book thing with Becky," I invited myself to join, hoping once again to take part in that great human experience of sharing thoughts and ideas with others without the restrictions of rules and deadlines that can bog one down.

What have I gotten out of book group? Some really great apple pie! And I have received what I was looking for: wonderful new friends, enriching discussions of a variety of authors' works and styles, and a better understanding of the power of the written word. We all have been moved at some point either by a description, viewpoint, or something unstated by an author. I have learned that although the words can't move on the page, they will forever remain liquid in interpretation by those who read them.

Becky: Gloria joined us just as we were beginning Adrienne Rich's *What Is Found There: On Poetry and Politics*, a book that could make you cry for the skill of it. While this selection edged more toward literary criticism, we never lacked for images or incredibly crafted phrases to discuss. Perhaps more than with any other book, the conversations around this book happened on a grander scale, on a deeper level, with a broader sweep. The feeling that each word had been specially selected, never carelessly dropped on the page, stayed with us throughout this reading.

Sandy: With Rich's book, it was as if our wish to be moved by a book, to be able to quote it to our friends and go back to it year after year was granted. I knew instantly that this was a book that would be with me for a long time and help me sort out life in these complicated, media-drenched times. The reason? Part of it is her insight into the artistic community as it tries to survive on the fringe of modern society and part is Rich's achingly beautiful prose. To be in the hands of such a master was an unexpected and well-remembered joy.

Gloria: Rich's book is definitely my favorite so far.

Becky: Unfortunately, such favorable reviews were not in order for our next selection, *Dakota* by Kathleen Norris. This book has become our whipping post and a standard against which almost anything will excel. Many other reviewers wearing the mantle of respectability from famous journals and newspapers would disagree. However, we found it to be one of the most strident works we'd read, written by someone we felt did protest too much. Definitely a discussion starter, our critique of Norris's work is the closest we've ever come to an outright flaying.

By July, we had recovered from the barrenness of *Dakota* and our group had added another member, Erika. As we took our books and iced tea to the beach and outdoor cafés, Sandy and I congratulated ourselves that the group had doubled in size in less than a year.

Erika: When Becky told me about the nonfiction book group she and Sandy had started, I was intrigued. Even as we spoke, I had twenty or so (and I only wish I were kidding) nonfiction books lying around my house waiting for me to pick them up and start reading. The problem was that although all of those books contained topics of interest to me, it was just too hard, required too much discipline to put down that really great murder mystery, or that fantastic science fiction book, and pick up something that would actually require some thought, some concentration.

Here was my opportunity. If I had a deadline, and if I had people with whom I could discuss these and other nonfiction works, then perhaps I could muster the motivation to crack those previously uncracked bindings.

It worked. I have found a way into the world of non. Good discussion and flying ideas lead me toward books that I would ordinarily never have stopped to peruse; and yet once I begin to read, all kinds of worlds, thoughts, and personalities open up and I am, more often than not, delighted!

Becky: One of the books that delighted some, but not all of us, was *The White Album* by Joan Didion, which, like *Soul of a New Machine*, served a historical purpose, as a primer on the sixties since all of us are too young to have been a real part of the events of that time. We marveled over Didion's ability to select just the right details for her lists, and her tendency as a Californian to be driven to distraction by the ebb and flow of water.

Next we methodically picked our way through Kansas and *PrairyErth* with William Least Heat-Moon. A few things set this book apart. The size, at 622 pages, was daunting and required us to think more than usual about where we should try to be in the book by our next meeting. The pace of this work was different too, more measured and even, like every Kansas county mile.

Presently, we're in the midst of *Surprised by Joy* by C. S. Lewis. Among us are a divinity school graduate with Unitarian leanings, a devout Catholic, a comfortably committed Congregationalist, and a former atheist making her way back into the spiritual fray. This mix should provide a rich and interesting context for discussions of this spiritual autobiography. Already we've wrangled with the definitions of joy—Lewis's and our own.

Sandy: One thing Lewis's book is teaching us is that four is not too few people to support wide-ranging views and lively discussions. Also, while our book group has some fairly specific aspects to it, like reading nonfiction, that other groups may not want to duplicate, there is a more basic concept that anyone can employ. When we did not find an established book group that would satisfy our interests and personal motivations, we simply started our own—something anyone can do.

Becky: As for me, did I find what I was searching for through this book group? You bet. I've surrounded myself with people who aren't put off by an animated, intense discussion about how a writer selects details. I am with individuals who know what it's like to read with pens in hand. I belong to a group whose members savor a well-proportioned trim size the way some people swill brandy in the light. I am among friends.

For the future, I'm confident that our group will thrive beyond its first anniversary, although the four of us now face the struggle of finding the point where our divergent schedules meet. The time spent together, when we can find it, is always rewarding. Everyone contributes equally. Each person brings a different perspective to the books, while maintaining a common commitment to the group. As such, this book group is truly a chorus of voices, and the result is richer than the sum of the parts.

The Book Ungroup

C. J. Arbor   **Chicago, Illinois**

A BOOK GROUP? No thanks. I can hardly think of anything duller, nerdier, or more pretentious than sitting in someone's living room (or should I say salon) dissecting the works of famous authors. Oh, I can see it now, my worst college nightmares revisited.

That deep and probing woman who always sat in the front row, "I believe that the imagery created by Shakespeare in *Othello* was more macabre than that in *Hamlet*."

Or the know-it-all guy who just *had* to tell the class all about his deep-sea fishing experience, which most certainly rivaled Mr. Hemingway's, and which made him the unqualified expert on the old man, as well as on the sea.

Worse, the arrogant teaching assistant (or for those who went to small colleges, professor) who would call on me *only* on days when I was visibly unprepared—as in, coming in late, no pen, no notebook (no shower, no deodorant . . .), slits-for-eyes—" Yes, you, please explain the relevance of the fact that Willy Loman sold shoes, instead of, say, ties." (With a tie, he could have hung himself quickly and saved us all a lot of misery . . .)

So why, now that I'm free of those kinds of restraints, now that I no longer have to posture or pose, now that I can choose to read what I want to read, *would I want to join a book group?*

Intellectual stimulation? Please! Try television's *McLaughlin Group.* Camaraderie? Well, the guys and gals on *SportsCenter* seem like friends and Luke and Laura have (happily) returned to my life. For the variety of foodstuff that would be present at the meetings? Like I need another excuse to eat?

Think of the winters in Chicago, where I live. For those without *The Weather Channel,* let me tell you, the windchill reduces residents to scurrying cockroach-like creatures, who, when forced to leave their warm nests, instantaneously find their limbs, their lips, their used Kleenex frozen solid. So why would persons in their right minds voluntarily leave their homes, apartments, one-room studios, or YMCA weekly rentals, to go out into the deep freeze to *talk about a book?*

I repeat: a book group? NO WAY!

Of course, I share book suggestions with friends, especially with Meg, Lee, and Dirk. Actually, I am most often the one doing the suggesting. I'll call Lee, who lives in Maine, and leave a message on her answering machine, "You've got to read *Animal Dreams.* It's by, uh, hang on a minute, let me check, oh, Barbara Kingsolver—she wrote *Bean Trees,* too. At first I thought it seemed stupid, but there was some real good stuff in it." In about a week, I'll receive a message on my machine from Lee, "CJ, I brought *Animal Dreams.* So far, it's good."

Empowered with that knowledge, I'll bring my copy (which is usually borrowed from my sister, who usually recommended it in the first place) to work and give it to Meg, who'll read just about anything. Dirk? Although he'll read about ten pages of absolutely anything, usually while sitting on the toilet, he's been known to finish only about fifteen books in his lifetime (wouldn't a book group love him). And that was before he moved to Florida where he can now golf year-round—I'm understandably more selective about the titles I share with him.

Then in about a month or so, I'll call Lee and in between complaining about our jobs, we'll talk about the most recent book we've read. Of course, usually by this time, I've forgotten 50 percent of the details, but she reminds me. "No CJ, Homero was the father, *not* the sister in Nicaragua . . ." About a week later, I'll come in (late) to work, and Meg's borrowed copy will be sitting on my desk, so I'll run into her office to hear what she has to say. It's often something to the effect of, "It was slow going at first, but by the end I didn't want to put it down." Then we'll look at each other and one of us will say, "Do you think Dirk would read it?" And most often we'll both agree, "No way."

Occasionally, though, Dirk has been included and has even finished the book. Most recently, he completed all of Donna Tartt's *The Secret History* (a page-turner, in spite of itself) and Mitch Albom's *The Fab Five* (a must read).

Oh, other people (they're often strangers) come in and out of our little circle, too. For instance, once Meg came into work and said, "This guy on the el this morning was reading a book that looked good. It had the coolest cover. It was called *Bastard out of Carolina*." Well, that was a good enough recommendation for us. Turned out the inside of the book wasn't too bad, either.

And then there was a book recommended by a friend, Valerie Martin's *Mary Reilly*—who could not have been drawn into that story from the minute they read about the girl and the rats? (Even Dirk read that part.) Mercifully, we all managed to complete our reading before we read that Julia Roberts had been cast in the lead role in the big-screen version. Talk about shattered illusions.

Sometimes you just want to laugh. Which is why, after stumbling upon Tama Janowitz's *The Male Cross-Dresser Support Group* in the library, and laughing out loud while reading it, I had to encourage everyone else to read it also. Well, no one wanted to buy it, and since I had dropped my library copy in the washing machine at the Laundromat, thereby ruining it for my personal circle of readers *and* for future library patrons, I couldn't even suggest that it be borrowed from the library. (At last check, it hadn't been replaced, despite my prompt and dutiful reimbursement to the library.) Finally, I gave up and bought a copy and *demanded* that it be read, first by Lee (she loved it) and then by Meg (she did too).

Then there was Susan Trott's *When Your Lover Leaves*, which is sadly out of print and crazily funny. The only copy we have has been circulating slowly. Lee dropped it in the sink, seriously damaging it (is there a connection between water and funny books?), so its future doesn't look bright. But it was swell while it lasted.

Laughter comes easily with anything by Tom Robbins, and I'm happy to report that Dirk has completed *Still Life with Woodpecker* and *Skinny Legs and All*. John Kennedy Toole's *Confederacy of Dunces* was also a laugh riot.

Of course a different kind of laughter accompanied other choices: Dominick Dunne's *A Season in Purgatory* (seemed more like hell), John le Carré's *The Night Manager* (so boring you had to laugh), John Feinstein's *Hard Courts* (editors, send your resumes to Villard Books—they obviously need a competent one), Maeve Binchy's *Circle of Friends* (so that's the kind of "novel" that makes The New York Times's best-seller list); and, basically, anything by John Grisham (who, to his credit, doesn't pretend he's any good).

At the opposite end, there's the somber, morose works of Anne Tyler. Will someone get this woman some uppers? Talented? Sure she is, but is there no end to the pain? From *Dinner at the Homesick Restaurant* to *Saint Maybe*, and just about everything in between, it seems like Ms. Tyler's novels should come equipped with rating codes: S (sad), VS (very sad), D (depressive), and DD (doubly depressing—as in don't even *think* about reading this unless you've just won the lottery).

There have been other flops—major ones. *Possession* was impossible to get through. I couldn't recommend it to anyone, though I did think of sending it to Dirk as a joke. Louise Erdrich's *Love Medicine* reminded me of one of my favorite arena basketball chants—OVER-RATED!— although Lee liked it well enough. How about Terry McMillan's *Waiting to Exhale*? The writing seemed on par with a decent Brady Bunch episode.

There have also been major disagreements. It seems that Toni Morrison's *Beloved* is a great book. So Lee tells me. I'm waiting for Meg to settle the argument. I loved *West with the Night* (ostensibly by Beryl Markham), but no one else got into its stories. It seems like I was also the only one who really loved Robert Boswell's *Mystery Ride*, not that anyone else hated it.

Other books have inspired us all. Lee *still* grows misty (literally) whenever she mentions Reynolds Price's *Kate Vaiden* (and she somehow finds a way to bring it up often in conversation); I usually respond that I agree with my book-lending sister—it makes me sort of sick that a man could have written that story, that he could understand a woman that well, but I loved it nonetheless. Speaking of women, Kate Chopin's *The Awakening* has got to be one of the coolest books ever written, and Maya Angelou's *I Know Why the Caged Bird Sings* is overwhelming proof that woman was meant to fly.

Cold Sassy Tree? Well, 'twas to my sister's credit that we all read that one. Olive Ann Burns just grabbed hold of our hearts with that story, and it's so sad that its sequel [sic] was such a letdown, or should I say nuclear meltdown.

Then there's Margaret Atwood. Mark my words, history will one day name her as the absolute best writer who ever wrote. (Or should I say, for the aspiring artists among us, the best writer who was ever published.)

So you see, book groups are an overrated commodity. Between Lee, Meg, and I, with occasional assistance from Dirk, we do fine. In fact, Lee and Meg recently met each other for the first time. The three of us sat down with some beer and talked. The subject of books never came up. Then, as we were breaking it up, Meg turned to Lee and said, "Did you die laughing at the *Male Cross-Dresser Support Group?* Lee hooted in response, while I remembered, "Man, I still have to mail that book to Dirk."

It's probably apparent by now that when we talk about these books, we seldom theorize or scrutinize. Perhaps we're constrained by geographical distance. Long-distance phone calls, usually to answering machines, don't inspire literary analysis, and teleconferencing doesn't seem a viable option. (Dirk, for one, can't figure out the time zones.) It's also probably safe to say that our depth of analysis would leave most book group members wanting more—unless "I loved it!" is deep enough for them. Oh, and we don't share meals, and we don't have *any* rules.

We're *definitely* not a book group. Works for us.

PART IV

Follow the Leader (Though in a Book Group, She's Probably Following You)

Book group leaders come in all forms—paid, unpaid, elected, unofficially appointed—and, as evidenced in this section, group members and their leaders tend to be fiercely loyal to each other. One of the many benefits of a leadered group is that it cuts the time spent on unrelated issues. If you're short on cash, but want a leader, check out your library. Library-sponsored groups (you'll find three in this section) are perhaps the most democratic book groups around—they're free of charge and open to everyone, even those who snooze through the discussion.

Becoming and Being— A Book Group Leader

Karen L. Thomson   **Evanston, Illinois**

" 'TIS A GIFT to be simple, 'tis a gift to be free, 'tis a gift to find out . . ." what one is eminently suited to be. It happened to me that I am a book group leader.

This vocation could, perhaps, have been predicted and even assigned to me at age twelve and I probably wouldn't have complained, but my path toward my vocation was instead a matter of steady discovery. Today, I just feel lucky that my lifelong love for reading and teaching and my antipathy for coercion and more than a modicum of institutional control should find itself at home in this niche of facilitating informal and intensely creative conversations about books.

There are typically two variations of the response to my vocational announcement. The first is something along the line of "You mean people actually pay you for that?" While the second goes something like "Oh how wonderful! I wish I could do something like that!"

The second response usually indicates that the person speaking has had some type of experience with a book or discussion group, and that the questioner has picked up on some of the excitement in my voice as I respond. The passion that I feel for my job is best communicated through stories

155

about how it happens and keeps happening after thirteen years. These are stories about art and connections.

The first story takes place during a discussion held at The Breakers, an independent living facility, where I meet with a group of older adults who demand good literature and give as much in discussion as they get. On this particular day, we were chewing over the symbols and meanings in "Babette's Feast," a wonderful story by Isak Dinesen about the spiritual power of art to transform and redeem human beings.

In the story, a French woman, Babette, spends all of her lottery winnings on a great feast that she prepares for her Danish employers and their guests, only one of whom is a connoisseur who can truly appreciate her efforts. The other guests, members of a small religious group that mistrusts sensual joy, experience the food as alchemical. The rich tastes and sensuality of Babette's French cooking bring such satisfaction that old hurts are forgiven and bitterness dissolves in the glow of pleasures that the meal provides. Their flagging love for God and each other is renewed.

Babette's feast has done what more traditional religious methods could not. The fantastic delights of her cooking cause renewal of her guests' exhausted spirits. Thus, she shows the power of art. When asked why she spent all her winnings on one meal, making her return to post-revolutionary France impossible, Babette replies, "Through all the world there goes one long cry from the heart of the artist: Give me leave to do my utmost!"

Our discussion at The Breakers that day ended on a note of celebration of the arts and the redemptive powers of creativity. The group responded to my last messages with the appreciative words, "And this is your art, Karen. You are an artist, too!" And I heard the truth of that moment. At least for that book group discussion, I had fulfilled my mission, my vocation as a book group leader. I had inspired joy and appreciation in these readers' hearts—for the work of literature, and even for the art of our connection in conversation. In kind, they had inspired appreciation in me. My response to them, "We are all artists! Thank-you."

This exchange reflected one of the truths I have learned about my work. If it is a good discussion, there is a sharing of insight that elicits a thank-you from me. It reminds me of my first shiatsu treatment. On that occasion, after a wonderful hour of deep acupressure that left me relaxed and full of joy, I was further astounded to hear a whispered "thank-you" from the person who had done all the work, to my way of thinking. And yet that thank-you made perfect sense—expressing the balance of giver and gift, the exchange of energy in any human interaction that is life enhancing to each.

As a book group leader, I labor over the intent of the author, agonize about appropriate ways to unlock conversation about the issues raised, and risk the possibility of hearing no answering voices, of seeing only tiredness that will not yield to inspiration, of sensing old anger that will not allow belief and hope to surface.

But when my gifts are received and my work is appreciated, an answering energy awakens and inspires me beyond what I came to present. It is about human connections through literature.

The second story is about what happened one recent Friday morning when I was sitting in a living room in a circle of about six women discussing *Mrs. Dalloway* by Virginia Woolf. After some initial talk about nonbook matters, we began to share our responses to the character of Clarissa Dalloway.

Clarissa is Woolf's dubious heroine who spends the day on which the book centers planning and living through a party she is giving that evening. As we began to warm up to Woolf and the discussion, I suddenly had a Woolf-like experience of being inside the conversation, while simultaneously being outside appreciating the complexity of interaction, memory, and experiences represented in the room.

I noticed the baby nursing noisily at the hostess's breast and the liveliness of the toddler grabbing at my loose papers and notes on Woolf, which were spread around me in a semi-circle, and I remembered my own sweet years of nursing babies and chasing small children. I noticed the snapping intensity in the eyes of the businesswoman, suited up to go to work, as she shared her insights about Clarissa Dalloway. I thought wonderingly of the many other discussions on *Mrs. Dalloway* that I had recently moderated, each so different in focus it was as if we were not discussing the same book. What a magical and rich book, I mused.

I also thought of my first book group discussion of Virginia Woolf, thirteen years earlier. It was another circle of women intent on understanding her vision. This group met at a local park district in a room designed and used for dance lessons. We sat around a card table in the middle of the mirrored room. My reference books on Woolf shared the limited table space with the cookies and wine brought for refreshment that evening.

I was in the middle of a lecture on Woolf's life, when all attention shifted from me to the mouse who had scurried up the back of one of our occupied chairs and was trying to reach the goodies on the table. While I was annoyed with the inter-ruption to my train of thought, it made for good storytelling and an almost immediate decision to move the discussions into our own homes, adding dimensions of culinary and personal comfort of which Woolf would have approved.

Moving back into the most recent Woolf discussion, with a warm mug of coffee at my elbow and six interested, if some-times distracted, Woolf readers, I realized that the moment was perfect—that this job was the one I had always wanted, complete in its satisfactions and its demands—that it was all about being in a place and time where *amidst* life, not apart from it, ideas and values could be shared and shaped. I under-stood that I had wanted literature to be connected to living in a very real way and this was it.

Edna O'Brien said once that "Books are the Grail for what is deepest, more mysterious, and least expressible within ourselves. They are our soul's skeleton." I like that. To my simple way of thinking, book group discussions are about books that are really about us, ultimately.

That Friday morning, Clarissa Dalloway's task of getting through life was also our own. That day, every day, and no matter what our individual responses to that challenge might be, the quest was still to affirm our connection and meaning to each other and to the unrelenting, if sometimes silent, self which is our voice. If Clarissa Dalloway put it all together, life and death, through a party, well, let's look at that and see how it is that we compose *our* meaning.

To criticize the British class system, as Woolf was certainly doing, to chronicle the changes in social meaning in Europe brought about by World War I, as Woolf also intended, is certainly grist for the mill, but the real power of the novel is in its artful way of asking us to look at our values, choices, and responses to questions of ultimate meaning. This is what makes the story of Mrs. Dalloway timeless and universal.

Franz Kafka said that "A book should act as an axe to the frozen sea within us." I like that, too. Both O'Brien's and Kafka's descriptions fit *Mrs. Dalloway.* I add my own criterion that a really good book must illuminate human experience, and so bring hope. Virginia Woolf was depressed and suicidal, and her novels are full of suicide and thoughts of aging and death, but they are not books of despair, because they tell the truth about human connections and reality. They inspire and excite us to the tasks of making meaning of our lives in the face of inevitable death. While asking us to examine the futility of war and passionless living, Woolf, by her own example, shows the hope gained by living creatively, be it through writing or giving parties. It is all about making connections, about becoming and being human.

I have digressed. I have preached hope and faith and vision and good books, when I have said I was telling a story about connections, about being a book group leader. But there it is. That is what I am. A digressor, an explorer into other voices through literature and conversation, a listener, a learner, an appreciator of human potential—the stuff of connections. I am a poet of voices, seeking to understand and illuminate the wonderful diversity of vision I see. I am a medium for voice.

You're a what? I am a book group leader.

For this group's reading list, see page 323.

Contemporary Books Discussion Group—Bettendorf Public Library

Hedy N. R. Hustedde   **Davenport, Iowa**

IN MANY WAYS, a book discussion group sponsored by a library is the best of all worlds. It tends to carry on as long as a library staff member is assigned to be its liaison, despite fluctuations in membership. Publicity is no problem; a meeting place is no problem; special deals on the purchase of books can often be arranged; audiovisual equipment is available; and participants are likely to be diverse in viewpoint, age, and background, making for lively discussions.

The Bettendorf Public Library's Contemporary Books Discussion Group officially began in 1961. I didn't join until 1989, when I also joined the library staff as a part-time circulation clerk and felt the need to broaden my reading experiences. After a couple of years as a member, I was promoted to being the group's library liaison, and I also began working on my master's degree in library science, which made for a fine mesh between my personal and professional life.

Currently, the group has thirty-one members, but that many have never shown up at any one meeting. Usually the number of participants hovers around twenty. Some of these people are what we call "founding" members who have stuck with the group for more than thirty years. Members range in age from their twenties to their seventies, and three-quarters of the group is female.

Participants come from all walks of life: journalist, minister, engineer, orthopedic surgeon, laboratory technician, parent, business teacher, English teacher, kindergarten teacher, special education teacher, salesperson, consultant, business executive, student. It is natural that many points of view are reflected in members' interpretations of what they read. This is a most valuable circumstance. When it was suggested that perhaps two groups should be formed from the one to prevent overcrowding in the library's small conference room, the idea was soundly defeated—nobody wanted to miss out on what anybody else had to say.

As long as I've been in the group, it has met on the second Wednesday evening of the month, September through May. Discussions have been known to continue out in the parking lot or at a local restaurant for those not satisfied at the conclusion.

Choosing books is a group effort. First, a volunteer committee of three to five members browses bookstores, reads reviews, asks friends and colleagues for recommendations, and comes up with a list of twenty titles that are available in paperback. The list is usually half fiction and half nonfiction, and despite the adjective "contemporary" in the group's name, it often includes classics like Mark Twain's *Roughing It* or Willa Cather's *My Antonia*. We also often include a play or a book of poetry, and we almost always read a prizewinner (Nobel, Pulitzer, National Book Award, or Booker).

After the list is compiled, the entire membership is then invited for a potluck meal at a member's home. We read the annotated list of titles there. At this time, members voice objections or make supporting statements for particular books. We vote for nine books by a show of hands.

Formerly, one infamous item was always included on the potluck menu—Artillery Punch. A mixture of, among other things, claret, bourbon, bitters, rum, and Rhine wine, I was given the recipe along with this admonition, "If you file it in the book group archives and don't serve it, I'm sure you're all better off." At recent potlucks, liquids of considerably less alcoholic nature have been the beverages of choice.

The potluck is usually well attended. While there, we get to know each other on a more personal basis, each member has a say in the choices for discussion for the next year, and we have yet another chance to talk about one of the loves of our lives—good reading.

Despite our attempts to be democratic, not everybody is always happy with the choice of book. One person was very disgruntled when we voted to read Rush Limbaugh's *The Way Things Ought to Be*. She came to the discussion, however, and got a rousing round of applause because it happened to be her seventy-fifth birthday. Her next statement, which we expected would acknowledge the applause, went something like this, "I have to say . . ." We nodded in encouragement, ". . . that I am still *ashamed* that this group chose that book to read!" We were somewhat deflated, but had to laugh in appreciation of her stubborn honesty.

Another member always reads the book aloud to her husband and said that there was a period in the seventies when the group was reading books that were so sexually graphic and so seemingly unnatural and immoral that her hair stood on end. Either the group's tastes have changed somewhat, writers aren't quite so graphic, or she's become immune, because her hair has always been in place of late.

I'm fond of remembering how some members initially didn't think Diane Ackerman's *A Natural History of the Senses* was so good, but after the discussion decided to purchase their copies. This same change of opinion has occurred with several titles and indicates the power of discussion.

At this time, books are paid for through the library's gift fund. Participants may purchase the books at a substantial discount or return them in as-good-as-mint condition to be sold in the library's semiannual book sale or to other local book discussion groups, of which there are several. The theory behind this generosity is to emphasize our library's dedication to free services and participation in programs as much as is possible. No one will be turned away from our discussion group because of not being able to afford to buy the books. Funding a book discussion group also helps fulfill the library's function of promoting lifelong learning.

New members are welcome at any time. Some stay for just one discussion and some become regulars. Sometimes students show up to take notes or tape the discussion because they happen to be studying the book we've read. This happened with Deborah Tannen's *You Just Don't Understand*.

Whenever the local colleges and arts council bring a major writer to our area for a series of readings, lectures, and workshops, we always read something by that writer. This was the case with Kurt Vonnegut, E. L. Doctorow, Marge Piercy, and Bharati Mukherjee, among others. Knowing something of them and of their work ahead of time enhanced their visits for us.

Periodically, we've enjoyed having a local expert lead a discussion on a book of choice (as happened with *My Antonia*, *The Great Gatsby*, and *Balkan Ghosts*). They are usually teachers who gladly share their special knowledge. In watching them, we are also given hints on how better to lead discussions ourselves.

For the most part, the discussions are led by volunteers from within the group. I rarely lead a discussion. But I always help the prospective leaders find information about the author, book reviews, etc., from the resources in our library. I also encourage them to check out Ted Balcom's exceedingly useful *Book Discussions for Adults*.

Props of all sorts are also appreciated. We snacked on Indian cookies (nankatai) and sesame crunch during the discussion of Bharati Mukherjee's *The Middleman and Other Stories* and on Czech kolaches during *My Antonia*. We've used transparencies with overhead projectors, shown short videos (for Michael Carey's *Honest Effort*), listened to audiotaped segments of author interviews (for Jonathan Kozol's

Savage Inequalities) and of programs conducted by authors (for Rush Limbaugh's *The Way Things Ought to Be*). We were treated to a simple and informative slide program on cell division as an introduction to Evelyn Keller's book about Barbara McClintock, *A Feeling for the Organism.* The person leading the discussion of Ralph Leighton's *Tuva or Bust!* brought a compact disc of incredible Tuvan throat singing, and he also managed to collect a whole set of oddly shaped Tuvan postage stamps for us to examine. That bit of extra effort is truly effective.

I do all the bookwork and scheduling and lend support in a number of ways. I cannot imagine not being a member of a book discussion group. It has been advantageous to me professionally and personally. I've heard other members make similar comments. We learn so much about ourselves from each other and from this literature, which is enhanced by our comments. What's more, we laugh a lot.

In the beginning, I think we join a discussion group because we care about literature. We keep coming back because we care about each other. In the end, the literature becomes us and we become the literature. That's what makes it great.

For this group's reading list, see page 276.

Confessions of a Bookaholic

Suzanne Hales **Kenilworth, Illinois**

HAVE YOU EVER entered a library, inhaling the musty perfume of thousands of books and felt euphoric? When you go to a bookstore, do the books seem to leap from the shelves into your hands? Do you have precarious piles of books covering all available surfaces in your home just waiting to be read? Does your spouse ever warn you that your house is about to collapse under the weight of books? If you've answered affirmatively, you have serious symptoms of a disease I suffer from, bookaholism. But don't despair. It's a healthy addiction.

Family legend says that I was born reading a book. I remember my brother saying, "I can't believe her. It's summer vacation, and she's reading books for school this fall!" A friend recently asked my husband if I was very busy giving book reviews or leading discussions. He replied, "If she's not off leading book groups, she has her nose in a book." His other favorite comment is, "Wind her up, and she talks books." Well, he knew what he was in for when he married me. After all, with a history like mine, I was destined for a lifetime affair with books.

It was only natural I would become an English teacher. (When I was in college in the sixties, women were either

165

teachers, nurses, or social workers.) I left the profession when my children were born. There I was in Brooklyn with two babies and reading trash for the first time in my life. It was pure escapism from colicky infants. I even read when I nursed. Then I panicked and feared my brain was turning to mush. I needed to get out and talk about good books with others.

Our family moved back to the Midwest and I became a book discussion leader for a bookstore that offered a series of discussions for its customers. Then I started leading several private groups. Before I knew it, I had my very own little book discussion business. I was saved from the jaws of mediocrity.

Another title I hold is "book enhancinator." A number of groups that usually have their own members leading the discussions call me in to help them get more out of challenging books such as *The Bone People* by Keri Hulme or A. S. Byatt's *Possession*. Some groups have me come in occasionally to lead a discussion, just to have a change of pace or to give their group a shot of adrenaline.

Still, I wanted to do more. I felt the need to inspire others to love literature. As a child, my mother nicknamed me Greta (as in Garbo), and in college I had majored in drama as well as English. The actress in me was crying to be let out. "Well, why not," I thought, "become characters from novels and biographies and make them come alive for others?" It worked. Audiences loved it.

I became, in costume, Nien Cheng in *Life and Death in Shanghai*, Katherine Hepburn in her story, *Me*, Miss Love Simpson Blakslee in *Cold Sassy Tree*, and many others, including Beverly Sills and Carol Burnett. I've even become men like Russell Baker and Robert Fulghum, who wrote *All I Really Need to Know I Learned in Kindergarten*. As Mr. Fulghum, I costumed myself in a black suit, bow tie, and wing-tip shoes, and told my audience they needed to use a leap of faith and imagine my full white beard.

I've traveled all over Illinois as the founder of the League of Women Voters, Carrie Chapman Catt, from her biography. I've also used several books to create a special program I call "A Celebration of Chicago Women." In it I portray, in authentic costumes, Mrs. Potter Palmer, Edith Rockefeller McCormick, Jane Addams, and Minna Everleigh, who ran one of Chicago's most famous brothels in the early twentieth century.

I work hard, travel far, charge too little, and reap great rewards by sharing my passion for literature in many ways with many others. I have not, thus far, become a "legend in my own mind." My audience keeps me honest about this. At a retirement home where I was giving a dramatic review, a woman in a wheelchair kept asking, "Who is she? Who did you say she was? Who?" Meanwhile, a jackhammer was drilling the cement floor in the hall. I thought it would be a disaster, but I continued on as the *Oldest Living Confederate Widow* telling all. (Someone did finally get the jackhammer to stop.) After my review, a nurse told me that the woman who had asked who I was, had not only smiled for the first time in years, she had actually laughed. Now, that's what I call reaping a fortune.

I've learned to expect the unexpected and not to lose my sense of humor. As I was reviewing Amy Tan's *The Joy Luck Club* in a private home, the owner's dog came up to me, woofed, and plopped down at my feet. I bent down and patted his head as if he were part of the story. In another private home, just as I reached a very moving moment about the killing of people in Sarajevo from Robert Fulghum's book *Maybe (Maybe Not)*, the television, which must have been on an automatic timer, blared on with the soap opera Days of Our Lives. Can you imagine competing with piped in music? That's just what happened when I was reviewing Kaye Gibbons's *Charms for the Easy Life*. I was dressed as Margaret, the granddaughter in the story, and was making my presentation at a luncheon meeting in a restaurant. It was on that occasion I overheard one woman commenting to another, "Even though I'm having difficulty hearing what she's saying, doesn't she remind you of the queen?" I still don't know if she meant I looked regal or frumpy!

If the costume I'm using to portray a character isn't too outlandish or doesn't prevent me from driving safely, I usually arrive wearing it. I arrived at a women's club dressed in southwestern garb—jeans, cowboy boots, Navajo jacket—to portray the character of Taylor Greer in Barbara Kingsolver's *Pigs in Heaven*. As I walked in the door, I said hello to a woman I recognized. She looked me over as if to say, "This woman is inappropriately dressed for the occasion." She then turned to another lady and said, "I wonder when Suzanne Hales is going to get here? Sometimes, even I wonder who I am. But so far I have managed not to mix up the characters in the books I am reviewing.

Occasionally someone in the audience forgets that I am only pretending. This happened when I was dressed in tennis whites as Alice Marble, who won Wimbledon in 1939 and was a spy in World War II, from her book *Courting Danger*. A gentleman told me I had great legs for a "woman my age." When I was reviewing for a group in Evanston, Illinois, as Audrey Meadows from her book *Love Alice, My Life as a Honeymooner*, I was asked, "Miss Meadows, are you visiting here because of Northwestern University?" I had brought my mother as a guest that day. A woman commented to her that Audrey Meadows had certainly aged well, and when my mother responded that I was not Audrey Meadows, but her daughter, the woman moved quickly away as if my mother were crazy. And someone recently confessed to me that when I had arrived at her book group to do a dramatic review as the character Maggie from Anne Tyler's *Breathing Lessons*, dressed in a polyester dress and a little hat with a veil that I had found at a rummage sale, she thought I must be a new member of the group. She said she felt genuinely sorry for anyone who would dress like that. She was relieved when I was introduced as the book reviewer and discovered I was in costume.

I have had to change clothes in less than desirable nooks and crannies. Stalls in ladies' rooms give little maneuvering area. I'd like to forget the day I had to fish my belt, an essential part of the costume I was wearing, out of the toilet. I've also received suspicious looks from women who come in to use the facilities and find some crazy woman dressed in a gown from the 1890s or looking like a 1920s flapper or putting on a wig. I have changed in furnace rooms, behind a stage with barely a curtain for privacy, in back rooms with filthy floors, under stairs, and even in a broom closet.

Doesn't this sound glamorous? And it's all for the love of books!

Hard Work and
Rich Rewards

Clare Peterson and
Marie Dench   **Philadelphia, Pennsylvania**

BOOK DISCUSSIONS BEGAN at Northeast Regional Library in 1966. At our library, the book discussions have both social and intellectual functions. The group members look forward to the time spent together, and the librarians who lead the discussions can interact with the group in a relaxed manner, in contrast to the hectic pace of reference transactions elsewhere in the library. The chance to share and enjoy ideas attracts the staff, even though the book discussions involve responsibilities above and beyond an already heavy workload.

How the Group Is Organized

The library is a logical setting for a book group. At Northeast, librarians volunteer to plan and lead the discussions. There are two book discussion series—fall and spring. Planning for each begins roughly six months in advance to allow time for publicity, placement of book orders, and other organizational tasks. The librarians discuss themes and titles, brainstorm about problems, and plan approaches to the material.

Anyone interested in starting a group should think seriously about how formal the group's operations will be. Obviously, the less formality, the less work. In a library setting, which involves intricate scheduling of staff and facilities, as well as advance orders for materials, the book discussion process demands an orderly routine.

At Northeast, two librarians lead each discussion. Pairing people has many advantages. Two people working together share ideas, split up the workload of background research, and give each other moral support if a problem comes up during a discussion. If one leader becomes ill, or cannot work the discussion because of some other emergency, the other is able to keep the series on schedule. Barring the inclusion of a partner, anyone working alone needs to keep arrangements fairly simple, and the group fairly small. Book discussions, for all the enjoyment and stimulation they provide, involve a lot of work.

Anyone wanting to establish his or her own group, outside the library, should ask friends, coworkers, and neighbors about their reading interests—this will give you a roster of eligible candidates from which to determine how much interest these people have in meeting to discuss what they read.

To find an established group to join, inquire at libraries, community centers, churches, or colleges that offer special workshops or noncredit courses.

Special Reading Interests

As it turns out, Northeast's book discussion patrons enjoy reading plays. Our members will try anything. Not that they necessarily like it—but they are willing to win a few and lose a few. However, in a book discussion questionnaire distributed nearly three years ago, the respondents made a point of asking for more plays.

Book Discussion "Bests"

Our most successful choices come in a variety of categories for us.

Best gamble on an unconventional book: *Lammas Night* by Katherine Kurtz. This story of the efforts made by England's White Witches to use their occult powers to ward off the Luftwaffe and save their country had the potential to upset people, but the group members took the book on its own merits and enjoyed two thoughtful discussions of it.

Best book that almost didn't make the cut: *Windwalker* by Blaine Yorgason. The leadership of the committee at the time hated this book, but a determined committee member held on to it. Her perseverance paid off handsomely, with two groups of satisfied patrons unable to stop discussing this moving story.

Best discussion of a book that no one (even the leaders) really liked: *In Search of Melancholy Baby* by Vasily Aksyonov. For a series on immigration, this book gave a perspective on the experiences of a latter-twentieth-century Russian immigrant. We were lucky to have such a book (especially since many newly arrived Russians use our library), but the author's smug, know-it-all attitude put everyone's teeth on edge. Nevertheless, we had fun imagining how we would function as newcomers to a strange country.

Best comment ever made about the book discussion series: This would have to be the compliment paid by a gentleman who told the leaders of the discussion of *Elmer Gantry* that he had attended another library's discussions, but was switching to Northeast Regional's because they are "more intellectually challenging."

Support Materials

Where appropriate, the book discussion leaders use other media to enhance the discussions. For instance, when we read *To Kill a Mockingbird*, we used scenes from the film (shown on video) to illustrate certain points we wanted to bring out. When appropriate, one discussion leader displays paper dolls which show what the characters in the book would have worn. Books related to the discussion theme are always on display for further reading on the subject at hand.

Other specific instances where we've used support materials, include:

1. A clothesline art exhibit of van Gogh and his contemporaries helped illustrate *Lust for Life*.

2. A full-length video showing of *The Great Impostor* complemented a similar book *Catch Me if You Can*.

3. Needleworked scarlet A's were given to those who attended discussions of *The Scarlet Letter* so that they could better understand the experience of wearing a badge of shame.

4. Selections from P.D.Q. Bach's *Oedipus Tex* gave the *Oedipus Rex* groups the real lowdown (literally) on Sophocles.

Tales of Woe

It hasn't been all smooth sailing. Several problems have plagued Northeast's series from time to time.

Low attendance has been one of these. We have adjusted both our scheduling and choice of material to attract a slightly younger group. With all due respect to the wonderful older readers who have supported the book discussions for nearly thirty years, we must acknowledge the need for new blood, particularly since we face the loss of our older patrons through illness, relocation to nursing homes, and, ultimately, death. If we can lure a few fresh kids in their forties and fifties into our group, we can anticipate more years of meaningful discussions.

Pushy members can be a problem. Most of the attendees are assertive enough to regain the floor from those who don't wish to yield it. Also, the leaders have developed a knack for seizing on comments made by the disruptive persons and using these remarks to segue back into the *group* discussion.

Those who haven't read the book are sometimes a problem. In most cases, those who are unprepared have enough sense not to draw attention to themselves. Frequently, these "auditors" simply want to sample the discussion to see if they want to participate more fully in the future. However, one woman who attended the discussion of Andrew Morton's *Diana: Her True Story* had not read the book, but came to the discussion for the sole purpose of proclaiming her vehement hatred for Prince Charles. One of the leaders later dubbed this woman the "Energizer Bunny," in honor of her persistence.

Then there are bodily functions. An evening discussion of *Mourning Becomes Electra* came complete with its own inebriated Irishman—an O'Neill soulmate, perhaps. Two women slept through an afternoon discussion of *Fried Green Tomatoes at the Whistle Stop Cafe*, one of them snoring like a locomotive. And then there is a certain evening male regular attendee who arrives promptly, greets everyone pleasantly, settles down, and, at regular intervals, emits thunderous belches. At the end of the discussion, he says a cordial goodnight. He rarely comments on the books, unless the belches mean something that the rest of the group cannot comprehend. However, this man did speak very eloquently during a session on Edith Wharton's *The Custom of the Country*, and belched only once. Forget Wharton's Legion of Honor and Pulitzer Prize—*this* is the tribute that really counts!

Organizational details gone awry can also muddle things up. Books sometimes go out of print, publicity flyers occasionally come back with major errors, and procedural questions can filter up or down from the library system's chain of command. These problems occur spontaneously, and we deal with them on an ad hoc basis.

Nuts and Bolts

As mentioned above, the volunteer librarians select a theme and flesh it out with appropriate books, which we both borrow from the library system and purchase in bulk in paperback. For this reason, we only use titles that are in print and in paperback. We schedule the use of two meeting rooms for the discussions, which occur at three-week intervals. The discussion dates cannot conflict with civic or religious holidays, library closings, or the vacation plans of the leaders.

Discussions last about ninety minutes, and begin with some background on the author's life and a few critical reviews of the book. The evening groups have a time constraint. They start at 7:30 P.M., but must end in enough time for the librarians and patrons to leave safely at the building's 9:00 P.M. closing time.

The discussion patrons sign in upon arrival and obtain the books for the next discussion. The setup resembles a relay race, with patrons checking in the books they have finished for that particular discussion, and checking out what they will need for the next discussion, three weeks away. The normal library borrowing period is three weeks; if the discussion patrons had to read their books in less time, they would complain bitterly. The afternoon patrons get a break in that they may remain behind after the discussion ends. The staff members have to leave to go to desk duty in their departments, but the patrons often remain behind, sometimes as long as an hour to share their thoughts about some of the more stimulating books.

Fulfilling a Personal Need, Too

No one has yet come forward with a story of how the discussions have saved them during a personal crisis, but we know that several of the regulars have lost spouses or others close to them, have retired, or have made other fundamental changes in their lives. We feel confident in saying that the discussions help these people keep active, maintain contact with other people with similar interests and tastes, and give them something to anticipate.

For this group's reading list, see page 303.

Frick and Frack at the Library

Laura Luteri and
Judy Bennett   **Mount Prospect, Illinois**

WHY IS IT that high comedy is usually delivered in pairs? Abbott and Costello, Laurel and Hardy, Edgar Bergen and Charlie McCarthy . . . Laura and Judy at the Library?

For the past four years, we have been bringing our brand of comedy to our Friends Evening Book Discussion Group on the third Wednesday of every month. Our regulars come each month to be entertained as much as to talk about the book, I think. We aren't sure what we're doing right, but we're having a lot of fun doing it. And, to my way of thinking, that's what makes it all worthwhile.

In the beginning there was an afternoon book discussion at our library, but it was losing momentum. Judy was president of the library board and I was the neophyte trustee. The library staff morale was low and the Friends group was suffering from terminal burnout after two unsuccessful referenda campaigns. It had become necessary to reduce library hours and jettison programs and services. When people requested a book discussion group that would meet in the evening, there was just no way the library was going to be able to fund it.

As I remember, it all started, as so many of the things I get myself into do, with the statement, "You know what would be neat ... ?" The next thing I knew, Judy and I had been volunteered to lead the book discussion sponsored by the Friends of the Library.

We meet in the library's conference room. Our books are borrowed through an interlibrary loan program from neighboring libraries and are checked out for one month. The discussion is advertised through the Friends' newsletters, as well as through the library's publicity.

We have a core group of about a dozen who come regularly, and new Friends are always welcome. Sometimes we have people who come just to see what we're about and other times new people come to discuss a specific book. We've had as few as four and as many as twenty attend depending on the book. Because it is a quasi-library program, we are always open to the general public, and we always try to make newcomers feel welcome. I usually start by making the introductions while Judy and the rest make side bets that I won't be able to remember everyone's name.

When Judy and I started it was the blind leading the partially sighted. I had gone to the afternoon discussion group just a couple of times. I don't think Judy had ever been in a book group. Our first choice was Robert Fulghum's *All I Really Need to Know I Learned in Kindergarten*. It was a terrific icebreaker because we went around the circle and encouraged participants to talk about how each of his little pieces reflected their own lives.

Our second book was Tom Wolfe's *Bonfire of the Vanities*. This was the first of our "Frick and Frack" routines. I liked the book, and Judy hated it. Judy and I share a sort of dynamic tension. When all else fails and the discussion lags a little, we square off. The group quickly takes up on one side or the other and the discussion takes on a life of its own. The fun part is that we're never sure who is going to side with Judy and who is going to side with me. Although there's a lot of good-natured teasing back and forth, we're all very careful to listen to each other's point of view and not to hurt feelings. We laugh a lot together.

Some of our best discussions have been on books one of us loved and the other hated. But we both agree on our outstanding successes (*Cold Sassy Tree* by Olive Ann Burns is now assigned reading for anyone who becomes a regular) and our total failures (*Thomas Jefferson* by Fawn Brody is our group's benchmark for our worst choice). Judy and I work with our library's readers' advisors and put together a list of books we think the group would like to read, and we also ask for suggestions from the group. We pirate information from anyone who will share it with us. We are very fortunate that Dee, one of our most loyal members, has a daughter who works in a bookstore in Seattle. She keeps coming up with great books for us to add to the list. It took Dee almost two years (Judy and I vetoed it originally) to convince us to read *The Bone People* by Keri Hulme, but it turned out to be a terrific discussion.

We read both fiction and nonfiction, but the group seems to enjoy fiction more. We try to set up the schedule about six months ahead so the library staff can line up the copies we need. Judy and I usually alternate months for choosing. That makes for better variety. If the selection is a success, I picked it. If the discussion is a dud, old-what's-her-face picked that one. Funny how it works out that way.

Our discussions are usually rather free-form. I come with a list of discussion questions, but on good nights I might not even look at the paper. Originally we were supposed to alternate months, but our schedules soon broke the order. Most months we touch base the afternoon before and ask, "Is it your turn or mine?"

Quite often if the story is one which most of the members have enjoyed and it has cinematic quality, we'll spend a few minutes casting the movie. We did this with *Bonfire of the Vanities*, and it was amazing. Not one of us thought of Tom

Hanks as the lead. When a book we talked about is filmed, we take a "road trip" to see it and discuss the film over dessert afterwards. Our verdict on *Jurassic Park*—read the book. Except for the *Name of the Rose* we usually agree that the books are better.

The average discussion runs an hour to an hour and a half. We then open up the floor to book reports. Each member is asked to tell us about what other books she has been reading since we last met. Some months this discussion of other reading matter is just as interesting as the book we came to discuss. We have discovered we have varied tastes, but we encourage each other to try new genres and authors. After Dee told us about the book, we all read *Bimbos of the Death Sun* by Sharyn McCrumb. I think someday we're going to have to discuss it just so we can see the reaction when it is advertised on the library's marquee at the intersection of two major highways.

I realized a while ago that we've all become close friends. When one of our regulars had the lead in a community dinner theater production that kept her from coming to the discussion, we surprised her by turning up as a group in the audience. We discuss our December selection over a potluck at Judy's house. When some scheduling conflicts and an illness in my family made me miss a couple of months in a row leaving Judy to fend for herself (with books I had picked), I realized how much I missed my friends.

This group may have started out as a Friends project, but it has become a project among friends.

Brown-Bagging and Mind Stretching

Ruth H. Kuehler   San Antonio, Texas

OUR BOOK DISCUSSION group started in 1979 under the direction of Dr. Coleen Grissom, who at the time was a professor of English and dean of students at Trinity University in San Antonio, Texas. It was her idea to structure the group as a noncredit, continuing education project for social and intellectual needs. Since then, Dr. Grissom, still an English professor, became president for student affairs and continues teaching one advanced English course each semester. She says she won't give up our reading group, if for no other reason than we keep her from being afraid of old age (many of us are senior citizens). She was born in 1934, and I'm afraid if she ever retires the group will never be the same.

We meet on Mondays from noon to two. There are six Mondays in each session, and we have three or four sessions a year, depending on Dr. Grissom's schedule.

Twelve to fifteen participants showed up for the first class in 1979, and we sat around a large conference table in the Gold Room of the Chapman Center for books and coffee. Now we have grown to approximately one hundred members, and we meet in a large room sitting at round tables in groups of six or eight.

181

Three original members still come to meetings, others have died and some have moved away, but the ranks keep filling up with women in their forties and fifties. And some of us oldies are still hanging on. One of our members, who has attended for years, was the first woman pathologist in the United States, and another the youngest woman to have ever graduated from Vassar. Almost all of the women are college graduates, many from Trinity University.

Our attendance is high all the time, and this is strictly due to Dr. Grissom. She is an accomplished leader, and keeps everything moving at a fast pace, calling on one after another as we raise our hands. She's a great show woman, putting on a performance of the highest quality. Everyone leaves class still energized and continuing the discussion nonstop with each other.

Dr. Grissom begins meetings by giving tidbits of information of interest to people who love fiction. Then she tells us something about the author of the day, always having done her homework thoroughly. Next, she may say something such as: "I would like you to talk about the style of the author and whether it enhances the novel, and if so, how? I know from experience most of you will decide to talk about what you want to talk about, but I'll do my best to keep you in line."

Then, as a show of hands quickly comes up, she calls on individuals, repeats their comments, and writes snatches of what they say on the blackboard.

She gave us the study sheet that runs at the end of this essay, and though she doesn't follow it during the discussion, it's very helpful for home reading.

Ours is a brown-bag meeting, since we meet during lunchtime. The University furnishes drinks. Dr. Grissom grabs a bite before she comes, telling us she stands in front of her microwave shouting at the potato in it to hurry up. The two hours fly. All of the women in the class are interesting—I haven't heard a dull one yet.

Dr. Grissom and the university take care of receptions for visiting writers, and we all get invited to these and sometimes even to the "Master Class." Over the years I've met many authors at these events, including Margaret Atwood, Joyce Carol Oates, John Updike, Jane Smiley, Toni Morrison, May Sarton, Susan Sontag, and John Irving.

Dr. Grissom chooses the books for our group and she tries to introduce us to new authors, as well as the classics. Sometimes she has a theme for a session, but often her selections are based on which books of value are available in paperback and can be readily obtained. She's also open to suggestions from members, but doesn't adhere to their choices too much.

Over and over I hear members say, "I didn't think the book this week was very interesting when I was reading it at home, but after hearing the discussion, I thought it was the most fascinating book I had read in years," or, "When Dr. Grissom had the discussion moving, I was sure I had read the wrong book. The one we were talking about was really great—once I learned how deep it really was."

What a mind stretcher this book group has been for me. I have met numerous interesting women and through them have enriched my life in other fields. Some have become very dear friends through the years.

Questions to Help Analyze Literary Style

(Illustrate your point by direct reference to the text.)

1. Is there anything strikingly different about the author's style?

2. Does she or he often use figures of speech?

3. Is there much wit and/or humor? Pathos?

4. Is there anything unusual about her or his methods of description?

5. Is there much dialogue? Is it natural? What is its purpose?

6. Do you feel the author is a close observer of life? Is she or he sensitive to life?

7. Does she or he ever moralize or seem didactic?

8. Is she or he particularly interested in moral problems? Social problems?

9. Does she or he succeed in evoking an emotional response on the part of the reader?

10. What are the themes? Are they universal or shallow ones?

11. Is the title related to the theme? Is it appropriate? Effective?

12. Is the setting essential to the story, i.e., are the particular times and places especially important?

13. Is an unusual amount of space devoted to establishing the setting? If so, what seems to be the reason?

14. Are the descriptions important either in establishing mood or atmosphere?

15. Is nature used to increase the effect of a scene?

16. Are there many changes of scene? Why or why not?

17. What is the basic conflict of the plot?

18. How is the exposition handled?

19. How is suspense created and maintained?

20. Is each chapter a unit? How does it begin? End? What keeps it going?

21. Is the hand of the author apparent in the plot, or is what happens the natural outgrowth of the circumstances, the characters, and their interactions?

22. Can the character development of the protagonist be readily traced? How and why did she or he change?

23. What use is made of minor characters?

24. Could any characters have been omitted? If so, why has the author included them?

25. What are the author's methods of character portrayal?

26. Who are the "essentially evil" characters? Do they have any redeeming qualities?

27. Who are the "essentially good" characters? Do they have any detracting qualities?

28. Do the characters seem more important than the action? Is what they are more important than what they do?

29. Is there foreshadowing? Is it "signposted" by the author?

30. What is the method of narration? (Chronological, flash-back, diary, letters, parallel events)

31. Are there episodes, incidents, or chapters that might have been omitted as far as the plot is concerned? If so, why did the author include them?

32. What makes the first scene a fitting beginning? Or isn't it?

33. What makes the last scene a fitting (or unfitting) ending?

34. Is the basic conflict of the plot completely and logically resolved?

35. What do you learn or assume to be the author's sense of morals or moral values?

36. Is there close integration of plot, character, setting, and theme?

37. What have you learned that will help you to live more finely (to paraphrase Arnold Bennett)?

A Conversation among Friends

Janet Tripp　　　　**Minneapolis, Minnesota**

BOOKS HAVE MORE to say to me since I joined my book group. Previously, the conversations I held with my books were a quiet dialogue. There were just two voices, mine and the book's. It was nothing like the communion that goes on now—full of exclamations, impassioned pleas, confession and campaigning, enlightenment, and exchange.

Our many voices open a dialogue between book, author, and reader that takes reading beyond a private intellectual endeavor. It places us all in a relationship, interconnected in a reading community. In the companionship of the group, my appreciation of the text is amplified, my relationship with the book transformed.

My book group is full of friends now, people who fourteen years ago were strangers in a continuing education for women class at the University of Minnesota. The class was offered to women interested in an education but not in working on a degree. Our focus was women's autobiography, and our teacher was English Professor Toni McNaron. At our last class meeting we read portions of our own autobiographies and came to a decision. This was too good to end.

Through our reading, we have become good friends. Fourteen years and 168 books after our original class we continue to read, discuss, and share our own writing each month. We do this self-consciously. Our lives as women are formed by our culture, by the books that we read. After twenty and forty and eighty years of shaping by male eyes, we are searching for a different pattern. In our reading we seek a balance to the outside world where men's words dominate the printed page and men's voices dominate the conversation. To this end, we read only books by women, and every six months we choose, at our leader's insistence, at least one poet, one writer from an earlier generation, and one author of color. Each member nominates one book and a vote is taken on which six books we'll read.

Book group keeps me abreast of the times. It leads me to books I'd never choose by myself. On one hand is the book and the author. On the other is me with my own history and expectations. In the middle is the book group—the balancing fulcrum. It is the ground on which my interpretation of the book is balanced with that of the others. I come away from group with an altered perception of the book—altered and enlarged as I see it through twelve sets of eyes and not my own alone.

Opening a new book is like the excitement of a flirtation. Something new, unknown, appealing yet unconsummated, promising endless pleasures. There is exhilaration in the feel of the book—its smooth surface, the small audible moment as the cover is opened and the pages first turned. The title sets up a question in my mind. It invites me in. On the jacket, admirers promote its virtues. I am hooked. Not yet in love, but attracted and willing to enter. Sometimes the promise is fulfilled.

Sometimes I am disappointed. There are books I haven't liked. But I'm never sorry for the investment of time. Each book has offered something. I've dealt with issues that did not concern me until I've found they mattered. I've read books about women who seemed like foreign creatures from another planet and ended up calling them friends. I've read books on subjects too painful for me to have chosen them and, consequently, have been moved to see things in a new light.

I open book group selections with a small reverence. It is someone's choice, meaningful to that woman, therefore deserving my attention, though it may not appeal to me, though it may be full of disappointment, frustration, and displeasure. I read it all. Then I go to group waiting to see what it is I missed, what it is the others saw and where inside was the pleasure—the word or phrase so carefully placed it brings a shiver to my spine, a tear rolling down my cheek. It is a revelation to go to book group, a revelation and a whole new conversation, different from the one I myself had with this book.

Sometimes these conversations have moved me into the larger world. They have prompted letters to the editor, donations to worthy causes, and on one memorable occasion even led me to a daughter.

Over the years we had read many books, such as Tsitsi Dangarembga's *Nervous Conditions*, Toni Morrison's *Beloved*, and Mariama Ba's *So Long a Letter*, in which the position of black women made me cringe for my privilege. It was at this juncture that I was offered the opportunity to help. The insight from these books and the empty room vacated by my college-bound son primed me to say yes when our pastor asked if we would consider taking in a young Ethiopian woman. She was stranded in this country with no support except an uncle who viewed her as a possession to be locked in for the summer and controlled in every aspect of her life. She lives with us now—proof that in a very real sense my book club has expanded my world and my family.

Some group conversations are memorable events in themselves: volatile and mind shattering. I remember the argument over *The Bone People* and the distaste of members whose personal experiences with alcoholism and child abuse pinpointed its romanticization in the novel. It led Toni to review the book critically for a local feminist journal, and it prompted Libby to write a letter to the editors rebutting Toni's critical reading. I remember the discussion after reading the Norwegian *Kristin Lavransdatter* when Toni, who is from Alabama, said it helped her understand Minnesota where the culture is so intertwined with its Scandinavian heritage.

Many of us remember one dramatic response to Margaret Drabble's *The Waterfall*. Janet was so disgusted with the alienated, neurotic, passive characters and their despairing, dreary, listless lives that at her turn in the circle, she tore what she felt was the one "worthwhile" page from the book and deposited the remainder into the fire that was roaring in the hostess's fireplace. There was shocked silence. We're not the kind of women to go in for book burnings. She had made her point.

Though we have strong feelings, we are a civilized group. There are some rules. We don't wear white gloves, flowered hats, and nylon stockings with seams snaking up the backs of our calves, but we are a polite group, well mannered and orderly. We are careful to show respect for the ideas in the book and for one another. There is no one correct interpretation of the book. We disagree often, but agree that these disagreements add zest to the discussion. We enter with an equality—one member with another. In the world outside our conversation, we are vastly different in age and station in life, in experience of inclusion or exclusion in mainstream culture. In group, we are equal. Though some of us live in exclusive neighborhoods in homes full of fine art and some of us cannot afford to replace a broken furnace, each opinion carries equal weight and is treated with respect. Books such as *Bastard Out of Carolina* deal with class issues and touch sensitive nerves. At this meeting women spoke with deep feeling and many with pain.

Two elements are key to our longevity. One is our leader, Toni McNaron, who keeps us on track. This is a paid position and she diligently monitors the time, moving us along and seeing to it that there is time at the end to read our own work. She contributes information about the author and literature of the period.

The other element is our structure of going around the circle, giving each woman uninterrupted time to speak. We explain our responses to the book, list our problems and disappointments, our connections and the pleasures we found within the pages. We read favorite passages aloud. Each woman has her time. She is forced to speak up, but the clock is ticking and no one is allowed to dominate. The time is shared.

Reading favorite passages aloud adds to our appreciation of the book. When we are in general agreement and everyone loves the book, reading aloud enlivens a discussion, which could otherwise be brief and without revelation. Hearing these passages, chunks of the novel are fixed in the reader's voice in my memory. They are framed like a jewel in its setting. I remember Ruth reading from *The Dollmaker* of the "icy-hearted refrigerator." I remember the image it created for us of the cold-hearted industrial world. Ruth has now moved to New York to care for her grandson, walk the streets like Grace Paley, and write and conduct walking tours of the neighborhoods. Still, when I describe the book to people, it is Ruth's voice I hear in my head reading lines to our circle of women.

My group puts me in a new relationship with the book. It extends the dialogue that is begun by the writer, continued in the text, heard by myself in the reading, responded to in the group discussion, and answered as we read our own work. We put ourselves in the position of writer.

The readings we share at the end of our group mark us as different from most book groups. These written responses increase the experience of dialogue we feel as we move back and forth between the book and our group. The conversation is deepened. Toni believes it is in this reading that the most empowering experiences occur. She says, "Every woman has a story. Our task is simply to create forums in which more and more women can get out more and more parts of their stories."

The first time we read together was the last day of our class at continuing education for women. Instead of discussing a text, we went around the circle and each read in turn from her own story.

Helmi, in her eighties at the time, read about her romance with her husband of many years. Helmi was a Finn from the Minnesota Iron Range, and Isadore was a Russian, a Jewish furrier who had come to New York to escape the Russian army. Helmi was headstrong and independent, free with her money. Isadore was a practical, business-minded young man who was aghast to learn that Helmi had not one penny saved despite her jobs in the St. Paul and Minneapolis libraries and at a private social agency for "wayward girls."

Money wasn't the only problem between the young married couple. She wanted a dozen children; he didn't care if they ever had any. He was troubled that Helmi was a gentile and that his beloved mother would not be able to accept her. He decided to take a long trip to Cuba to think things out. Helmi went home to visit her family.

She read to us, "So he went and I went. My parents were calm, unruffled Finns who took things as they are without any hoopla, and I had a lovely visit. When I returned to Minneapolis, my brother-in-law and I met the thinker at the train, came home and had a gala lunch opening gifts brought by the traveler. As soon as my brother-in-law left, I was thrown on the bed with great joy and no protection and no discussion of should we or should we not have a family. Nine months later there was Libby—a gift of love, and later two more gifts of Sara and Arnold."

This cycle of communication—author-book-reader-group-writer—is completed when we trade seats with the author, write and then read our own work to the group. We hear letters to children and friends, letters to the editor, essays, short stories in progress, poems and memoir, personal reflections and, occasionally, a published piece. From this new perspective as writer, we enter our reading on another level. We hear with a finely turned ear.

There are many large problems in this world and not many large pleasures. My book group, however, is one such pleasure. The books that we read link us one to another, a small experience of the joyful dialogue that is life.

For this group's reading list, see page 328.

PART V

See, It's Really *More Than Just a Book Group*

You don't have to dig too deep to uncover all the things besides thoughtful discussion that book groups offer their members. Book groups can reflect problems in society and culture. And they can do their part in helping to overcome both. For instance, in this section you'll find a piece about why Eastern Europeans don't join book groups and one that illuminates why American men don't. Surprisingly, the reasons aren't so different.

Meeting Bill

Katheryn
Krotzer Laborde   **River Ridge, Louisiana**

THIS STORY STARTS with three single, bored, twentysome-
things, looking for intellectual stimulation and a reason to
gather on a regular basis.

I doubt we would have met Bill any other way.

One muggy September night, Doug called out of the blue,
saying he wanted to form a book discussion group. At about
the same time Gina, claiming her brain was turning to mush,
came upon the same idea. The three of us got together, added
some others, and our group was born.

Altogether there were about ten of us: all with liberal arts
educations we failed to use in occupations that bored us. We
decided to meet every other Tuesday, and drew up a preliminary book list. We agreed to read Kate Chopin's *The
Awakening*—something short to get us started—for our first
official meeting, set two weeks from that night.

The big night came. Five people showed up.

"We need some outsiders, some new blood," Gina said,
and we agreed. I designed eye-catching flyers that we placed
in a few coffeehouses around New Orleans. They didn't go
unnoticed: I received one death threat (complete with heavy

breathing) and one query from a guy named Bill, whom I told to read Anne Rice's *Interview with the Vampire* for Tuesday.

I told the three who showed up that night of our solitary response. We ordered coffee and scones and agreed that, should this Bill turn out to be weird—remember that death threat?—we'd change our meeting spot and conveniently forget to inform him.

We looked around anxiously. Doug eyed his watch and announced the newcomer was already fifteen minutes late and would perhaps never show. Then, as if on cue, the door edged open and a chubby man carrying a worn paperback looked around anxiously.

I called out to him and motioned to an empty chair. He sat, blinking several times as we introduced ourselves.

None of us were prepared for Bill, to be quite honest. He was older by a good fifteen years, for one thing, sporting more than a few gray hairs. He was pudgy and soft and had an intense squint. As the night wore on, he rubbed his palms along his thighs frequently and constantly pushed up his glasses. When he got nervous, he stuttered. Softly.

But he knew books—the great and the insignificant, the classic and the just published. And while his ways bordered on timidity, his comments were insightful. "If you d-don't mind," he said after the third meeting, "we need to revise this b-book list. W-w-why should I read something suggested by someone who's not even here?" He was right, of course, since the group had already lost more than half of its original, enthusiastic core.

I opened my book and recorded the new list on the back cover. Some suggestions stayed the same: Deanne still wanted to read *Cold Sassy Tree*; Gina suggested *The World According to Garp*; Doug insisted we would love *Murder in the Smithsonian*; and I maintained that a discussion of *Edie*, accompanied by a viewing of the cult film *Ciao! Manhattan*, would give greater insight to a decade that most of us had seen through Mr. Rogers's eyes.

Bill looked to the ceiling before speaking. "W-well, those are OK, but there are a few books I know of that I think you'd like." *The Unbearable Lightness of Being. Justine. The Last Temptation of Christ.* ("The movie's coming out soon," Doug said. "Oh, but there's no way the movie could be as beautiful as the book," Bill countered, and, of course, he was right.)

Deanne left the group before we could get to her book, so we never read it. Nothing against Olive Ann Burns, but we found ourselves adding to and deleting from the official list so often that I never bothered to retype it. All Gina had to say was, "García Marquez's new book is in paperback," and we found ourselves adding *Love in the Time of Cholera* to the list. I can still remember the heated discussion over the success of that book's ending, with the men defending its romantic beauty, and Gina and I denouncing it as sentimental. What wouldn't be after reading President Clinton's favorite book—*One Hundred Years of Solitude?*

On more than one occasion, I noticed people staring as we debated a particular point. *In Cold Blood* led to a discussion of capital punishment. We couldn't pick a mutual favorite from the *Best American Short Stories* anthology. Bill was the only one to enjoy *Forrest Gump* (but now that it's made it to the big screen, I'm tempted to read it again). I recall being the lone defender of *A Cannibal in Manhattan.* And on one night, we were ten minutes into a discussion before realizing Bill had read Steinbeck's *Cannery Row* rather than *Tortilla Flats,* the book *he* had suggested.

As weeks passed, we got to know Bill better than we originally would have thought possible. He told us stories about a younger, thinner Bill who wore his hair long and hitchhiked across the country. Occasionally he would talk about how he had waited out the Vietnam War in Canada, or how his trench coat and bike were, at one time, his only possessions. He mentioned that while his estranged wife was living in Alabama, he still worked for his father-in-law as a roofer. Though we all hated our jobs, we felt the worst for Bill since his was obviously tearing him apart. We saw him as a teacher. A wonderful teacher.

And a frustrated writer. I still can remember him telling us about living in a boarding house that was occupied, for the most part, by old people. It wasn't until one of the tenants— an old, lame man whom he used to visit—died that Bill discovered the man was the estranged husband of the woman who ran the house. "I've always wanted to write about that, but I've never known how," he said.

Actually, we all wanted to write, so in addition to our bimonthly book meetings, we added a few writing sessions. On these nights, each handed his or her notebook to another who would write an opening sentence. We would take these sentences and build upon them for an hour, then spend the next hour reading our work aloud over second cups of coffee.

Once, I handed my notebook to Bill, who wrote: *When I was a kid, I remember riding down the highways out west and seeing little white crosses on the side of the road where there had been an accident.*

It occurred to me that Bill, in many ways, was still that little boy traveling the highways of this country, not really settled or satisfied. Fiction must have offered an escape to him from a life I could barely imagine. I knew he wasn't what you would call a happy person, but I also knew that our group offered some sort of salvation to him. He looked forward to our meetings, and was often not only the first to arrive, but the last to rise from his chair when we were through.

One night, Bill announced the roofing company had gone bankrupt, and that he was out of a job and broke. His wife was willing to take him back, he said, and he would be leaving at the end of the week. He was telling us good-bye.

Though it didn't have to be, that was the last meeting for all of us. Doug was considering a move to Miami, and Gina, a career change. I had been accepted to graduate school, which I knew would take me away from the group in time.

It was time to move on.

A good five years have passed since the group disbanded. My MFA diploma hangs neatly on the wall. I'm married now, and a mommy to boot. I've lost touch with Doug, but Gina and I still get together to discuss books, or life in general. We're ready to form another group—a new group. Sure, we have names of people we'd like to ask to join, but we're working on flyers to stick in our favorite bookstores.

We're hoping to find Bill.

I still half-expect to find him sitting on the coffeehouse porch, book open. Sometimes I think I see him in a crowd—quickly, peripherally—the way one sees someone who has passed away. I remember asking a limousine driver if his name was Bill, which he denied. Being drunk on champagne and the excitement of my wedding day, I decided that my eyes were playing tricks on me.

If I ever do see him again, I'll tell him that I've made the jump: I'm a writer now. That I'm still working on that story about the little white crosses on the side of the road. And that I'd like to write that other story for him, the one about the boarding house. It's a hard story to write, but I know one day I'll find the words.

And I'll name the main character Bill.

Dangerous Book Groups

Susan P. Willens   **Washington, D.C.**

DURING THE YEAR I just spent as a Fulbright professor of literature in a small city in eastern Slovakia, I became close friends with several women who had lived there all their lives. Now, in their early forties, these educated, English-speaking women are established in their professions and their family lives, ready to branch out beyond the doctor's practice, the interpreter's travels, the mother's schedule. "Bored, that's what I am," said Dagmar. "How much gossip can I endure? How many conversations with my sister-in-law?" Zuzana concurred. As much as they love their families and work, an intellectual void, which their sporadic English lessons did not quite fill, was yawning before them.

"Why not start a book group?" I asked and described how my long-running groups in Washington, D.C., had provided just that chance that they were looking for, to talk about books with interesting men and women. Blank faces. "No," they finally chorused, "no one would come."

In the conversation that followed, I discovered one more of the many differences between Slovak culture and American culture that grow from the long authoritarian domination of the East. No one would come to a book group meeting because for years meetings were places where people observed each other's ideological development. Right thinking meant promotion, summer holidays, opportunities for one's children. Wrong thinking—even apathy—meant delayed privileges, thwarted plans, or quiet exile. Now, after the Velvet Revolution, the memory lingers, and people shun meetings.

Zuzana and Dagmar are both readers of fiction in several languages and loved discussing with me any of the writers whose works we'd all read, especially Steinbeck and Hemingway. But those discussions were with me—a safe outsider. Even if they could build on these conversations and persuade their friends that the thought police have relaxed, that book groups could be exploratory, open to conversations and tentative ideas, with no one reporting on anyone else, there was still a corollary holdover from the bad old days. They claimed that their friends had lost the habit—maybe had never had it—of expressing personal opinions in public. "Even the women I meet all the time at my children's school, stop talking when I bring up anything beyond the teachers or the lunches," Dagmar complained.

In the United States, book groups meet in a particular psychological area, halfway between the private zone of household and family, and the public zone where strangers conduct the affairs of the world, stores, offices, civic services of all kinds. In between we have another region, where we meet acquaintances to discuss our children's play groups, the work of our church or synagogue, the safety of our neighborhoods, the protest before the city council. This is where we attend to the work of the bar association, the alumni association, Alcoholics Anonymous, or the board of a charity; it is the home of the PTA and the political club, the tennis association, the AIDS awareness group, the ecology newsletter—and the book club.

The authoritarian system in Slovakia, and, I assume, most of Eastern Europe, spoiled this psychological area as well. Because a centralized planning structure was responsible for all the questions that citizens in a democracy manage in this middle region, people have neither the interest nor the skills to solve problems with others who are not family or friends on one hand, or strangers on the other. Furthermore, the past makes them reluctant to confide in a mere acquaintance, for fear that, as in the old days, that acquaintance might report the confidence. Although the old system has died, its ghost haunts those who endured it for so long.

Book groups as we know them depend on the members' capacity to trust each other, to permit half-formed, unorthodox, revolutionary, even wrong, ideas to be stated, considered, debated, used, or discarded. They depend on our comfort with acquaintances with whom we share, not our whole lives, but just this interest, reading and discussing books.

Now, if anyone can shake loose from old habits, my Slovak friends can do it. As we talked about the possibility of their forming a small book group—maybe among those few who can read and discuss in English or maybe among those who want to read Slovak or other literature together, maybe with other women or other professionals—they seemed more hopeful that such an experiment is at least worth a try. I expect to hear from them in the fall that a few friends have gathered for the adventure of discussing their reading.

I am not suggesting a covert way for eastern Europeans to imitate us in the United States. They have many strengths in their culture and we have many weaknesses in ours. Not all the good is on the side of the West. At the same time, I learned—as I did all the time I was there—how precious are our patterns of democratic debate, informal assembly, and continuous learning, as evidenced by the thousands of book groups across the United States.

If my friends could overcome the hurdles on their way to a book group, they could gain access to ideas for debate and exploration now that their formal schooling is over. They might find a place to practice the skills of free assembly and open discussion that they have lost. And I find myself hoping that conversation about books can bring energy, excitement, and collegiality to areas of the world that have been deprived of them for so many years.

As a result of my being in Eastern Europe for a year, my book group in Washington, D.C. wants to read books that will teach us more about that part of the world. A partial list of our readings on this topic includes: *Mendelssohn Is on the Roof,* Jiri Weil (Czech novel); *The Castle,* Franz Kafka (Czech novel); *The Captive Mind,* Czeslaw Milosz (Polish essays); *One Day in the Life of Ivan Denisovich,* Alexander Solzhenitsyn (Russian novella); *The Encyclopedia of the Dead,* Danilo Kis (Serbian stories).

Where Are
All the Men?

Bob Lamm   New York City

LET'S BEGIN WITH Louisa May Alcott and Amy Tan.

In early 1995, I came across a brilliant and devastating op-ed piece in the *New York Daily News* by Fran Wood, that paper's managing editor for features. Wood wondered why droves of women and virtually no men were going to see the latest Hollywood version of *Little Women*. Wood noted that most of the men who did see the film didn't "get it" and didn't cry even when Beth died. Moreover, Wood added, even if the men did cry, they wouldn't dare admit it, because such an admission would violate the "Guy Code."

Wood's column reminded me of a discussion in a reading group in 1994 when the film version of *The Joy Luck Club* came out. Virtually all of us (seven women, two men) were fans of Amy Tan's writing. The movie was a big hit in the group, and many of us spoke of crying and crying throughout it. A few of the women finally concluded that any man who *didn't* cry a lot while watching that movie wasn't worth knowing.

I believe that the issues of crying, reading, and joining book groups are all related. If we understood why men don't read *Little Women* or *The Joy Luck Club*, why men don't see the film versions of these great works, why men don't cry

204

when they do, then we would understand why men don't join book groups.

So, to begin with an oversimplified statement, men don't join reading groups because it would violate the Guy Code. Many men have been conditioned—in our sexist, homophobic society—to be suspicious of reading and socializing and to be downright terrified of showing and sharing feelings. Because of that powerful conditioning, men look at book clubs as an inherently feminine and feminist enterprise and as one more form of "women's work" that should be avoided at all costs.

I will explore this further by addressing three interrelated questions: 1) Why are men significantly less likely than women to read books? 2) Even when they read books, why are men significantly less likely than women to read serious fiction? 3) Even when they read serious fiction, why are men significantly less likely than women to join book groups?

But first, a word about my qualifications for this task. I'm a freelance writer, coauthor of an introductory sociology textbook for college students, and I've taught classes on "Men, Masculinity, and Sexism" at Yale, Queens College, and the New School for Social Research. I love lots of things in the Guy Code, among them playing competitive sports, watching sports on television, and playing poker. I also love lots of things *not* in the Guy Code, including daytime soap operas, cooking, and talking about actual feelings. I've been in a number of book groups, one of them a wonderful men's study group on early feminist political writings.

Why Are Men Significantly Less Likely Than Women to Read Books?

In my early twenties, I was a nursery school teacher for about two years. In my experience, many little boys love books, just as many little girls do. At age four or five, the thrill of having a parent or teacher read you a story surely crosses gender lines. But socialization into traditional masculinity, into traditional masculine notions of career and fatherhood, means that most boys are pushed very early on into giving up their creative impulses, their spontaneity, and their sense of play.

Competitive male sports remain acceptable as a training ground for the battles of the corporate world, the factory floor, and the actual battlefield. But many boys who love painting, creative writing, strumming a guitar, or even reading for sheer pleasure (rather than high grades) receive messages that such activities are frivolous and somewhat unmanly.

Even worse, of course, are the pressures on boys who love dolls or sewing or dance classes, in a society where terror of homosexuality remains intense. Parents, teachers, religious leaders, and others zealously watch boys to ensure that they will become appropriately "masculine"—in other words, not like women (as if that would be so terrible!) and not like gay men (who are stereotyped and condemned for being too much like women). How many boys each year stop painting or sewing or even reading because someone has called them a "faggot" for doing so?

It's true that not every boy experiences this type of socialization. I grew up in an upper-middle-class, suburban, Jewish subculture where my skills in academic tasks were viewed as much more important than my deficiencies as an athlete. But even in subcultures that encourage boys to read and value educational achievement, the instrumental value of schooling is often prized far more than the inherent value of being well read. If any boy in my circle had failed his classes because he was reading novels and poetry all night rather than studying for exams, his parents' priorities would have become very clear, very fast.

It's true as well that some boys subject to traditional masculine conditioning nevertheless find the strength and courage to remain true to themselves and pursue their creative dreams. They become dancers, sculptors, violinists, poets, novelists, and professors of literature. Still, despite these exceptions, many boys succumb to the intense weight of the Guy Code and lose a great deal of their humanity as they "mature" and become men.

Ironically, one of the costs of maintaining power and dominance in a sexist society is that men distance themselves from many creative highs, including the satisfaction of reading. There is a great joy, a great peace, that comes from living for a time inside a wonderful book. Any of us who have ever said "I just couldn't put it down" know that feeling deep inside. Too many men are missing that pleasure.

Even When They Read Books, Why Are Men Significantly Less Likely Than Women to Read Serious Fiction?

Reading *any* book or magazine can spark emotions if you are open enough. But the themes and issues of serious fiction inevitably focus on all those murky, reflective, internal, interpersonal aspects of life that men tend to find threatening. Just as most men would rather see *Die Hard 12* than *Little Women*, they will absorb themselves in the most brutal detective novels, the most technological science fiction, or the most dehumanizing pornography—rather than a compelling novel about people's thoughts and feelings that would make them actually *feel* something.

It is sometimes argued that men prefer escapist entertainment to more challenging art and literature because they face painful pressures to perform on the job and therefore need to escape. Yet many women hold exactly these types of jobs *and* are the primary or only caregivers for their children. And somehow they read serious novels despite all that! Does anyone experience more pressure to perform than a single mother who works outside the home? But, more so than men, these single mothers "escape" to Louisa May Alcott or Amy Tan, rather than to mindless fiction or *Lethal Weapon 25*.

The lives of too many men focus on escaping from their own emotions and the emotions of others. If a man's life has that orientation, he is not likely to fill his leisure time with serious novels that make emotional demands on him. (Just as he may be likely to avoid *human beings* who make emotional demands.)

Even When They Read Serious Fiction, Why Are Men Significantly Less Likely Than Women to Join Book Groups?

Many older book clubs were established at a time in which voluntary associations were overwhelmingly all-male or all-female. Book clubs were often composed of full-time home-makers, women who were barred from most avenues of intellectual or professional life and even from voting. For such women, book clubs provided intellectual stimulation and a sense of community; they were also an admirable experiment in self-education in a society that placed little value on women's education.

Since women had second-class status, it is hardly surprising that men looked with disdain on any enterprise created by and comprised of women. Consequently, book clubs began, in men's eyes, as a "feminine" pastime, as another example of "women's work" to be ignored or patronized. Given that history, those of us in the book groups of the nineties should remember and honor those women who pioneered this grand experiment—women who made a commitment to their own intellectual growth and to each other.

In the nineties, however, many of the women in reading groups are committed to careers and work nine to five or longer hours. Yet, these women still read books, still read serious fiction, still join book groups more often than equally hardworking male counterparts. Many women *prefer* women-only groups. In our sexist society, it is important to support their right to that time and space and community in women's groups. At the same time, some women diligently attempt to recruit men for book groups but meet with little success.

I suspect that while men of earlier generations avoided book clubs because they were viewed as too *feminine*, men of the nineties do the same because contemporary reading groups are seen as too *feminist*.

On the obvious level, many women in current book groups (including groups open to men) *are* explicitly feminist. These women prefer to read women writers, are tired of male domination of mixed groups, and will surely challenge the misogyny of male authors or group members. Since most men want their sexism to remain unchallenged, staying out of reading groups makes a certain kind of sense.

On a more subtle level—as was well examined in an article in *Ms.* magazine by journalist Robin Neidorf—reading groups are inherently feminist in important ways even when members avoid that identification. The structure and group process of many book groups borrow from the best of the participatory democracy of the sixties and the women's consciousness-raising groups of the seventies.

Many groups meet in the informal, personal settings of people's homes, which adds to the intimacy of the book group experience. There is generally strong emphasis on each member's opinion and on minimizing competitive frictions. While some groups have leaders or facilitators, many do not. Often there are few or no rules, there is a give-and-take atmosphere, and personal reactions and revelations are accepted or even encouraged.

All this stands in dramatic contrast to the kinds of formal, structured, "objective," impersonal groups that many men prefer. Indeed, book groups often have no hierarchy, no status positions, no experts, no trophies, prizes, or tangible rewards. Just the vague, spectacular reward of meeting people you like and respect in an intimate setting to share insights, experiences, food, and drink.

In a better, saner world, the desire to spend an evening sharing food and conversation and reactions to great literature would have nothing to do with gender. In a better, saner world, men would look forward to Amy Tan's next novel and to the next Hollywood version of *Little Women*. They would even cry when touched by brilliant novels or cinema or theater. In a better, saner world, all those little boys who love having someone read to them would *never* lose their passion for words and stories and ideas and fantasies and feelings and books.

I don't know if I'll live long enough to see that better, saner world. But in the nineties—in a world with too many video games and not enough literacy—I believe that each book group, in its own quiet way, is fighting a valiant fight. Each book group is bringing us closer to a world where everyone, even adult men, will escape to great literature.

Gentle Reader

Noëlle Sickels   **Los Angeles, California**

I DO NOT belong to a book group. I was once a member of a short-lived, four-woman group in Philadelphia; we read three books before unraveling, not from lack of enthusiasm for our enterprise, but because we failed to see in time that our group needed conscious protection from the pull of the other strands in our lives.

In spite of the undeniable fact that I love to read and to talk about books and although during a recent visit to Manhattan I sat in on a long-running group and found it welcoming, stimulating, and very enjoyable, I do not plan to start a book group, either, at least not in the foreseeable future. The New York group was discussing *Middlemarch* (before the television series), which coincidentally, I had just read a year earlier. Hence, I was able to insert my two cents worth about the irritability quotient of the pious Dorothea.

So what am I doing worming my way into a collection of essays on book groups? I am here to try to explain why it means so much to me to know that such groups are flourishing across the nation, creating their own nonelectronic Internet, complete with the hum of ideas and feelings aroused by the thoughtful and intricate perusal of books.

I am a writer. I have tackled every form of writing except the limerick, but my mainstay is fiction, both long and short. Writing is, paradoxically, both an extremely solitary occupation and an activity that presupposes the existence of an "other"—the unknown reader. As a writer, I do not write to seduce or even, necessarily, to please this reader; nevertheless, by the very nature of writing, I am constantly addressing her, inviting her to walk with me a while, to trust me enough to follow my map even if the ground is familiar, to see what I notice and listen to what I hear, to open her heart to invented pains and joys as fully as she does to those in real life, sometimes, perhaps, even more fully.

The kind of readers who choose to join book groups are a writer's dream come true, the perfect hiking companions through the writer's claimed landscape. Metaphorically speaking, they know enough of botany and geology to appreciate the curve of the hills, the shadowy undergrowth of the fens, and the sweep of the beaches. They see the forest and the trees. They have, too, a firm purchase on human nature, both their own and various fictional representations of it, so they are able to judge a story's people (and a person's story) with acumen and sympathy.

But above all else, they care. They take the time and the energy needed for caring and give it to a book as they would to a friend. They invest their reading and their discussions of what they have read with true passion. They are willing to spend their emotions and their intellect with openhanded generosity. A casual observer of one lively book group meeting remarked with amazement on the involvement of the members with the book at hand, the fervor of their opinions, as if, he said, the characters under discussion "were real people they knew." Though it was not meant as a compliment, I think that group can take it as such, for it is testimony to their success as readers.

It seems to me that the members of book groups think like writers. They are acute observers. To each book, they bring what they already know of both books and life, and, as importantly, they bring an openness to learning something new—not learning in a dull, moralistic sense, but learning as discovery. They are willing to let what is unformed within them well up and take shape in answer to words on a page. Indeed, they invite this to happen. For the writer, these things occur as the words come out; for the reader, they occur as the words go in. The book group member then takes an extra step, entering with a kind of joyous bravery the fray of explaining her reactions, harnessing yet more words, her own and those of her fellow members, to expand and extend the reading experience, and, in an intangible but substantial way, the book itself.

I have modest aspirations. I do not covet a place on the best-seller list or the movie of the week. What I want for my poems and short stories and novels and essays is an engaged audience. (Not, perhaps, such a modest aspiration, after all.) Engaging them is part of my job, of course, but it is a great boost to my spirits to know that readers exist who fervently seek engagement—readers who will bring to my work as deep an attention as I spent in producing it.

I struggle to find the right words, the most effective sequence of events, the most appropriate form, and the essential truth of my characters because I must do so to satisfy myself. But close to that, so close as to be simultaneous, I do it to communicate my vision, to share my versions of storytelling and living and language.

I do not know who will pick up the anthology that contains my story, when someone will read my poem in a literary journal, or where someone will curl up with my novel. I cannot know, either, what secrets, bitter and sweet, those readers carry in their backpacks as they trudge through my contrived territory, nor how they will spread their own meanings on my tale—whether they will choose to lay their bedrolls on granite or moss. What I do know is that if this reader—this intimate stranger—is in a book group, half the battle is won, for my writing will have its day in court before a jury that weighs justice with both head and heart. Critical but patient ears and eyes will be turned my way. Private lives will be suspended for a brief span to make room for the lives I have devised. I couldn't ask for more. I don't.

So, to all book group members everywhere, leaning across crumb-strewn tables toward one another or circled in a living room with books open on your laps and arguments or laughter in the air, I say, keep up the good work. For it is work, and it is good, what you are doing. Even if the authors you discuss never know a single word of what you have said, even, in fact, if the authors are dead, you are contributing to their vitality and to the longevity and reality of their creations. You are patrons of the arts, spending the invaluable coin of your minds and your sentiments. Actions may speak louder than words, but words matter. They matter very much. You, gentle reader, stand witness to that.

A World Open to Chance

John McFarland　　　　　**Seattle, Washington**

"YOU WALK DOWN the street. You see somebody that looks interesting. You strike up a conversation. You check it out," one of us said. The other three nodded in agreement. We'd all been there. "You clear a place for chance to operate with your men, and you see where it takes you. Why would you want it to be any different with your book group?"

Who of us could argue with that? Thus it was that the four of us, all gay men, chose serendipity and experimentation as the guiding principles in forming our book group. We were convinced that being open to chance influences would protect us from what we saw as the forces that would doom such a venture. Just as they should be avoided in budding romances, the stodgy, the routine, and the pretentious were to be guarded against at all costs in book group. We trusted that diversity of membership, with the promise of new blood constantly recharging the mix, would be our insurance. Our only rule was that there were no rules. That was our beginning and we greeted it with all the hope and anticipation that we brought to meeting anybody hot and promising that we ran into in our world open to chance.

Our group had sixteen members at first: men and women, gay and straight, all voracious readers with eclectic tastes. Once that group assembled, of course, we established ground rules in the great tradition of participatory democracy. We would meet on the last Wednesday of the month. The meeting would start at 7:30 P.M. sharp and would include discussion of that month's book with time set aside for the selection of the next month's book. The meeting would rotate through our various residences and the only thing served would be brewed decaf coffee. We kept it simple.

Then, with the simple ground rules in place, the eternal dance of small group dynamics took over. It became clear very quickly that we had a strong and sizable literary contingent among us. These people knew their books, were up on the latest trends, and were passionate in their advocacy of certain books.

In a group that went whichever way the wind blew, this contingent took over from the get-go. But none of us argued with the fact that these people contributed an untold knowledge of books. They raised the level of books we read and held the discussions to a high standard. They also did everybody's homework since they had enough book suggestions to last us into the next century.

But on the whole, we all had to admit that the discussions of these high-caliber books weren't exactly hot stuff no matter how much we liked the books themselves. Louise Erdrich's *Love Medicine* was a prime example. Here was a rich and satisfying collection of short stories about Native Americans on and off a reservation in the desolate landscape of North Dakota—the electric private reading experience that we all pray for. But it left us with little to say to each other besides "beautifully written," and "profoundly affecting."

Love Medicine was not alone in our experience. Over and over again, we found that a praiseworthy novel or story collection did not stimulate substantive discussion. We were there to share our reading experiences, not husband them like priceless jewels. We wanted debates and dynamics and explorations, not just consecration of high art that didn't need our added blessing. The trick was how to get to that sharing.

To solve our problem, we resorted to experiments. During one summer when everybody in the group was planning a trip, we decided to take a three-month hiatus from meeting and to read a classic, the longer the better, to fill the months we were apart. We chose Leo Tolstoy's *Anna Karenina*.

When we reunited in the fall, the group did have a lively discussion, but not in the way any of us could have predicted. Though we didn't depart radically from the "liked it/didn't like it" trap that we fell into when it came to modern American fiction, people's passionate involvement with Tolstoy's masterpiece made them reveal aspects of their tastes that were news to the rest of us. "Next to this novel, every-thing else looks bland," was one comment. Another person enjoyed the portrait of Russian life, but declared, to gasps of astonishment, "Anna is a shallow character." Yet another said, "I liked this, but I have no interest in reading another word he wrote."

Although people did reveal themselves in relation to *Anna Karenina*, we couldn't deny that novels were not the best basis for discussion. Yet all of us were fanatic novel readers and wanted to include them among our selections.

It was time for another experiment. This time it was an attempt to mix in more nonfiction with our fiction choices. And soon we selected Richard Rodriguez's *Hunger of Memory*, a book that addressed the issue of bilingual programs in U.S. education. As we assembled, people mumbled that they *hated* this book. We felt that Rodriguez had been set up as a Hispanic spokesperson fronting for conservatives who wanted bilingual education programs to die. We wanted to put our fists through the wall at what a dishonest piece of work this was. Then the formal discussion began.

Much to our surprise, we found that the points Rodriguez made provided an excellent framework for thought-provok-ing policy debate whether we agreed with his point of view or not. The book inflamed readers in our group like no other one we had read so far, yet it was the basis for the single most exciting discussion in the first two years of our group.

Despite all the benefits the group reaped from the literary contingent, there was a very real downside to their dominance. We lost some of our members who didn't like the "serious" direction in which things were drifting. After the defections, there were new and healthy grumblings that "certain people's" tastes were shutting out other valid alternatives. Once again, it was time for an experiment.

To force people to voice their choice, we declared that those who had chosen a book recently should sit back while others proposed a book. Although this approach was unusually regimented for us, it did break up the sense of literary uniformity that was settling over the group.

Things went along fine with this method for a while. Until we chose Don DeLillo's *The Names*, that is. What appeared to many of us as the simple story of a vacation on an unnamed mysterious Greek island awash with spy-like activities, incensed others. The anti-forces declared that they found the novel not to be of interest—empty, silly, and macho posturing. That assault drove the pro-forces to defend their position. As the debate got ugly, opinions grew more polarized. And there we were facing the reality that although our group itself was diverse, our choices of what to read were shutting down diversity in choice and response.

We kicked this problem around for a while. It seemed that people wanted guarantees. They wanted to know ahead of time that investing time in reading a book and coming to the two-hour meeting would be interesting. But as we all knew, gay men and lesbians especially, there are no guarantees.

After much wrangling, we settled on a device long used by *The New York Review of Books*: pairing books according to some common criterion and thus creating a de facto forum. This choice provided many options for our diverse membership: we could read one book and not the other; we could read some of one, hate it and close it, and then move on to read all of the other; we could read them both, be insatiable and studly, and compare and contrast them or generally lord it over our less energetic colleagues. By this time we were so used to experiments, what did we have to lose with another one? We went for it.

Since it was late September when we had this discussion and our next meeting would be just before Halloween, we put a seasonal spin on our experiment. We selected Anne Rice's *Interview with the Vampire*, the first installment of her vampire chronicles that nobody had read but many had heard was solid storytelling, and Stephen King's *Salem's Lot*, a tale of horror set in autumnal New England and a bone thrown to those members with less exalted tastes.

As it turned out, each novel was excellent on its own terms, and full of surprises in the bargain. Anne Rice's was funkier than its literary reputation suggested, and Stephen King's was a lot more literary and well written than its trashy reputation implied. The discussion of how these two writers got their effects turned into one of our best about novels. It gave us hope that we wouldn't have to give up fiction as a group.

This successful combination, which happened by chance, seemed to make people less hesitant about suggesting titles. The burden of selecting a book to impose on everybody was lifted. Now you had only 50 percent responsibility and, as we would find out, often a less-than-sterling book set off its partner to great advantage. The key was selecting matches that would lead to creating a dynamic discussion. Now every time was an experiment. And since the selection process became interesting in its own right, people seemed more willing to come to meetings even when they had no interest whatsoever in the books being discussed. They came because the future always held promise and possibility.

It was a new variation of the reason why we all go out, and why we give strangers the benefit of the doubt. It was as if each of us believed in the depth of our throbbing hearts that right around the corner there would be that one glorious book to change our lives.

The list section of this book highlights some of the books we paired together in experiments that paid off in ways that we all want our romances to pay off.

For this group's reading list, see page 301.

Transported

E. Shan Correa   Honolulu, Hawaii

ONCE, WHEN I wrote a science fiction story called "The End of the Road," I carried it along to my book group. That group was, I'm certain, the best book group in existence. We all loved reading and loved each other, so how could it have been otherwise? We had long since accepted that the first half hour of our discussions needed to be nonstructured, a euphemism for "we'll never get down to business right away anyway, so why try?" That was when we shared news, triumphs, rejections (Angie and I were both writers who shared most of those), support, and kindness. Sometimes Angie and I tried out new poetry or short prose during our nonstructured time. That morning I read "The End of the Road."

Now when I wrote that story, I hated it. Not the story. I'm still fond of the short-short about an elderly, childless couple who found a baby, took it home, then faced some very strange circumstances when the infant spoke to them. What I hated was myself for writing in a genre I found unfamiliar and, I'll admit, slightly inferior to the more "literary" fiction I fancied I wrote. I blamed my new computer for enticing me into foreign territory, and myself for relishing the way my characters reacted to the extraordinary events in their tired, ordinary lives.

Our unofficial group leader loved my little fantasy. Helen, a bulky woman with straight hair and a plain face adorned only by constellations of freckles, was our most perceptive reader. Her ordinary appearance masked an extraordinary mind, and her insights into our readings sometimes left us shaking our heads. Helen's tastes in literature were eclectic, encompassing ancient tomes and, it turned out, future worlds. I especially admired her quirky sense of humor, so I preened mightily when she laughed at what she termed the "whimsy" in my story.

Helen immediately suggested that we read the science fiction anthology she'd just finished, *Writers of the Future, Volume V*. As she dug about in her capacious rattan beach bag for the book, the other five of us exchanged weak smiles. We didn't read science fiction and fantasy. "I vaguely remember liking some Ray Bradbury and Isaac Asimov a hundred years ago in junior high," Angie admitted, "but I think I grew out of it."

"Speculative fiction can be a real kick," Helen countered. She produced a thick, slick, black-and-silver paperback with a white butterfly-like creature on the front. At closer glance, the creature centered between gossamer wings and beneath three antennae was a comely, nude woman. A moon of some sort floated on the black behind her, and a space traveler gazed up at her from his newly-downed craft. Definitely alien stuff.

Angie squinted at the cover's large white letters: "L. Ron Hubbard presents the best new SF of the year . . ."

"Forget it," we said. The name on the cover held no pleasant associations for us. "No way, Helen," we said. "You can give sci-fi a fancy name, but it's still juvenile and stupid."

We took a vote.

And in spite of our protests, we agreed to read the anthology of "speculative fiction."

Why? Maybe because we realized that our criticism was shallow. Or because our group was, at last, ready to give more than lip service to the premise that no literary genre was inferior in and of itself . . . that the author's creativity and skill mattered, not the subject matter.

More likely, the reason for Helen's prevailing was Helen, herself, who smiled and nodded, her gray-blue eyes sparkling as she waited for each of us to have our say. She had never steered us wrong, not even when she decided we should read a "western" and Walter Van Tilburg Clark's *The Oxbow Incident* blew away our preconceptions about bloody, mindless cowboy sagas.

I voted yes for reading sci-fi. But I also bought a floral-quilted book cover for paperbacks when it appeared auspiciously at a craft fair—bought it to cover *Writers of the Future*. On the bus, I kept the book closed when a friend sat down close enough to peek at the pages. And I felt something akin to guilt when, late at night, I read one of the book's stories and let myself be transported by a magical healer into the Realm of Mistrel.

"She died just before dawn," the tale began. "I closed the book I had been reading—*Estavio's Moral Tales*—and placed it atop the pile of volumes that leaned perilously against my chair." Damiano, the old queen's attendant in Mark Matz's fantasy "Despite and Still," drew the drapes. "We had wanted to see the sunrise, but now I had no affection for that sight." He smoothed the queen's hair with her favorite carved rosewood hairbrush, pulled the satin quilt to her quiet breast, and left the room. In the antechamber were lords, ladies, and Prince Giovan, the firstborn and heir: "The boy's face was frozen in a perfect mourning mask, but how his eyes were rich with exaltation!"

Damiano was bereft, but not witless. He knew that he, "the queen's whore," was in danger. He left immediately for remote Salentina and chimerical adventures as the thrall of a marauding sea king. I followed him, transfixed by his escapades and his healing magic, delighted by the author's lyrical style and skill.

While reading other selections in the book, I was transformed into a bag lady named Maude who found a magical wallet, a courageous Jewish woman named Rachel in an artificial world, a fledgling attorney encountering gothic adventures on the Iowa farm of the grotesque Nomaler family. Reading earlier and later volumes in the series transported me into the body and soul of a vampire (what a lonely soul that was!). I survived in a world of ice and devastation. I shuddered when a red-eyed thing howled in the night for me.

Although each story in the series was not as captivating as "Despite and Still," the overall quality was excellent, especially considering that the authors were not professionals. (For instance, author Marc Matz "supervises the financial management of his family's cosmetics company.") The works were selected each year from the winners of an open contest. I knew better than to submit "The End of the Road." Helen's encouragement to the contrary, I was quite humbled.

When our group met again, I found I was not alone in my enthusiasm for our latest reading. The discussion that day was one of the richest ever. Helen never gloated over our conversion; instead she suggested an Ursula LeGuin novel for a later time—and a romance novel that had captured her fancy.

Reading, we're told, is broadening. Yet on my own I had always selected books which roamed within the borders of the prose and poetry land where I felt comfortable. True, I had come to enjoy the best in music and art from all eras and all genres, but I was snobbish when it came to certain literary types. It took a beloved book group—and a Helen—to stretch me out of my complacency, to beam me up, to transport me to new and exotic realms.

PART VI

What to Read: Book Groups Share Their Reading Lists

You probably could look at a group's reading list and come up with a fairly accurate picture of how the group operates. As more than one essay writer noted in the earlier sections of this book, you are what you read. So, here's your chance—comb these lists (presented in alpha order by contributor) and you'll receive not only an embarrassment of rich reading ideas, but also a peek into the psyches of twenty-eight thriving book groups.

Oberlin Book Club List

Jeanne Bay and Shirley Johnson   Oberlin, Ohio

"SHIRLEY'S BOOK CLUB" (so named by the Oberlin Cooperative Bookstore because Shirley did all the arranging with them for selecting and ordering books) is just entering its fourth decade. The founding group began by discussing Betty Friedan's *The Feminine Mystique* and then branched out into many other areas. Subjects? These vary considerably, as you can see from our lengthy reading list. Sometimes we have a theme—minorities, women authors, mother-daughter relationships; sometimes we focus on tried-and-true authors—Cather, James, Faulkner. But whatever we read, as Shirley pointed out in a recent Co-op Book Store article about local book clubs, "When we talk about books, we reveal something about ourselves."

Woman in the Dunes, Kobo Abe
A Natural History of the Senses, Diane Ackerman
Second Chances, Alice Adams
Twenty Years at Hull House, Jane Addams
A Death in the Family, James Agee
Who's Afraid of Virginia Woolf?, Edward Albee

Of Love and Shadows, Isabel Allende
I Never Sang for My Father, Robert Anderson
Winesburg, Ohio, Sherwood Anderson
I Know Why the Caged Bird Sings, Maya Angelou
The Lark, Jean Anouilh
Surfacing, Margaret Atwood
Powers of Attorney, Louis Auchincloss
Dog beneath the Skin, W. H. Auden, and Christopher Isherwood
Emma, Pride and Prejudice, and *Northanger Abbey,* Jane Austen
Growing Up and *Good Times,* Russell Baker
Père Goriot, Honoré Balzac
Kepler, a Novel, John Banville
Nightwood, Djuna Barnes
End of the Road, John Barth
Love Always, Ann Beattie
Virginia Woolf: A Biography, Quentin Bell
The Victim, Saul Bellow
Love Is Not Enough, Bruno Bettelheim
Lying, Alva Myrdal, and *A Daughter's Memoir,* Sissela Bok
Lost Honor of Katharina Blum, Heinrich Böll
A Man for All Seasons, Robert Bolt
Ficciones, Jorge Luis Borges
Miracle at Philadelphia and *Yankee from Olympus,* Catherine Bowen
The Death of the Heart, Friends and Relations, and *The Little Girls,* Elizabeth Bowen
Three Short Novels, Kay Boyle
The Desegregated Heart, Sarah P. Boyle
Joan of the Stockyards and *Mother Courage,* Bertolt Brecht
Tenant of Wildfell Hall, Anne Brontë
Jane Eyre and *Shirley,* Charlotte Brontë
Wuthering Heights, Emily Brontë
A Closed Eye, Anita Brookner
Still Life, A. S. Byatt

Women in Fiction, edited by Susan Cahill

Exiles, The Plague, The Stranger, Caligula, and *The Just Assassins,* Albert Camus

The Homemaker, Dorothy Canfield

The Education of Little Tree, Forrest Carter

House of Children, Joyce Cary

Death Comes for the Archbishop, My Antonia, O Pioneers!, The Professor's House, and *Sapphira and the Slave Girl,* Willa Cather

Uncle Vanya and *Three Sisters,* Anton Chekhov

The Awakening, Kate Chopin

Taipan, James Clavell

Chéri, Colette

Family Happiness, Laurie Colwin

Mrs. Bridge, Evan S. Connell

Lord Jim, The Secret Agent, Heart of Darkness, Youth, and *Typhoon,* Joseph Conrad

Stop-Time, Frank Conroy

The Road from Coorain, Jill Ker Conway

Great Short Works, Stephen Crane

A Woman's Place, Anne Crompton

Madame Curie, Eve Curie

Memoirs of a Dutiful Daughter, Simone de Beauvoir

Moll Flanders, Daniel Defoe

White Noise, Don DeLillo

Year of the Zinc Penny, Rick DeMarinis

Bleak House and *American Notes for General Circulation,* Charles Dickens

White Album, Joan Didion

Pilgrim at Tinker Creek and *An American Childhood,* Annie Dillard

Seven Gothic Tales and *Out of Africa,* Isak Dinesen

Lincoln Reconsidered, David H. Donald

Crime and Punishment and *The Idiot,* Fyodor Dostoevsky

Sister Carrie, Theodore Dreiser

World without End, Francine du Plessix Gray

The Visit, Traps, The Pledge, and *The Physicists,* Friedrich Durrenmatt

A Matter of Principle, Donald Dworkin

Disturbing the Universe, Freeman Dyson

The Solace of Open Spaces, Gretel Ehrlich

Middlemarch and *The Mill on the Floss,* George Eliot

The Invisible Man, Ralph Ellison

Silence, Shusaku Endo

The Trojan Women, Euripides

Five Smooth Stones, Ann Fairbairn

Absalom, Absalom!, Light in August, Sartoris, The Sound and the Fury, The Unvanquished, Go Down Moses, William Faulkner

Joseph Andrews, Henry Fielding

The Great Gatsby, F. Scott Fitzgerald

Madame Bovary, Gustave Flaubert

Mary Wollstonecraft, Eleanor Flexner

The Good Soldier, Ford Madox Ford

Howards End, The Longest Journey, A Passage to India, and *A Room with a View,* E. M. Forster

Love in Full Bloom, edited by Margaret Fowler and Priscilla McCutcheon

The French Lieutenant's Woman, John Fowles

Thaïs, Anatole France

Man's Search for Meaning, Victor Frankel

My Mother, Myself, Nancy Friday

The Feminine Mystique, Betty Friedan

The Art of Loving, Erich Fromm

Overhead in a Balloon, Mavis Gallant

One Hundred Years of Solitude, No One Writes to the Colonel and Other Stories, The Autumn of the Patriarch, and *Love in the Time of Cholera,* Gabriel García Marquez

Nickel Mountain, John Gardner

North and South, Elizabeth Gaskell

The Balcony, Jean Genet

Lafcadio's Adventures, André Gide

The Trouble in One House, Brendan Gill
Electra, Jean Giraudoux
The Odd Women, George Gissing
Schools without Failure, William Glasser
The Inheritors, *Lord of the Flies*, and *The Spire*, William
  Golding
The Vicar of Wakefield, Oliver Goldsmith
World of Strangers and *A Sport of Nature*, Nadine Gordimer
Final Payments, *Men and Angels*, and *On the Other Side*, Mary
  Gordon
The Keepers of the House, Shirley Grau
I Never Promised You a Rose Garden, Hannah Green
In this Sign, Joanne Greenberg
Praying for Sheetrock, Melissa Greene
The Best and the Brightest, David Halberstam
In Search of Salinger, Ian Hamilton
Growth of the Soil, Knut Hamsun
Seduction and Betrayal, Elizabeth Hardwick
Jude the Obscure, *The Mayor of Casterbridge*, *Tess of the
  d'Urbervilles*, and *Under the Greenwood Tree*, Thomas
  Hardy
The Other America, Michael Harrington
Decision, Richard Harris
The Go Between, L. P. Hartley
The Marble Faun and *The House of Seven Gables*, Nathaniel
  Hawthorne
The Transit of Venus, Shirley Hazzard
Writing a Woman's Life, Carolyn Heilbrun
Catch 22, Joseph Heller
Pentimento, Lillian Hellman
No Man's Land: the Last of White Africa, John H. Heminway
Siddhartha and *Steppenwolf*, Hermann Hesse
The Deputy, Rolf Hochhuth
Private Memoirs: Confessions of a Justified Sinner, James Hogg
Hazards of New Fortune and *The Rise of Silas Lapham*,
  William Dean Howells

A Doll's House, Hedda Gabler, and *Rosmersholm,* Henrik Ibsen
The Remains of the Day, Kazuo Ishiguro
Soledad Brother, George Jackson
The Ambassadors, The Aspern Papers, Portrait of a Lady, Washington Square, The Turn of the Screw, Wings of the Dove, The American, The Golden Bowl, and *Spoils of Poynton,* Henry James
Pictures from an Institution, Randall Jarrell
Country of the Pointed Firs, Sarah Orne Jewett
Heat and Dust and *Out of India,* Ruth Prawer Jhabvala
Foxybaby, Elizabeth Jolley
Fear of Flying, Erica Jong
Portrait of the Artist As a Young Man and *Dubliners,* James Joyce
The Trial, Franz Kafka
Sound of the Mountain, Yasunari Kawabata
Freedom or Death, Nikos Kazantzakis
Annie John and Lucy, Jamaica Kincaid
The Bean Trees, Barbara Kingsolver
The Woman Warrior and *China Men,* Maxine Hong Kingston
A Not Entirely Benign Procedure, Perri Klass
Age of Longing and *Darkness at Noon,* Arthur Koestler
Obasan, Joy Kogawa
On Death and Dying, Elizabeth Kübler-Ross
Laughing Boy, Oliver LaFarge
The Leopard, Giuseppe di Lampedusa
The Quest, Elizabeth Langgasser
Sons and Lovers, The Plumed Serpent, and *Women in Love,* D. H. Lawrence
Martha Quest and *The Golden Notebook,* Doris Lessing
Balm in Gilead, Sara L. Lightfoot
The Watch that Ends the Night, Hugh MacLennon
The Natural, Bernard Malamud
The Autobiography of Malcolm X, Malcom X with Alex Haley
Man's Fate, André Malraux
Death in Venice, Thomas Mann

Nectar in a Sieve, Kamala Markandaya
Bird of Life, Bird of Death, Jonathan Maslow
The Folded Leaf and *They Came Like Swallows,* William Maxwell
Memories of a Catholic Girlhood, Mary McCarthy
Principles of American Nuclear Chemistry, Thomas McMahon
Testing the Current, William McPherson
Blackberry Winter, Margaret Mead
The Confidence-Man, Herman Melville
Growing up Female in America, edited by Eve Merriam
Death of a Salesman, Arthur Miller
Spring Snow, Yukio Mishima
Dangerous Dossiers, Herbert Mitgang
Love among the Cannibals, Wright Morris
Song of Solomon and *The Bluest Eye,* Toni Morrison
The Flight from the Enchanter and *The Severed Head,* Iris Murdoch
Speak Memory, Vladimir Nabokov
India—A Wounded Civilization and *A Bend in the River,* V. S. Naipaul
The Vendor of Sweets, R. K. Narayan
Portrait of a Marriage, Nigel Nicholson
The Octopus and *McTeague,* Frank Norris
Expensive People, Joyce Carol Oates
Three Plays, Sean O'Casey
White Lantern, J. Leonard O'Connell
A Good Man Is Hard to Find, Flannery O'Connor
Tell Me a Riddle, Tillie Olsen
Mourning Becomes Electra, Eugene O'Neill
Keep the Aspidistra Flying, George Orwell
My Michael, Amos Oz
Close Company: Stories of Mothers and Daughters, edited by Christine Park and Caroline Heaton
I Remember, Boris Pasternak
A Short History of a Small Planet, T. R. Pearson
Manchester Fourteen Miles, Margaret Penn

Naked Masks, Luigi Pirandello
The Bell Jar, Sylvia Plath
Presidential Elections, Nelson W. Polsby and Aaron
  Wildavsky
The Old Order, Katherine Ann Porter
My Name is Asher Lev, Chaim Potok
Swann's Way, Marcel Proust
Quartet in Autumn, Barbara Pym
The Negro in the Making of America, Benjamin Quarles
Beyond Vietnam, Edwin Reischauer
Smile Please, Jean Rhys
Rabble in Arms, Kenneth Roberts
Survive the Savage Sea, Dougal Robertson
Housekeeping, Marilynne Robinson
Jean Christophe, Romain Rolland
Parallel Lives, Phyllis Rose
Boss, Mike Royko
Autobiography (Volume 1), Bertrand Russell
Home, Witold Rybczynski
*The Man Who Mistook His Wife for a Hat and Other Clinical
  Tales* and *A Leg to Stand On*, Oliver Sacks
Mrs. Stevens Hears the Mermaid Singing and *History of a Man*,
  May Sarton
Memoirs of a Fox-Hunting Man, Siegfried Sassoon
A Fine Romance, C. P. Seton
Major Barbara, *Heartbreak House*, and *St. Joan*, George
  Bernard Shaw
And Quiet Flows the Don, Mikhail Sholokhov
Orphans, Real and Imaginary, Eileen Simpson
Spinosa of Market Street, Isaac Bashevis Singer
Walden Two, B. F. Skinner
A Thousand Acres, Jane Smiley
The Russians and *Power Game*, Hedrick Smith
The Expedition of Humphry Clinker, Tobias Smollett
Cancer Ward and *The First Circle*, Alexander Solzhenitsyn
Electra, Sophocles
Memento Mori and *A Far Cry from Kensington*, Muriel Spark

Salt Line, Elizabeth Spencer
The Education of a WASP, Lois M. Stalvey
Angle of Repose, The Spectator Bird, Crossing to Safety, and
    Where the Bluebird Sings, Wallace Stegner
Three Lives, Gertrude Stein
Rosencrantz and Gildenstern Are Dead, Tom Stoppard
Never Done, Susan Strasser
Pioneer Women, J. S. Stratton
Alice James, Jean Strouse
Lie Down in Darkness, William Styron
The Kingdom and the Power, Gay Talese
The Joy Luck Club, Amy Tan
Angel, Elizabeth Taylor
Old Forest and Other Stories and *A Summons to Memphis,* Peter
    Taylor
The White Hotel, D. M. Thomas
Lark Rise to Candleford, Flora Thompson
The Eco-Spasm Report, Alvin Toffler
Anna Karenina and *War and Peace,* Leo Tolstoy
Middle of the Journey, Lionel Trilling
Barchester Towers, Anthony Trollope
A Connecticut Yankee in King Arthur's Court, Mark Twain
The Accidental Tourist and *Breathing Lessons,* Anne Tyler
Kristin Lavransdatter, Sigrid Undset
On the Farm, John Updike
A Far-Off Place, Laurens Van der Post
Galapagos and *Slaughterhouse Five,* Kurt Vonnegut
The Color Purple and *The Third Life of Grange Copeland,* Alice
    Walker
American Originals, Geoffrey Ward
All the King's Men, Robert Penn Warren
A Handful of Dust and *Decline and Fall,* Evelyn Waugh
Marat/Sade, Peter Weiss
The Hearts and Lives of Men, Fay Weldon
The Optimist's Daughter, Thirteen Stories, and *Golden Apples,*
    Eudora Welty
The Devil's Advocate, Morris West

The New Meaning of Treason and *The Real Night*, Rebecca
    West
Roman Fever, *The Age of Innocence*, and *The House of Mirth*,
    Edith Wharton
Points of My Compass, E. B. White
Solid Mandela, Patrick White
One Generation After, Elie Wiesel
Incline Our Hearts, A. N. Wilson
The Quest for Christa T., Christa Wolf
Look Homeward Angel, Thomas Wolfe
Mrs. Dalloway, *To the Lighthouse*, *The Waves*, and *Three
    Guineas*, Virginia Woolf
A Coin in Nine Hands, Marguerite Yourcenar
The Masterpiece, Émile Zola

Book List

Ellie Becker   **Santa Fe, New Mexico**

1988

The Unbearable Lightness of Being, Milan Kundera. Men,
women, love, freedom, necessity, political repression, moral
truth. Elicited either strong like or dislike.

Beloved, Toni Morrison. Haunting, deep discussion of
humanity, mother, dignity, truth, the black woman's experience. Profound.

In a Different Voice, Carol Gilligan. Questions about dividing
up and determining moral choices on the basis of gender.

Love in the Time of Cholera, Gabriel García Marquez. Lost in the magic of García Marquez, surreal. Where will Fermina and Florentino end up? Or will they end?

1989

The Drama of the Gifted Child, Alice Miller. Implications for our own children, for all children. How do we raise whole human beings?

The Woman That Never Evolved. Sarah Blaffer Hrdy. Why are female reproductive organs hidden? Does the female primate choose the father of her offspring? Which tends more toward monogamy, male or female? Who's in charge here, anyway?

A Room of One's Own, Virginia Woolf. Difficult, but worth it.

Jacob's Room, Virginia Woolf. Almost incomprehensible.

Breathing Lessons, Anne Tyler. Disappointing. Superficial. As one member noted, doesn't say much for the Pulitzer.

1990

Ceremony, Leslie Marmon Silko. Extraordinary. Moving. Violent.

Caring: A Feminine Approach to Ethics and Moral Education, Nel Noddings. Better scholarship than the Gilligan. Cogent. Moral Choices. Are imperatives ethical?

The Road from Coorain, Jill Ker Conway. A pleasing biography. The effects of constraint, bias, education, and harsh landscape on a woman of courage.

The Bone People, Keri Hulme. Strange, almost eerie. Unusual style—the literal part is difficult, but a deeper level is experienced.

Woman at Otowi Crossing, Frank Waters. Uninspired by the writing, intrigued by the time, place, history, and woman. Desire to read other versions by other authors.

Sons and Lovers, D. H. Lawrence. Vintage Lawrence: mother, woman, love, violence. Is anyone likeable in this book?

The Mill on the Floss, George Eliot. Dissatisfying. Much inferior to *Middlemarch.* Cop-out ending.

1991

Crossing to Safety, Wallace Stegner. Sensitive and perceptive writer. We know the people Stegner wants us to know.

Ake: The Years of Childhood, Wole Soyinka. Lukewarm. Somewhat engaging story of a childhood, confusing place.

Composing a Life, Mary Catherine Bateson. Rather self-righteous, self-justifying. Only relatively affluent women portrayed.

Madame Bovary, Gustave Flaubert. Another woman with circumscribed choices, who has to die for being distinct, for doing what men do.

Anna Karenina, Leo Tolstoy. See *Madame Bovary.*

Their Eyes Were Watching God, Zora Neale Hurston. Dialect, gut-level speech and action. Deceptively simple. Had to read more Hurston.

A Midwife's Tale: The Life of Martha Ballard, Based on Her Diary 1785–1812, Laurel Thatcher Ulrich. The forming of America, with families as production units. Primarily work, more work, and death. Realization: at this same time, Mozart was composing in Vienna.

1992

Mrs. Caliban, Rachel Ingalls. A little book, a deep discussion. Is Larry real? Does it matter? Mysterious, frightening, unforgettable. Had to read more Ingalls.

Stones for Ibarra, Harriet Doerr. Intelligent and perceptive. A little too sparse to be entirely satisfying, but that's probably the point.

Mama Day, Gloria Naylor. Unusual. Told from varying points of view and it works. Magic and love. Had to read more Naylor.

The House of Mirth, Edith Wharton. Wonderful portrayal of New York turn-of-the-century society and constraints on women. See *Madame Bovary* and *Anna Karenina*.

The Charterhouse of Parma, Stendhal. Love and politics. No one was much impressed.

Mrs. Dalloway, Virginia Woolf. One of Woolf's more accessible works. Discussion about Clarissa's happiness, sincerity, marriage. Yes.

As I Lay Dying, William Faulkner. Grim. Rough. Hopeless. Clearly a master.

Eichmann in Jerusalem, Hannah Arendt. Profound questions. Who is ultimately morally accountable?

Iron John, Robert Bly. Terrible scholarship. Sloppy writing. Almost humorous. The same old story—men, take charge, be "real" men, don't take any crap from women.

Women Respond to the Men's Movement, edited by Kay Leigh Hagan. Anthology of responses from varied and articulate women. Diverse points of view. Lively discussion.

1993

A Thousand Acres, Jane Smiley. A brilliant undertaking. This one *deserved* the Pulitzer. We can never know the why of meanness, of blind ego; we can only witness the devastation it sows.

King Lear, Shakespeare. Read in conjunction with *A Thousand Acres.* Those who have taught Lear for years began to look at him and his daughters in a different light.

Angle of Repose, Wallace Stegner. The title reflects a metaphor that wraps itself around past and present stories, intricately interwoven. Rest and repose are not easily found. An engaging read, a sweeping story.

The Mismeasure of Woman, Carol Tavris. Feminist critique of the consequences for women when Man is the measure of all things. A pretty thorough going over of the beauty myth, the medical/psychological professions, and women's sexuality. In the end, we wished for more clarity about where Tavris lands on the gender sameness/difference question.

The Messiah of Stockholm, Cynthia Ozick. It is post-Holocaust Europe. A Jewish man may or may not have reinvented his past. Engendered a difficult and ultimately illuminating discussion.

Villette, Charlotte Brontë. A dark book with an unusual point of view and an oddly modern aspect. As one reader put it, "Who is this woman and why would anyone love her?"

The Spoils of Poynton, Henry James. It's about furniture and love, but also about the corruption of money, the power of art, and the poisonous influences of the two on the principal characters. A stroke of other-than-human justice ends this tale.

The Abyss, Marguerite Yourcenar. A philosophical novel that describes, in often-beautiful prose, the life of a medieval physician/scholar/alchemist who is not limited by the thinking of the church or that of the era he moved within.

The Book Group Book, edited by Ellen Slezak. Yes, we really read this as a group. And it changed the way we thought about ourselves as a group, broadening our perspective and giving us new direction.

1994

The Things They Carried, Tim O'Brien. There you are, wherever O'Brien wants you to be: immersed in a heavily mined jungle quagmire; crossing a Canadian river; watching your nine-year-old best friend die. Yet all the stories are the same story, trying to remember the same truth. In this book, the coward is the one who goes to war.

Ordinary Love and Good Will, Jane Smiley. An aching restlessness pervades these tales of two very different families, forever changed by single jarring incidents. Illusion clashes with the realities of intention, commitment, and love. What can we give our children? What do they inherit?

The Lost Honor of Katharina Blum, Heinrich Böll. An attractive housemaid falls in love with a wanted criminal she's just met—and things are definitely not as simple as they seem.

Girl, Interrupted, Susanna Kaysen. Personal narrative account of an eighteen-year-old woman's sojourn in a psychiatric hospital in the late sixties. Riveting descriptions illustrating the thin line between sanity and madness. Beautiful prose. The book asks difficult questions.

Paris Trout, Peter Dexter. Despite its genteel complexion, the small town of Cotton Point, Georgia, contains an undercurrent of violence and greed. A senseless crime launches the story of a paranoid psychotic—otherwise known as one of Cotton Point's best—and the shattering of a town that will never be the same.

Listening to Prozac, Peter D. Kramer. Thinly disguised paean to Prozac, ostensibly exploring the concepts of self, mood, and personality. Lots of dense text regarding research and biochemical processes. Importance and discussion value lie in the implications of Kramer's perspective for the malleability of the human personality.

Woman in the Dunes, Kobo Abe. A man hunting beetles is held captive in a town of sand. Sensual and existential.

1995

A Lost Lady, Willa Cather. Before we could figure out why she was lost, we tried to figure out what it was that caused every male in her sphere to be so taken with Mrs. Forrester. She was strong and full of life, yes, but she was also reckless, full of artifice, and linked romantically with a scoundrel. Her fall paralleled the end of the era of western expansion.

The English Patient, Michael Ondaatje. A multitextured novel with stunningly beautiful prose. This is a rich work of art: compassionate portraits of damaged people, poetry, romance, mystery, and philosophy. Those of us who haven't already read this twice plan to reread it.

Feminist Book Discussion Group Book List

Henri Bensussen   San Jose, California

1985

Another Mother Tongue, Judy Grahn
The Color Purple, Alice Walker
The Mists of Avalon, Marion Zimmer Bradley
Lesbian Nuns: Breaking the Silence, Rosemary Curb and Nancy Manahan
Ancient Mirrors of Womanhood, Merlin Stone
Other Women, Lisa Alther
The Wanderground, Sally Gearhart

1986

Sisterhood is Global, Robin Morgan
Zami: A New Spelling of My Name, Audre Lorde
The Kin of Ata Are Waiting for You, Dorothy Bryant
Choices, Nancey Toder
When God Was a Woman, Merlin Stone
A Reckoning, May Sarton
Goddesses in Everywoman, Jean Shinoda Bolin
The Ladies, Doris Grumbach

Sinking, Stealing, Jan Clausen
Gyn/Ecology, Mary Daly
Necessary Losses, Judith Viorst
Confessions of a Failed Southern Lady, Florence King

1987

Medicine Woman, Lyn Andrews
The House at Pelham Falls, Brenda Weather
Sisters of the Road, Barbara Wilson
Long Time Passing: Lives of Older Lesbians, Marcy Adelman
Elsa: I Come with My Songs, Elsa Gidlow
Confessions of Madame Psyche, Dorothy Bryant
The Handmaid's Tale, Margaret Atwood
Odd Girl Out, Ann Bannon
Going Out of Our Minds, Sonia Johnson
Their Eyes Were Watching God, Zora Neale Hurston
Soul Snatcher, Camarin Grae

1988

Memory Board, Jane Rule
Salt Eaters, Toni Cade Bambara
Unlit Lamp, Radclyffe Hall
Woman on the Edge of Time, Marge Piercy
Women and Nature, Susan Griffin
Beloved, Toni Morrison
Over the Hill: Reflections on Ageism Between Women, Baba
  Copper
Outrageous Acts and Everyday Rebellions, Gloria Steinem
The Chalice and the Blade, Riane Eisler
Mundane's World, Judy Grahn

1989

Through Other Eyes, Irene Zahava
Lesbian Couples, D. Merilee Clunis and G. Dorsey Green

The Woman Who Owned the Shadows, Paula Gunn Allen
Lesbian Ethics, Sarah Lucia Hoagland
All Good Women, Valerie Miner
Why Can't Sharon Kowalski Come Home, Karen Thompson
Womonseed, Sunlight
Daughters of Copper Woman, Anne Cameron
Wildfire, Sonia Johnson
Kindred, Octavia Butler
A Passion for Friends, Janice Raymond

1990

Cat's Eye, Margaret Atwood
The Price of Salt, Claire Morgan
Lesbian Love Stories, Irene Zahava
She Came in a Flash, Mary Wings
Borderlands/La Frontera, Gloria Anzaldua
The House of the Spirits, Isabel Allende
Cassandra, Christa Wolf
The Joy Luck Club, Amy Tan
The Female Man, Joanna Russ
A Restricted Country, Joan Nestle

1991

The Beet Queen, Louise Erdrich
The Temple of My Familiar, Alice Walker
This Bridge Called My Back, Cherrie Moraga and Gloria
    Anzaldua
Gaudi Afternoon, Barbara Wilson
A Little Original Sin, Millicent Dillon
Lesbians at Midlife, B. Sang, J. Warshow, and A. J. Smith
Final Session, Mary Morell
The Wounded Woman, Linda Leonard
Macho Sluts, Pat Califia
The Gilda Stories, Jewelle Gomez

The Ship That Sailed into the Living Room, Sonia Johnson
Trash, Dorothy Allison

1992

Woman of the 14th Moon, Dena Taylor and Amber Coverdale
    Sumrall
The Search for Signs of Intelligent Life in the Universe, Jane
    Wagner
Fried Green Tomatoes at the Whistle Stop Cafe, Fannie Flagg
Margins, Terri de la Pena
Odd Girls and Twilight Lovers, Lillian Faderman
The Education of Harriet Hatfield, May Sarton
Closer to Home: Bisexuality and Feminism, Elizabeth Weise
Two-bit Tango, Elizabeth Pincus

1993

Backlash, Susan Faludi
Lucy, Jamaica Kincaid
Lovers, edited by Amber Coverdale Sumrall
The Kitchen God's Wife, Amy Tan
Animal Dreams, Barbara Kingsolver
Her, Cheri Muhanji
Stone Butch Blues, Leslie Feinberg
Herland, Charlotte Perkins Gilman
Mrs. Dalloway, Virginia Woolf
Life Savings, Linnea Due
Hamlet's Mother, Carolyn Heilbrun
Alma Rose, Edith Forbes

1994

Little Altars Everywhere, Rebecca Wells
The Road from Coorain, Jill Ker Conway
Trees Call for What They Need, Melissa Kwasny

Superstars, Dell Richards
Refuge, Terry Tempest Williams
Dancing Jack, Laurie Marks
Forty-Three Septembers, Jewelle Gomez
Mary Reilly, Valerie Martin
Daughters of Darkness, edited by Pam Keesey
Eleanor Roosevelt, Volume I, 1884–1933, Blanche Wiesen Cook

Selected Book List—Tacoma Park and Bowie, Maryland, Book Clubs

Barbara Bernstein   Bowie, Maryland

Fiction

Map of the World, Jane Hamilton. Two women trade babysitting, and tragedy sets in motion a chain of events with profound effects on everyone.

Other Women's Children, Perri Klass. The events in a pediatrician's life as they interweave with and affect her work at the hospital.

Of Such Small Differences, Joanne Greenberg. Profoundly moving novel about a community of people who are both deaf and blind.

Before and After, Rosellen Brown. When a teenage boy is suspected of murder, his mother wishes to hide nothing and his father tries to protect him. Members discussed how they would react to this situation.

When Nietzsche Wept, Irvin Yalom. Description of a therapeutic relationship between Nietzsche and Joseph Breuer, a doctor in the late nineteenth century. Describes how psychotherapy feels and might have been invented.

Family Pictures, Sue Miller. The impact of an autistic child on the rest of the family, set in an era when mothers were largely blamed for a child's autism.

The Thanatos Syndrome, Walker Percy. Story about a criminal plot involving psychoactive drugs—led to a fascinating discussion about the use of drugs in modern life.

Waiting to Exhale, Terry McMillan. Female bonding runs deep in this story about four professional black women and their lives, loves, and searches for men.

The Joy Luck Club, Amy Tan. A look at the relationships between several Chinese mothers and their daughters in a culture of close-knit family bonds.

Animal Dreams, Barbara Kingsolver. A beautiful story with a Native American theme about maturing and finding happiness in one's own backyard.

The Beans of Egypt, Maine, Carolyn Chute. Offbeat story about lives of poverty and squalor in America.

The Accidental Tourist and *Dinner at the Homesick Restaurant*, Anne Tyler. A travel writer who hates to travel and a restaurant for people who'd rather not eat out. Tyler's twists and eventful plots make both these novels fascinating reading.

Cold Sassy Tree, Olive Ann Burns. An excellent coming-of-age story about a teenage boy in a small town and his relationship with his grandfather.

A Thousand Acres, Jane Smiley. A slice of life on a midwestern farm. Beautifully written, but depressing.

Nonfiction

City of Joy, Dominique LaPierre. In Calcutta, India, the human spirit surmounts incredible physical hardships and dire poverty. Squalid, depressing, and uplifting at the same time.

Life and Death in Shanghai, Nien Cheng. The hardships of a well-educated Chinese woman jailed for more than six years in solitary confinement during the Cultural Revolution.

From Beirut to Jerusalem, Thomas Friedman. The history of the Arab-Israeli conflict and the efforts to resolve it.

Home Fires, Donald Katz. A troubled family with children growing up in the sixties.

Common Ground: A Turbulent Decade in the Lives of Three American Families, J. Anthony Lucas. Several Boston families are followed through many generations, setting the stage for the conflict surrounding integration of public schools.

You Just Don't Understand: Women and Men in Conversation, Deborah Tannen, Ph.D. Men use language to establish independence and status while women use language to establish intimacy and connection. With this premise the author explains some classic gender conflicts such as why men don't want to ask for directions and women do.

Living in the Labyrinth, Diana Friel McGowin. A woman recounts early descent into Alzheimer's.

Lost in Translation: A Life in a New Language, Eva Hoffman. A psychologically rich autobiographical account of a youngster who moves from Poland to Canada (and ultimately to the United States). The language and culture were so different that the author couldn't find English words for her "Polish feelings."

Book List

Mary Nell Bryant   **Washington, D.C.**

WASHINGTON, D.C., is not a city know for the stable composition of either its population or its institutions. Yet transience, elected or otherwise, has not defeated a group of readers who, for the past twelve years, have gathered at each other's homes to share a love of books, ideas, and friendship. Certainly, the composition of the group has changed and will change more over time, with people moving in and out just as they do in the city. Yet the institution, the book group, thankfully stays put.

We refer to it as "Book Group." Not "a book group," not "the book group." Perhaps the generic nature of the name reflects the quality of the group which has enabled it to weather changes in family status, careers, jobs, and even administrations. That quality is flexibility—an ability to bend and adapt (almost effortlessly) to the differing needs and interests of a changing membership. We have no hard and fast rules regarding what, when, how, and where. While some might find this frustrating, we find it leaves the door open to explore books of all kinds, from all eras, and from all parts of the world as the spirit of the moment moves us.

The following list, in chronological order, shows the quixotic nature of the group and suggests the spontaneity and fun that we have had in our literary explorations. May it launch you on some rewarding explorations of your own!

The Edible Woman, Margaret Atwood
Thérèse Raquin, Émile Zola
Democracy, Henry Adams
Mrs. Dalloway, Virginia Woolf
I Know Why the Caged Bird Sings, Maya Angelou
The Age of Innocence, Edith Wharton
Autobiography of Alice B. Toklas, Gertrude Stein
The Warden, Anthony Trollope
Short Stories of John Cheever, John Cheever
Searching for Caleb, Anne Tyler
Vagabond, Colette
The Scarlet Pimpernel, Emmuska Orczy
All about Jeeves, P. G. Wodehouse
O Pioneers!, Willa Cather
Pale Horse, Pale Rider, Katherine Anne Porter

Small Changes, Marge Piercy
Dinner at the Homesick Restaurant, Anne Tyler
The Color Purple, Alice Walker
Aunt Julia and the Scriptwriter, Mario Vargas Llosa
In Memory of Old Jack, Wendell Berry
Innocents Abroad, Mark Twain
Excellent Women, Barbara Pym
Minor Characters, Joyce Johnson
The Master and Margarita, Mikhail Bulgakov
Happy to Be Here, Garrison Keillor
The Ambassadors, Henry James
Optimist's Daughter, Eudora Welty
The Wide Sargasso Sea, Jean Rhys
Jane Eyre, Charlotte Brontë
A Mother and Two Daughters, Gail Godwin
Light in August, William Faulkner
Spring Snow, Yukio Mishima
Bartelby the Scrivener, Herman Melville
The Book of Laughter and Forgetting, Milan Kundera
Blue Highways, William Least Heat-Moon
Out of Africa, Isak Dinesen
A Passage to India, E. M. Forster
During the Reign of the Queen of Persia, Joan Chase
Enormous Changes at the Last Minute, Grace Paley
Bright Lights, Big City, Jay McInerney
The Lost Honor of Katharina Blum, Heinrich Böll
West with the Night, Beryl Markham
Parallel Lives, Phyllis Rose
One Writer's Beginnings, Eudora Welty
The Reivers, William Faulkner
Desert Rose, Larry McMurtry
Mrs. Palfrey at the Claremont, Elizabeth Taylor
Swann's Way, Marcel Proust
Transit of Venus, Shirley Hazzard
Housekeeping, Marilynne Robinson
Down among the Women, Fay Weldon
The Moviegoer, Walker Percy

Journal of a Solitude, May Sarton
A Room of One's Own, Virginia Woolf
The Sot-Weed Factor, John Barth
Fifth Business, Robertson Davies
Here to Get My Baby out of Jail, Louise Shivers
Confessions of a Failed Southern Lady, Florence King
Hotel du Lac, Anita Brookner
Stones for Ibarra, Harriet Doerr
Accidental Tourist, Anne Tyler
House, Tracy Kidder
An Unsuitable Job for a Woman, P. D. James
Cannery Row, John Steinbeck
Lonesome Dove, Larry McMurtry
Villette, Charlotte Brontë
July's People, Nadine Gordimer
Last September, Elizabeth Bowen
The Power and the Glory, Graham Greene
The Old Forest and Other Stories, Peter Taylor
Monkeys, Susan Minot
What's Bred in the Bone, Robertson Davies
Song of Solomon, Toni Morrison
Death Comes for the Archbishop, Willa Cather
The Beet Queen, Louise Erdrich
Cakes and Ale, Somerset Maugham
Madame Bovary, Gustave Flaubert
The Scarlet Letter, Nathaniel Hawthorne
Family and Friends, Anita Brookner
Life and Death in Shanghai, Nien Cheng
A Yellow Raft in Blue Water, Michael Dorris
Miss Peabody's Inheritance, Elizabeth Jolley
Interview with the Vampire, Anne Rice
Of Love and Shadows, Isabel Allende
Dancing at the Rascal Fair, Ivan Doig
An American Childhood, Annie Dillard
Crossing to Safety, Wallace Stegner
Baltasar and Blimunda, Jose Saramago
Annie John, Jamaica Kincaid

Moon Tiger, Penelope Lively
Love in the Time of Cholera, Gabriel García Marquez
The Lover, Marguerite Duras
Mrs. Bridge, Evan S. Connell
Paris Trout, Peter Dexter
A Country Doctor, Sarah Orne Jewett
Dead Souls, Nikolai Gogol
Song of the Lark, Willa Cather
A Late Divorce, A. B. Yehoshua
Changing Places, David Lodge
The Whiteness of Bones, Susanna Moore
A Far Cry from Kensington, Muriel Spark
The Sheltering Sky, Paul Bowles
The Joy Luck Club, Amy Tan
Lost in Translation, Eva Hoffman
The Wanderer, Alain Fournier
The Road from Coorain, Jill Ker Conway
The Remains of the Day, Kazuo Ishiguro
Pride and Prejudice, Jane Austen
The Lion, the Witch, and the Wardrobe, C. S. Lewis
All Hallow's Eve, Charles Williams
Beloved, Toni Morrison
Palace Walk, Naguib Mahfouz
Waterland, Graham Swift
Ake: The Years of Childhood, Wole Soyinka
The American Senator, Anthony Trollope
Friend of My Youth, Alice Munro
Angle of Repose, Wallace Stegner
The Diary of Helena Morley, translated by Elizabeth Bishop
Possession: A Romance, A. S. Byatt
Widows' Adventure, Charles Dickinson
The Beautiful Mrs. Seidenman, Andrzej Szczypiorski
Cat's Eye, Margaret Atwood
Patrimony: A True Story, Philip Roth
The Bigamist's Daughter, Alice McDermott
Jasmine, Bharati Mukherjee

Ordinary Love and Good Will, Jane Smiley
The Kitchen God's Wife, Amy Tan
A Thousand Acres, Jane Smiley
*A Life of Her Own: The Transformation of a Country Woman in
    20th Century France,* Emilie Curles
Flaubert's Parrot, Julian Barnes
In This House of Brede, Rumer Godden
Wartime Lies, Louis Begley
How the García Girls Lost Their Accents, Julia Alvarez
Justine, Lawrence Durrell
Heat and Dust, Ruth Prawer Jhabvala
Kim, Rudyard Kipling
A Sensible Life, Mary Wesley
All the Pretty Horses, Cormac McCarthy
Ever After, Graham Swift
The Spoils of Poynton, Henry James
Young Men and Fire, Norman Maclean
The Stone Angel, Margaret Laurence
October Light, John Gardner
The Volcano Lover: A Romance, Susan Sontag
Mystery Ride, Robert Boswell
Animal Dreams, Barbara Kingsolver
Postcards, E. Annie Proulx
Two Lives, William Trevor
Kristin Lavransdatter (Parts 1 and 2), Sigrid Undset

Classics Book Club List

Edmund de Chasca   **St. Louis, Missouri**

OUR GROUP IS devoted to reading great world literature of the
past. To ensure that we would not gravitate toward the merely
recent, we rule out any book published after 1900. This has

been violated only twice, once by an uninitiated new member who insisted we read Campbell's *The Hero with a Thousand Faces,* and once by consensus for Joyce's *Ulysses.*

This may seem arbitrary, but, like unknown places on a map, we wanted to know what lay behind names like Augustine, Dante, and Pepys. We had heard about *Confessions, La Vita Nuova,* and the *Diaries.* Why not travel there and read the author's words firsthand?

The list that follows represents about four years of reading. In many cases, we have been unable to finish the text in the six weeks or so we allow ourselves, but at least we have gained familiarity with the book. Some of the authors disappointed expectation; others exceeded it. All have been worth encountering.

Those interested in starting a similar group will find good reading lists in Britannica's *Great Books of the Western World,* Clifton Fadiman's *Lifetime Reading Plan,* Everyman's Library, and the Harvard Classics. We avoid abridgements, condensations, and modernizations whenever possible.

Selected Poems, Thomas Wyatt

The Oresteia, Aeschylus

The Consolation of Philosophy, Boethius

The Praise of Folly, Erasmus

The Last Chronicle of Barsetshire, Anthony Trollope

"De Senectude," "De Amicitia," and *De Officiis,* Cicero

La Vita Nuova, Dante

Faust, Goethe

Troilus and Cressida, Chaucer

The Hero with a Thousand Faces, Joseph Campbell

Hecuba, Electra, and *The Trojan Women,* Euripides

Mort D'Arthur, Thomas Malory

Thus Spake Zarathustra, Nietzsche

The Canterbury Tales, Chaucer

Ulysses, James Joyce

Apologia Pro Vita Sua, John Henry Newman

Orlando Furioso, Lodovico Ariosto

Ethics, Aristotle

Gargantua and Pantagruel, François Rabelais
Endymion, John Keats
The Ring and the Book, Robert Browning
Discourses, Epictetus
Diary, Samuel Pepys
"The Rape of Lock," "An Essay on Criticism," "An Essay on Man," Alexander Pope
The Awakening, Kate Chopin
"Apology," "Crito," "Phaedo," "Lysis," "Euthyphro," "Protagoras," "Phaedrus," "Symposium," "Theatetus," Plato
The Autobiography of Benvenuto Cellini, Cellini
Don Juan, Byron
The Blithedale Romance, Nathaniel Hawthorne
Confessions, Augustine
The Satyricon, Petronius
Chronicles, Froissart
Ethics, Spinoza
Life of Johnson, Boswell
La Vida Es Sueno, Calderon

Bemidji Book Club Reading List

Alice V. Collins   **Bemidji, Minnesota**

1985

Wuthering Heights, Emily Brontë
Growing Up, Russell Baker
Lutefisk Ghetto, Art Lee
Love and War, John Jakes

1986

Hunt for Red October, Tom Clancy
Iacocca, Lee Iacocca
A Distant Mirror, Barbara Tuchman
Ironweed, William Kennedy
Walking Drum, Louis L'Amour
The Agony and the Ecstasy, Irving Stone
On Wings of Eagles, Ken Follett
The Diary of a Provincial Lady, E. M. Dellifield
The Adventures of Huckleberry Finn, Mark Twain

1987

Strange Encounters, Mike Wallace
The Haj, Leon Uris
Nutcracker, Shana Alexander
Common Ground, Anthony Lucas
The Beans of Egypt, Maine, Carolyn Chute

1988

Pride and Prejudice, Jane Austen
The Red and the Black, Stendhal
Grand Opening, Jon Hassler
Silent Partner, Judith Greber

1989

Taming of the Shrew, Shakespeare
Hatchet, Gary Paulsen
Walden, Henry David Thoreau
Vanity Fair, William Thackeray
Accidental Tourist, Anne Tyler
Les Misérables, Victor Hugo
Cold Sassy Tree, Olive Ann Burns
Lonesome Dove, Larry McMurtry
84, Charing Cross Road, Helene Hanff

1990

Killing Time in St. Cloud, Judith Guest
Spring Moon, Bette Bao Lord
Crossing to Safety, Wallace Stegner
Love Medicine, Louise Erdrich
Love in the Time of Cholera, Gabriel García Marquez
Indian Givers, Jack Weatherford
The Sun Also Rises, Ernest Hemingway
Type Talk, Otto Kroeger

1991

Jubilee, Margaret Walker
Billy Bathgate, E. L. Doctorow
Big Rock Candy Mountain, Wallace Stegner
Once Upon a Time on the Banks, Cathie Pelletier
Pilgrim at Tinker Creek, Annie Dillard
A River Runs Through It, Norman Maclean
When Rabbit Howls, Trudy Chase
The Power and the Glory, Graham Greene
A Cup of Christmas Tea, Tom Hegg

1992

Necessity of Empty Spaces, Paul Gruchow
Death in Venice, Thomas Mann
Rabbit Run, John Updike
Ashana, E. P. Roesch
A Is for Alibi, Sue Grafton
The Oldest Living Confederate Widow Tells All, Allan
    Gurganus
Walking Across Egypt, Clyde Edgerton
Mark of the Maker, Tom Hegg
Secret Garden, Frances Hodgson Burnett

1993–94

Callander Square, Anne Perry
Bridges of Madison County, Robert James Waller
The Firm, John Grisham
Follow the River, James Thom
H Is for Homicide, Sue Grafton
A Thousand Acres, Jane Smiley
My Antonia, Willa Cather
Rising Sun, Michael Crichton

1994–95

Gulliver's Travels, Jonathan Swift
Trinity, Leon Uris
Twelfth Night, Shakespeare
Honor among Thieves, Jeffrey Archer
The Odyssey, Homer
The Age of Innocence, Edith Wharton
Mousetrap, Agatha Christie
I Know Why the Caged Bird Sings, Maya Angelou

North Tarrytown Book Group List—The First Ten Years

Nancy Cooper　　　　　　　　North Tarrytown, New York

The House of the Spirits, Isabel Allende
Bastard out of Carolina, Dorothy Allison
I Know Why the Caged Bird Sings, Maya Angelou
Cat's Eye and *The Robber Bride*, Margaret Atwood
The Book Class, Louis Auchincloss
Mansfield Park, Jane Austen

New York Trilogy: City of Glass, Paul Auster
With a Daughter's Eye, Mary Catherine Bateson
In the Heat of the Day, Elizabeth Bowen
Testament of Youth, Vera Brittain
Wuthering Heights, Emily Brontë
Hero with a Thousand Faces, Joseph Campbell
Black Ice, Lorene Carey
Wise Children, Angela Carter
Death Comes for the Archbishop, Willa Cather
During the Reign of the Queen of Persia, Joan Chase
Life and Death in Shanghai, Nien Cheng
The Awakening, Kate Chopin
Memoirs of a Medieval Woman, Louise Collis
Goodbye without Leaving, Laurie Colwin
The James Joyce Murder, Amanda Cross
The Divine Comedy, Dante
The Leopard, Giuseppe di Lampedusa
An American Childhood, Annie Dillard
Stones for Ibarra, Harriet Doerr
A Yellow Raft in Blue Water, Michael Dorris
The Brothers Karamazov, Fyodor Dostoevsky
The Realms of Gold, Margaret Drabble
The Lover, Marguerite Duras
Alexandria Quartet, Lawrence Durrell
Middlemarch, George Eliot
Love Medicine, Louise Erdrich
As I Lay Dying, William Faulkner
The Good Soldier, Ford Madox Ford
Passage to India and Maurice, E. M. Forster
The Brontës, Antonia Fraser
The Old Gringo, Carlos Fuentes
Forsythe Saga, John Galsworthy
Love in the Time of Cholera, Gabriel García Marquez
The Finishing School, Gail Godwin
A Sport of Nature and July's People, Nadine Gordimer
The Power and the Glory, Graham Greene
The Book of Ruth, Jane Hamilton

Writing a Woman's Life, Carolyn Heilbrun
The Mambo Kings Play Songs of Love, Oscar Hijuelos
Their Eyes Were Watching God, Zora Neale Hurston
Binstead's Safari, Rachel Ingalls
The Remains of the Day, Kazuo Ishiguro
Portrait of the Artist As a Young Man, James Joyce
Billy Phelan's Greatest Game and *Quinn's Book*, William
    Kennedy
The Bean Trees, Barbara Kingsolver
The Woman Warrior, Maxine Hong Kingston
The Book of Laughter and Forgetting, Milan Kundera
The Diviners, Margaret Laurence
Lady Chatterley's Lover, D. H. Lawrence
The Golden Notebook, Doris Lessing
Moon Tiger, Penelope Lively
Palace Walk, Naguib Mahfouz
West with the Night, Beryl Markham
In Country, Bobbie Ann Mason
Peter the Great, Robert Massie
So Long, See You Tomorrow, William Maxwell
All the Pretty Horses, Cormac McCarthy
Memories of a Catholic Girlhood, Mary McCarthy
Truman, David McCullough
PrairyErth, William Least Heat-Moon
The Secret Passion of Judith Hearne, Brian Moore
Beloved and *Jazz*, Toni Morrison
Dance of the Happy Shades, Alice Munro
A Severed Head, Iris Murdoch
The Return of Eva Peron, V. S. Naipaul
Megatrends, John Naisbitt
The Women of Brewster Place, Gloria Naylor
Solstice, Joyce Carol Oates
Wise Blood, Flannery O'Connor
The English Patient, Michael Ondaatje
How to Make an American Quilt, Whitney Otto
Touch the Water, Touch the Wind, Amos Oz

Cannibal Galaxy, Cynthia Ozick
The Street, Ann Petry
Going down Fast, Marge Piercy
Kate Vaiden, Reynolds Price
The Shipping News, E. Annie Proulx
Parallel Lives, Phyllis Rose
A Woman of Egypt, Jehan Sadat
A Thousand Acres, Jane Smiley
A Far Cry from Kensington, Muriel Spark
The Man Who Loved Children, Christina Stead
Crossing to Safety, Wallace Stegner
Revolution from Within, Gloria Steinem
The Joy Luck Club, Amy Tan
You Just Don't Understand: Women and Men in Conversation,
    Deborah Tannen, Ph.D.
A Summons to Memphis, Peter Taylor
Kristin Lavransdatter, Sigrid Undset
Losing Battles, Eudora Welty
The House of Mirth, Edith Wharton
A Room of One's Own and *Three Guineas,* Virginia Woolf

Between the Covers Book Club List

Nancy J. Court   **Grand Rapids, Michigan**

BETWEEN THE COVERS began in 1980. Our thirteen female members have read more than 160 books. Although focusing on recent fiction, our yearly book choices have also included nonfiction, classics, humor, and autobiographies. The following list includes those books that provided stimulating discussions and hours of joyful reading.

Classics

East of Eden, John Steinbeck. Monumental novel of good and evil and the passionate lives of two turbulent American families. One of Steinbeck's best. A favorite.

Rebecca, Daphne du Maurier. Successful novel of romance and mystery. The author is a virtuoso at conjuring up suspense, tragedy, and romance.

Maurice, E. M. Forster. A must-read classic in our current homophobic age. Written around 1913, this novel of a young homosexual in the elegant world of Cambridge University was not published until 1971. Very moving.

My Antonia, Willa Cather. Story of a pioneer woman and life as an early settler. Author's anger at loss of earlier values sets the tone.

Lady Chatterley's Lover, D. H. Lawrence. World-famous love story is a masterpiece. Want to read more Lawrence.

Pulitzers

A Thousand Acres, Jane Smiley. Shakespeare fans will love the *King Lear* parallels in this twentieth-century version of tragic family passions. Exposure to large-scale midwestern farm life.

The Color Purple, Alice Walker. Issues of racism, child abuse, and universal truths about intimate relationships in another time and culture. Memorable.

A Confederacy of Dunces, John Kennedy Toole. Unforgettable slob extraordinary, Ignatius Reilly, has been told by his mother that it is time to get a job. Comic and tragic. Toole committed suicide in 1969 at age thirty-two. His mother had his novel published in 1980.

Lonesome Dove, Larry McMurtry. Epic masterpiece of the American West. Wonderful characters and story. Read this book.

About Women

The Road from Coorain, Jill Ker Conway. Thoughtful autobiography of the first woman president of Smith College. Set in the harsh Australian landscape and a male-dominated society. This author's reflections are highly recommended.

Written by Herself, edited by Jill Ker Conway. Collection of autobiographies of American women. Why weren't these women mentioned in our American history classes? Inspiring.

West with the Night, Beryl Markham. Autobiography of a female pilot in Africa in the early thirties. Beauty, humor, and wisdom pervade this lovely book.

Libby, Betty John. This extraordinary book is presented by Libby Beaman's granddaughter. Through Libby's diaries and letters (1879–80), we travel with the first nonnative woman to go to the Alaskan Pribilof Islands, just outside the Arctic Circle.

Life and Death in Shanghai, Nien Cheng. Who needs fiction? Nien Cheng's autobiography of imprisonment during the Chinese Cultural Revolution in the mid-sixties is powerful, nonstop reading. Fascinating insights into Mao's China during a time when the United States was preoccupied with Vietnam and our own cultural revolution.

Miscellaneous

A Gift from the Sea, Anne Morrow Lindbergh. Lindbergh's reflections on a woman's life and the values of one's inner life in a hectic, pressured world. Timeless. For reading in a quiet space.

House of Light, Mary Oliver. Poetry explores the connectedness of humanity to the elemental forces of nature. Oliver can make us see what she sees and believe what she believes. Deceptively simple. Profound truths.

Happy to Be Here, Garrison Keillor. Those with adolescent sons will hoot at "Local Family Keeps Son Happy." Witty short stories that will make you happy to be in Keillor's world.

Kaffir Boy, Mark Mathabane. True story of a black youth's coming of age in apartheid South Africa and his triumph over a life of degradation and hopelessness. Powerful.

Nonfiction

The Immense Journey, Loren Eiseley. Nature book intertwines scientific information with Eiseley's vision of life's mysteries. Beautiful.

A Season on the Brink, John Feinstein. If you are going to read only one sports book in your life, read about a year with Bobby Knight and the Indiana Hoosiers. Unique. Discussable.

Nicholas and Alexandra, Robert K. Massie. Brilliant piece of history that reads like a novel. A life drama more interesting than fiction.

Freedom at Midnight, Larry Collins and Dominique LaPierre. Epic portrait of Mahatma Gandhi is a riveting page-turner. Highly recommended.

Confessions of a Medical Heretic, Robert S. Mendelsohn, M.D. Mix the author's premise that annual physicals are a health risk and that hospitals are dangerous places for the sick with two nurses and two physicians' wives and what do you get? One of the most memorable book discussions in the fifteen-year history of our group.

The Disuniting of America, Arthur M. Schlesinger. Examination of the contemporary controversy over multiculturalism and education with the premise that multiculturalism will undermine our republic. Great discussion.

General Fiction

The Dollmaker, Harriet Arnow. This Michigan author tells a powerful story of a courageous Kentucky woman thrust into the ugliness and confusion of wartime Detroit. Arnow is a brilliant storyteller.

Prince of Tides, Pat Conroy. This novel of Tom Wingo and his troubled sister spans forty years. The South Carolina low country is enchanting. Humor, tragedy, powerful emotions. A favorite.

Run with the Horsemen, Ferrol Sams. Novel of a southern farmboy's growing up years in the Great Depression. Porter Osborne Jr., will become a household name because everyone will want to read the book that keeps you laughing out loud. Warmth and humor. First in a delightful trilogy.

The Kitchen God's Wife, Amy Tan. Wonderfully satisfying story of a Chinese woman. Better than Tan's first novel, *The Joy Luck Club.*

Fried Green Tomatoes at the Whistle Stop Cafe, Fannie Flagg. The negative critiques of this novel were dead wrong. One of the most entertaining narratives that has arrived in the last ten years. "Dot Weems' Weekly" is a jewel. Funny and wise.

Ishmael, Daniel Quinn. Unusual dialogue between a gorilla and a man. Will change your thinking about the role of humans as a species on this planet.

Their Eyes Were Watching God, Zora Neale Hurston. This classic of black literature has had a recent revival. As a black woman in the late thirties, Hurston was given little recognition as a writer. Rich text is written in the dialect of its time and culture. A must read for book groups.

To Dance with the White Dog, Terry Kay. An unusual and unforgettable story about elderly Sam Peek, who recently lost his wife, and the mysterious white dog, invisible to all but Sam.

Follow the River, James Thom. History lives in this adventure novel of twenty-three-year-old Mary Ingles, kidnapped by Indians in 1755. The story of this courageous pioneer woman who walked one thousand miles of wilderness to return to her own people.

Crossing to Safety, Wallace Stegner. Sensitive story of two couples and their long-term give-and-take friendship. Universally loved.

The Education of Little Tree, Forrest Carter. Tears and laughter intertwine while reading this tender story of a Cherokee boy in Tennessee in the thirties. Delightful for children, adolescents, and adults.

The Bean Trees, Barbara Kingsolver. Story of a young woman who finds herself the unlikely mother of an abandoned Native American child. Funny and heartwarming. Want to read more Kingsolver.

The Ginger Tree, Oswald Wynd. Compelling story of a young Scotswoman in Peking in 1903 and her bittersweet romance with a young Japanese nobleman. A favorite.

The Handmaid's Tale, Margaret Atwood. Powerful story about the world of the near future and the question of who controls women's bodies. Chilling. A must for book groups.

The Bridges of Madison County, Robert James Waller. Recordsetting, bestselling sleeper guarantees a lively evening. Heated discussion between those who get swept away by Harlequin romances and those who oppose "bodice ripper" rip-offs.

My Name is Asher Lev, Chaim Potok. Another winning story from Potok about the choice of a young man torn between his compelling drive to create art and his Jewish tradition and heritage.

Black Rain, Masuji Ibuse. Story of a Japanese man in the days immediately following the bombing of Hiroshima. Powerful.

A Prayer for Owen Meaney, John Irving. Storytelling genius Irving gives us a most unusual hero in Owen Meaney. Disturbing and wonderful. Had to read more Irving.

Hot Flashes, Barbara Raskin. Reunion of four extraordinary modern women. Portrays cultural changes from the forties to the eighties with humor. Perfect for the premenopausal group.

The Beans of Egypt, Maine, Carolyn Chute. Quirky, fascinating story of America's rural underclass. Beans are all over America living in mobile homes on the wrong side of the tracks. Comic and tragic.

Fifteen Years of Books: Women's Book Group—San Diego

Barbara Kerr Davis   **Exeter, California**

The House of the Spirits, Isabel Allende
I Know Why the Caged Bird Sings, Maya Angelou
Hunter's Horn, Harriet Arnow
Surfacing, *The Handmaid's Tale*, and *Cat's Eye*, Margaret Atwood
Emma and *Sense and Sensibility*, Jane Austen
Virginia Woolf: A Biography, Quentin Bell
Death of the Heart, Elizabeth Bowen
A Weave of Women, E. M. Broner
The Tenant of Wildfell Hall, Anne Brontë
Providence, Anita Brookner
Cold Sassy Tree, Olive Ann Burns
The Professor's House and *My Antonia*, Willa Cather
During the Reign of the Queen of Persia, Joan Chase
The Awakening, Kate Chopin
Duo, My Mother's House, Sido, The Ripening Seed, Chéri, and *The Last of Chéri*, Colette
Another Marvelous Thing, Laurie Colwin
Memoirs of a Dutiful Daughter, Simone de Beauvoir

Play It As it Lays, Joan Didion
An American Childhood, Annie Dillard
Out of Africa and *Seven Gothic Tales*, Isak Dinesen
Stones for Ibarra, Harriet Doerr
The Garrick Year, *The Millstone*, and *The Realms of Gold*,
  Margaret Drabble
The War: A Memoir and *The Lover*, Marguerite Duras
Semi-Attached Couple/Semi-Detached House, Emily Eden
The Mill on the Floss and *Middlemarch*, George Eliot
Tracks and *Love Medicine*, Louise Erdrich
Serve It Forth, M. F. K. Fisher
Fried Green Tomatoes at the Whistle Stop Cafe, Fannie Flagg
Howard's End, E. M. Forster
Two Under the Indian Sun, Jon and Rumer Godden
Greengage Summer, Rumer Godden
The Mind Body Problem, Rebecca Goldstein
Burger's Daughter and *July's People*, Nadine Gordimer
Final Payments, *Men and Angels*, and *The Company of Women*,
  Mary Gordon
A Woman of Independent Means, Elizabeth Forsythe Hailey
The Duchess of Bloomsbury Street and *84, Charing Cross Road*,
  Helene Hanff
She Had Some Horses, Joy Harjo
Transit of Venus, Shirley Hazzard
Writing a Woman's Life, Carolyn Heilbrun
Little Foxes, *Pentimento*, and *Scoundrel Time*, Lillian Hellman
The Cloud Catchers, Ursula Holden
The Bone People, Keri Hulme
Dreams of Sleep, Josephine Humphreys
Their Eyes Were Watching God, Zora Neale Hurston
The Sun Dial, Shirley Jackson
Unnatural Causes and Innocent Blood, P. D. James
Country of the Pointed Firs, Sarah Orne Jewett
Good Behavior, Molly Keane
The Bean Trees, Barbara Kingsolver
The Woman Warrior, Maxine Hong Kingston

The Left Hand of Darkness, Ursula K. LeGuin
Metropolitan Life, Fran Lebowitz
A Note in Music, Rosamund Lehman
Memoirs of a Survivor and *The Summer Before the Dark,* Doris
  Lessing
West with the Night, Beryl Markham
Shiloh and Other Stories, Bobbie Ann Mason
The Member of the Wedding, Carson McCullers
That Night, Alice McDermott
Blackberry Winter, Margaret Mead
Autobiography, Golda Meir
Beloved, Sula, and *Tar Baby,* Toni Morrison
The Philosopher's Pupil, Word Child, and *The Sea, the Sea,* Iris
  Murdoch
The Women of Brewster Place, Gloria Naylor
Bellefleur, Joyce Carol Oates
Yonnondio, From the Thirties, and *Tell Me a Riddle,* Tillie
  Olsen
The Little Disturbances of Man, Grace Paley
Close Company: Stories of Mothers and Daughters, edited by
  Christine Park and Caroline Heaton
The Portable Dorothy Parker, Dorothy Parker
Machine Dreams, Jayne Anne Phillips
Vida, Marge Piercy
Woman on Paper, Anita Pollitzer
The Old Order, Katherine Anne Porter
A Few Green Leaves, The Sweet Dove Died, and *Excellent
  Women,* Barbara Pym
Wild Sargasso Sea, Jean Rhys
The Vampire Lestat, Anne Rice
Housekeeping, Marilynne Robinson
The Country Waif, George Sand
The House by the Sea and *The Small Room,* May Sarton
The Story of an African Farm, Olive Schreiner
The Killing Ground, Mary Lee Settle
Transformations, Anne Sexton

Sassafras, Cypress, and Indigo, Ntozake Shange
A Far Cry from Kensington, Muriel Spark
The Autobiography of Alice B. Toklas, Gertrude Stein
The Joy Luck Club, Amy Tan
Angel, Elizabeth Taylor
Singing Sands and *The Daughter of Time*, Josephine Tey
Celestial Navigation, *The Accidental Tourist*, and *Breathing Lessons*, Anne Tyler
Kristin Lavransdatter, Sigrid Undset
Meridian, *The Third Life of Grange Copeland*, *The Color Purple*, and *The Temple of My Familiar*, Alice Walker
The Lives and Loves of a She-Devil, and *Hearts and Lives of Men*, Fay Weldon
Delta Wedding and *Ponder Heart*, Eudora Welty
Run Softly, Go Fast, Barbara Wersba
The Age of Innocence, Edith Wharton
The Sugar House and *Beyond the Glass*, Antonia White
A Room of One's Own, *Mrs. Dalloway*, *The Waves*, and *To the Lighthouse*, Virginia Woolf
Memoirs of Hadrian, Marguerite Yourcenar

Faculty Folk Novel Discussion Group Book List

Irma Dunninger and
Ruth Ann Stump   **Haslett, Michigan**

THESE ARE SOME of our favorite selections from the past twenty-three years.

The Age of Innocence and *Ethan Frome,* Edith Wharton
Animal Dreams, Barbara Kingsolver
Beloved, The Bluest Eye, and *Jazz,* Toni Morrison
The Book of Daniel, E. L. Doctorow
Crossing to Safety and *Angle of Repose,* Wallace Stegner
Fifth Business, Robertson Davies
Fried Green Tomatoes at the Whistle Stop Cafe, Fannie Flagg
Giants in the Earth, Ole Edvart Rölvaag
Obasan, Joy Kogawa
Quartet in Autumn, Barbara Pym
Southern Discomfort, Rita Mae Brown
Sport of Nature, Nadine Gordimer
The Good Terrorist, Doris Lessing
The Diviners and *The Stone Angel,* Margaret Laurence
The Dollmaker, Harriet Arnow
The Bostonians, Henry James
The Handmaid's Tale, Margaret Atwood
The Slave, Isaac Bashevis Singer
The House of the Spirits, Isabel Allende
The Color Purple, Alice Walker
The Joy Luck Club, Amy Tan
To Dance with the White Dog, Terry Kay
The Quiet American, Graham Greene
My Antonia, Willa Cather
The Chosen, Chaim Potok
The Middle Ground, Margaret Drabble
Stones for Ibarra, Harriet Doerr
The Tin Can Tree, Anne Tyler
Their Eyes Were Watching God, Zora Neale Hurston
The Hunter's Horn, Harriet Arnow
Fifth Business, Robertson Davies
My Son's Story, Nadine Gordimer
"...And Ladies of the Club," Helen Hooven Santmyer
Chilly Scenes of Winter, Ann Beattie

Alpha Kappa Alpha BookLovers Reading List

Flora J. Eikerenkoetter   **Media, Pennsylvania**

OUR BOOK DISCUSSION group focuses mainly on the issues presented by African American writers. Our aim is to examine the issues these writers present within the parameters of our own experiences. Each reader responds to the content as well as to the personal feelings and ideas that are awakened by the book. These shared experiences enhance our goal of personal growth. The books we read include historical and modern perspectives about people of color from around the world.

Annie John, Jamaica Kincaid
Brothers and Keepers, John Edgar Wideman
Family, J. California Cooper
Clover, Dori Sanders
Joy, Marsha Hunt
Fences, August Wilson
The Chaneysville Incident, David Bradley
Your Blues Ain't Like Mine, Bebe Moore Campbell
I Saw the Sky Catch Fire, T. O. Echewa
A Question of Power, Bessie Head
Before and After, Rosellen Brown
A Gathering of Old Men, Ernest Gaines
Middle Passage, Charles Johnson
Joe Turner's Come and Gone, August Wilson
Long Distance Life, Marita Golden
I Been in Sorrow's Kitchen and Licked out All the Pots, Susan
    Straight
A Lesson before Dying, Ernest J. Gaines
Disappearing Acts and *Waiting to Exhale,* Terry McMillan
Lure and Loathing, Gerald Early

Brothers and Sisters, Bebe Moore Campbell
Beloved and *Jazz*, Toni Morrison
The Street, Ann Petry
Sweet Summer, Bebe Moore Campbell
Praisesong for the Widow and *Brown Girl, Brownstones*, Paule
  Marshall
Their Eyes Were Watching God, Zora Neale Hurston
The Color Purple, Alice Walker
A Woman of Egypt, Jehan Sadat
Linden Hills, Mama Day, and *The Women of Brewster Place*,
  Gloria Naylor
Sally Hemings, Barbara Chase-Riboud
Ant Hills of the Savannah, Chinua Achebe
The Good Mother, Sue Miller

Poetry List

Peggy Heinrich   **Westport, Connecticut**

Some of Our Favorite Contemporary Poets

Elizabeth Bishop, Robert Bly, Lucille Clifton, Nikki
Giovanni, Stanley Kunitz, Li-Young Lee, Susan Mitchell,
Sharon Olds, Mary Oliver, Theodore Roethke, Charles
Simic, Gary Snyder, William Stafford, Derek Walcott

We've Also Been Enthusiastic About

Eavan Boland, Billy Collins, Rita Dove, Stephen Dunn,
Louise Erdrich, Carolyn Forche, Tess Gallagher, Seamus
Heaney, Galway Kinell, Maxine Kumin, Derek Mahon,
Stephen Mitchell, Richard Wilbur, James Wright

We've Been Divided About

John Ashbery, Raymond Carver, Robert Creeley, Allen Ginsberg, Dana Gioia, Brad Leithauser, Cynthia Macdonald, James Merrill, Alicia Ostriker, Adrienne Rich, Anne Sexton, Mark Strand, Mona Van Duyn

We Haven't Overlooked Wonderful Foreign Poets

Yehuda Amichai, C. P. Cavafy, Czeslaw Milosz, Pablo Neruda, Octavio Paz

Nor Have We Ignored the Long-Established Poets

Robert Browning, Emily Dickinson, John Keats, Percy Bysshe Shelley, William Wordsworth, Walt Whitman

Or Those Bright Lights of This Century

W. H. Auden, Hart Crane, e. e. cummings, T. S. Eliot, Robert Frost, Robert Graves, Amy Lowell, Robert Lowell, Edna St. Vincent Millay, Marianne Moore, Ezra Pound, Rainer Maria Rilke, Wallace Stevens, Dylan Thomas, William Carlos Williams, William Butler Yeats

We spent a dozen meetings reading Derek Walcott's "Omeros" and not only found it well worth the time, but were sorry when it ended. That started us on another long-term project, Dante's "Inferno." We used the recent 1993 edition with translations by twenty contemporary poets. While we enjoyed the project, we felt that John Ciardi's 1954 version more than held its own against the competition.

Our Long, but Partial, List of Contemporary Poets Includes

Diane Ackerman, A. R. Ammons, Amiri Baraka (LeRoi Jones), John Berryman, Joseph Brodsky, Gwendolyn Brooks, Amy Clampitt, Jane Cooper, Alfred Corn, Federico García Lorca, Louise Gluck, Jorie Graham, Linda Gregg, Emilyn Grosholz, Thom Gunn, Marilyn Hacker, Donald Hall, Michael Harper, Robert Hass, Robert Hayden, Richard Howard, Ted Hughes, Richard Hugo, Colette Inez, Josephine Jacobsen, Erica Jong, Donald Justice, X. J. Kennedy, Jane Kenyon, Etheridge Knight, Philip Larkin, Denise Levertov, Philip Levine, John Logan, William Matthews, J. D. McClatchy, William Meredith, W. S. Merwin, Carol Muske, Robert Pinsky, Sylvia Plath, Stanley Plumly, Sonia Sanchez, Louis Simpson, Dave Smith, W. D. Snodgrass, Gary Snyder, Gerald Stern, James Tate, Quincy Troupe, Jean Valentine, Nancy Willard, C. K. Williams, Charles Wright

And We Intend to Look into These Newer Voices

Claribel Alegria, Victor Hernandez Cruz, Marie Howe, Linda McCarrison, Sandra McPherson, Naomi Shihab Nye, Jimmy Santiago Baca, Sherod Santos, Cathy Song, Sekou Sundiata, Daisy Zamora

Contemporary Books Discussion Group Book List—Bettendorf Public Library

Hedy N. R. Hustedde   Davenport, Iowa

1988–89

Mortal Choices: Ethical Dilemmas in Modern Medicine, Ruth Macklin. An ethicist at Albert Einstein College of Medicine uses medical case histories to show how philosophers can help doctors make difficult moral decisions. This book motivated me to draw up a living will, copies of which now reside with my doctor, lawyer, parents, and husband.

What's Bred in the Bone, Robertson Davies. "What's bred in the bone will come out in the flesh" is the proverb at the base of this richly textured novel about a famous art expert. A complex and inventive work by an esteemed Canadian author.

Against All Hope, Armando Valladares. A Cuban political prisoner for twenty-five years, the author maintained a relentless resistance to his tormentors despite excruciating conditions and increasing physical paralysis. His poetry, smuggled out of Cuba, led to his cause being taken up by groups such as Amnesty International.

Roughing It, Mark Twain. A record of several years of travel to, in, and around Nevada by one of America's foremost humorists.

The Modern Tradition, collected by Daniel Howard. A short story anthology.

The Closing of the American Mind, Allan Bloom. Bloom decries the state of higher education in the United States. Though his case concerning humanities deserves serious consideration, many critics decry Bloom. This made for a lively discussion.

Slaughterhouse Five, Kurt Vonnegut. The author's black humor on the subject of human stupidity is evident in this novel about the bombing of Dresden.

The Haunted Mesa, Louis L'Amour. A combination of western and occult adventure, with the former given a decided edge. The hero, investigating the mystery of a race of vanished cliff dwellers, "crosses over" into a fourth dimension, which turns out to be another frontier.

The Discoverers, Daniel Boorstin. Humankind's endless adventure in unraveling the mysteries of the universe and the many "discoverers" who have added to our cumulative wisdom are the subjects of this work.

1989–90

The Power of Myth, Joseph Campbell with Bill Moyers. The ways in which mythology illuminates the stages of life. Most of us found our individual faiths strengthened by reading this book, even though it challenged and questioned them.

Manufacturing Consent: The Political Economy of the Mass Media, Edward S. Herman and Noam Chomsky. Argues that America's government and its corporate giants exercise control over what we read, see, and hear. A disturbing picture of a news system that panders to the interests of America's privileged and neglects its duties when the concerns of minority groups and the underclass are at stake.

Foreign Affairs, Alison Lurie. What makes this novel such a delight is the author's feel for the comedy of the human situation in which growing up and learning to love defeats our most cherished preconceptions about ourselves.

The Book and the Brotherhood, Iris Murdoch. Murdoch's twenty-third novel begins at a midsummer ball at Oxford where a group of friends have gathered. Years ago, these friends had financed a political and philosophical book by David Crimond, a monomaniacal Marxist genius. Crimond's actions touch off a crisis and, by night's end, the vindictive ghosts of the past have invaded the present.

Man of the House: The Life and Political Memoirs of Speaker Tip O'Neill, Tip O'Neill with William Novak. For its evocation of the early Boston days alone, this book deserves to be a hit. The politically-hooked reader will hear, in the background, the voice of derby-hatted John Kelly calling, "Up, up the Speaker!"

The Flight of the Iguana, David Quammen. Naturalist Quammen's essays are compiled into a lively book. How many of us have studied the face of a spider or spent an hour thinking about earthworms? Quammen has and shares his observations with us.

The Trial of Socrates, I. F. Stone. Stone's portrait of Socrates sharply contrasts with popular hagiographies and will interest a wide range of readers, although Socratic experts will find much to argue with. Categorized as fiction, but smacks of fact. It was the first and only time I've seen a member of the group get so riled that he slammed the book flat on the table exclaiming, "I don't like it!!!"

1990–91

Life and Death in Shanghai, Nien Cheng. A woman of wealth and privilege, Cheng was imprisoned in 1966 at the onset of the Cultural Revolution. She spent more than six years in solitary confinement, refusing to confess to false charges against her. Her intelligence, independent spirit, and determination shine through this revealing memoir.

A Yellow Raft in Blue Water, Michael Dorris. In consecutive narratives, three generations of Native American women offer varying perspectives of their lives on a Montana reservation.

Warrior Queens, Antonia Fraser. Lively, readable history with new insights into some familiar figures and provocative introductions to national heroines little known in the West.

The Thrill of the Grass, W. P. Kinsella. Best known for his novel *Shoeless Joe,* on which the film *A Field of Dreams* was based, the author visited our area for a series of lectures, readings, and workshops. The short stories in this volume are all related to baseball.

Wordstruck, Robert MacNeil. In this fond memory of his Nova Scotia boyhood, the cohost of the MacNeil/Lehrer NewsHour recalls the beginnings of a lifelong love affair with language.

Singular Rebellion, Saiichi Maruya, translated by Dennis Keene. When a middle-aged, electronics executive marries a beautiful, young model, he finds out that her grandmother, a convicted murderer just out of jail, is part of the deal. The novel's humor revolves around being modern and being Japanese.

The Man Who Mistook His Wife for a Hat and Other Clinical Tales, Oliver Sacks. The author, a neurologist who describes himself as equally interested in people and in diseases, as scientist and as romantic, has written twenty-four case histories of patients he has treated. Intriguing reading for those who are interested in various permutations of neurological disease.

Angle of Repose, Wallace Stegner. A young married couple goes west at the turn of the century so the husband can pursue his engineering career. He experiences a series of failures, some because of his own weaknesses, some because of his overzealous sense of integrity. The tale is told by his grandson, a noted historian who has lost a leg and a wife.

The Joy Luck Club, Amy Tan. Common threads of chance and fate are woven intricately through stories of four Chinese mothers and their American daughters revealing their struggle for assimilation. A real tearjerker.

1991–92

The Remains of the Day, Kazuo Ishiguro. The story takes place in the summer of 1956 and concerns the insular, fading world of the perfect English butler. A winner of Britain's highest literary award, the Booker Prize.

Jefferson and Monticello: The Biography of a Builder, Jack McLaughlin. A National Book Award nominee in nonfiction, this book is scholarly and immensely readable. Reveals new insights into Jefferson's personality through a detailed examination of his home.

Panther in the Sky, James Alexander Thom. A vigorous and imaginative recreation of the life of the Shawnee Chief Tecumseh (1768–1813).

From Beirut to Jerusalem, Thomas Friedman. A winner of the National Book Award for nonfiction, this book is tough on both the PLO and the Israelis. We agreed that more than anything any of us had read, it clarified and helped us understand the situation between the Israelis and Palestinians in the Middle East.

A Feeling for the Organism: The Life and Work of Barbara McClintock, Evelyn Keller. A clear and exciting picture of one of the most remarkable scientists who ever practiced genetic biology.

You Just Don't Understand: Women and Men in Conversation, Deborah Tannen, Ph.D. Even in the closest relationships, women and men live in different worlds made of different words. This discussion was filled with much laughter as personal anecdote after anecdote was related—all categorically supporting Tannen's ideas.

East is East, T. Coraghessan Boyle. A Japanese sailor jumps overboard off the coast of Georgia, encountering, among other things, a writers' colony and much culture shock. Well, the shock goes both ways.

This Boy's Life: A Memoir, Tobias Wolff. Brings to life the stuff of boyhood and captures fifties America as well. Parts of the story seemed so fantastic that some of us questioned the author's veracity.

The Oldest Living Confederate Widow Tells All, Allan Gurganus. A ninety-nine-year-old widow tells her husband's war stories and more from her bed in a charity rest home in Falls, North Carolina, to a visitor with a tape recorder. Some participants didn't finish this long book. Others were so taken by it, they read it twice! The nonfinishers were persuaded to keep reading postdiscussion. It was worth it.

1992–93

Father Melancholy's Daughter, Gail Godwin. The world of Margaret Gower, daughter of the rector of St. Cuthbert's Church in Romulus, Virginia, changes forever when Margaret is six. On that day, her mother walks away from her life as a rector's wife never to return. A moving and spiritual novel.

How to Make an American Quilt, Whitney Otto. Set in a small, central California town, the novel chronicles the local quilting circle and its eight members. This book held special meaning for our group members who quilt. We bind ourselves to each other in many ways, including quilting and discussing books together.

Amusing Ourselves to Death, Neil Postman. The author contends that today's public media are designed to do little more than entertain. He laments the decline of print intelligence and the people's ability to read reflectively and judge the quality of arguments. He examines how Aldous Huxley's *Brave New World* prediction that people can be controlled by inflicting pleasure may be true.

Without Feathers, Woody Allen. This is Jewish, big city, East Coast humor—something we small town, primarily Christian, midwesterners find worth delving into. The title comes from Emily Dickinson's observation that, "Hope is the thing with feathers."

A Natural History of the Senses, Diane Ackerman. A grand tour of the realm of the senses in prose that is sensual in and of itself. One can tell that Ackerman is a poet at heart. Two years later, I am still quoting from this book and giving it as a present to deserving friends.

Honest Effort, Michael Carey. Carey is a farmer who lives near Farragut, Iowa, but was raised on the East Coast. His poems are very accessible to people not familiar with or even interested in poetry. His poetry delighted us so much, I arranged for him to give a reading at our library.

Braided Lives, Marge Piercy. This novel concerns the lives of two women who grew up in the fifties and the major theme is abortion. As in most of Piercy's work, politics and feminism loom large.

Savage Inequalities, Jonathan Kozol. Kozol takes us into schools across the country describing what is happening to children from poor families in the inner cities and less affluent suburbs and, justifiably so, we are made to feel ashamed. He doesn't just shame us though, he also galvanizes us to change the educational system and its gross and consistent inequalities.

Second Nature: A Gardener's Education, Michael Pollan. Allen Lacy, author of many gardening books, says this book is about gardening, but only in the same way that Dante's Divine Comedy is about getting lost in the woods. Pollan has a lot to say about the overlapping, sometimes conflicting, moral and political borders of nature and culture.

1993–94

Getting Even and *Side Effects*, Woody Allen. A continuation of last year's readings from *The Complete Prose of Woody Allen*. One group member was reading in bed late into the night, and while he managed not to wake his wife by laughing out loud, he laughed so hard he shook the bed and woke her up anyway.

The Living, Annie Dillard. Set in Bellingham, Washington, from 1855–97, with a large cast of vivid characters, this novel gave us prairie dwellers a different view of trees. Dillard did a lot of primary source research—reading letters and diaries—to be as authentic as possible with language, dress, food, and attitudes.

The Last Word and Other Stories, Graham Greene. This volume gathers previously uncollected stories from the entire range of Greene's career, 1923 until 1989. One, "A Branch of the Service," had never been printed before. Greene's religious and moral conundrums are always thought provoking.

The Way Things Ought to Be, Rush Limbaugh. *The New York Times Book Review* proclaimed that, "However concocted, this is a work for its time . . . right wing populism, an American perennial, is in bloom, and at the moment Mr. Limbaugh is its gaudiest flower." We had our largest attendance of the year at this discussion. Many of us voted to read this book because we knew we never would read it on our own.

A River Runs Through It, Norman Maclean. Vivid images of the Big Blackfoot River in Montana; convincing evidence of the parallels between fly-fishing and life; painstaking and painful semiautobiographical analysis of family relationships; writing so subtle and beautiful that the reader laughs and cries almost without knowing why. The last sentence is ultimately memorable, "I am haunted by waters."

The Middleman and Other Stories, Bharati Mukherjee. The author sees immigrants to America from Asia, the Middle East, and Latin America as a wave of pioneers who will change their new homeland just as inexorably as the Europeans changed America in the nineteenth and early twentieth centuries. These stories evoke the longing and confusion of both the newest immigrants and the long-time residents. Mukherjee makes us see things through completely different eyes.

Tuva or Bust! Richard Feynman's Last Journey, Ralph Leighton. Tuva is Tuvinskaya, a notch in northwest Mongolia. What Ralph and Richard go through to try to get to Tuva in incredible. Leighton gives the reader ideas for where to get answers—from libraries to corresponding with government officials, movie stars, and musicians, to examining maps everywhere, even on shower curtains and piggy banks at K-Mart. We learned a little about Feynman, who won a Nobel Prize in physics, and a lot about Tuva and Tuvans, a place and a people most of us well-read individuals had never heard of before.

Midaq Alley, Naguib Mahfouz. This Egyptian author is the winner of a Nobel Prize in literature. This story concerns the inhabitants of an alley in Cairo in the forties—their comings and goings, births and deaths, timelessness.

My Antonia, Willa Cather. A classic of pioneer America. A Bohemian immigrant girl copes with all the hardships of her life on the Nebraska prairie of the late nineteenth century.

1994–95

Jump and Other Stories, Nadine Gordimer. This South African author is one of the few women to win a Nobel Prize in literature. This collection of stories was cited by the committee awarding the prize. It gives us access to many lands, from suburban London to the veldt in South Africa.

The De-Valuing of America, William Bennett. The author is a patriot and an individualist. Rush Limbaugh thinks he's great (he's quoted on the cover of the paperback edition). They both value America. Bound to be plenty of heated discussion on this one.

The Shipping News, E. Annie Proulx. Darkly humorous and very moving, this novel won both the Pulitzer Prize and the National Book Award. After a series of tragedies in Brooklyn, homely and hesitant Quoyle moves with his two young daughters to Newfoundland, his ancestral family home. He gets a job reporting the shipping news for a local newspaper and meets a bevy of eccentric, lovable (and not so) characters.

Balkan Ghosts: A Journey Through History, Robert Kaplan. A timely study of the countries in the Balkan peninsula, written in travelogue style, insightful and informative. A must for those who would like to understand the plights of these emerging countries in Eastern Europe.

Breaking Barriers: A Memoir, Carl T. Rowan. The author grew up in severe poverty in McMinnville, Tennessee, but through luck and hard work managed to obtain a position at the cutting edge of power and social change. Rowan's blatant opinions and scathing denunciations make this memoir both controversial and fascinating.

Cavalry Maiden: Journals of a Russian Officer in the Napoleonic Wars, N. A. Durova, translated by Mary Zirin. This book was one of the first autobiographies printed in Russia (1836) and explores a man's world as seen through the eyes of a woman who masqueraded as a man for ten years so she could be a soldier in the Russian Army. (We chose to read it because Ralph Leighton had recommended it in *Tuva or Bust!*, a book we read last year.)

The Great Gatsby, F. Scott Fitzgerald. The leader of this discussion had done extensive research on Fitzgerald and believes that this is Fitzgerald's most complete and quintessentially American novel with its portrayal of the promise and pathos of wealthy society, specifically in New York City and Long Island.

Jesus: A Life, A. N. Wilson. The author claims that the Jesus of history and the one of faith are really two separate beings with two separate stories. He tells the historical story in an incisive, insightful way, leaving faith to the spiritual realm.

The English Patient, Michael Ondaatje. Winner of a Booker Prize. In this novel, four people come together in a deserted Italian villa during the final moments of World War II: a young nurse whose energy is focused on her last dying patient; the patient who is an unknown Englishman and survivor of a plane crash; a thief whose skills made him both a hero and a casualty of war; and an Indian soldier in the British army who is an expert at bomb disposal.

The List

Stephen A. Huth   **Oak Park, Illinois**

THE LIST IS not complete. We don't keep records of the books we read, but the majority are listed below. The notes are even more incomplete, and mostly represent my rather random recall of the book club years.

Accidental Tourist, Anne Tyler (one of several books we have read which later was adapted as a movie—we've *meant* to view one of these as a group, but I guess our group spirit does not extend to film)
Adventures of Augie March, Saul Bellow
The Age of Innocence, Edith Wharton
All the Pretty Horses, Cormac McCarthy
An Artist of the Floating World, Kazuo Ishiguro

Beans of Egypt, Maine, Carolyn Chute (we now call every book about a strange family "The Beans of . . ." and add a place from the new book)

Beet Queen, Louise Erdrich

Beloved and *Bluest Eye,* Toni Morrison

Bonfire of the Vanities, Tom Wolfe

Book of Daniel, E. L. Doctorow (his books have proved poor for discussion)

Braided Lives, Marge Piercy

Breathing Lessons, Anne Tyler

The Brethren, Bob Woodward and Scott Armstrong

Bright Lights, Big City, Jay McInerney (we compared to *Generation X* in style)

Burger's Daughter, Nadine Gordimer

Call it Sleep, Henry Roth (one of many books that struck a resonant chord in just one club member—he had never heard of the book and was amazed by it—in sum, what I think is the real value of a book club)

A Canticle for Liebowitz, Walter Miller (the first science fiction we read as a group; most enjoyed the book, but circumstances intervened and only three people showed up for the discussion—more have come to discuss universally disliked books)

China Men, Maxine Hong Kingston (we later discussed in conjunction with *The Joy Luck Club*)

Cities on a Hill, Frances FitzGerald (allowed for lots of talk about current issues—as we have come to realize over the years, nonfiction books generate discussion more easily than fiction)

Clan of the Cave Bear, Jean Auel

The Color Purple, Alice Walker

A Confederacy of Dunces, John Kennedy Toole

The Confidence-Man, Herman Melville (to this day I am derided for choosing this as our first book—how we continued after that we are not sure)

Crows, Charles Dickinson (a local journalist whom we invited to our club—he couldn't make it, but sent a nice note and a signed copy of his next book)

Devil's Stocking, Nelson Algren

Dinner at the Homesick Restaurant, Anne Tyler

Einstein's Dreams, Alan Lightman (great surprise for many, but surprisingly difficult to discuss; we discussed the book almost as much before and after the formal discussion as during it)

A Fan's Notes, Frederick Exley

Far Pavilions, M. M. Kaye

Fifth Business, Robertson Davies (consistently one of the best-liked authors)

From Beirut to Jerusalem, Thomas Friedman

Generation X, Douglas Coupland (better received than you might expect from a baby-boomer group; we viewed it as a growing-up novel)

God Knows and *Good As Gold,* Joseph Heller

Gorky Park, Martin Cruz Smith

Growing Up, Russell Baker

The Handmaid's Tale, Margaret Atwood

Hocus Pocus, Kurt Vonnegut (most of us like his writing, but we have found it difficult to discuss)

Home Fires, Donald Katz (brought us back to the discussion of *Cities on a Hill* and the formation of cults)

I Know Why the Caged Bird Sings, Maya Angelou

Ice Age, Margaret Drabble

Immortality, Milan Kundera

In Memory of Junior, Clyde Edgerton (we saw similarities to *The Storyteller,* because of the importance of storytelling to life)

Ironweed, William Kennedy

Jasmine, Bharati Mukherjee

The Joy Luck Club, Amy Tan

Libra, Don DeLillo (a great fantasy read about the Kennedy assassination in 1963, even for conspiracy phobes)

Life and Death in Shanghai, Nien Cheng
Lincoln, Gore Vidal
Linden Hills, Gloria Naylor
Listening to Prozac, Peter D. Kramer
Loon Lake, E. L. Doctorow
Love Medicine, Louise Erdrich
The Man Who Mistook His Wife for a Hat and Other Clinical Tales, Oliver Sacks
Manticore, Robertson Davies
Mariette in Ecstasy, Ron Hansen (gave book club members who were raised as Catholics a chance to show off and gave others the chance to marvel at a strange subset of behaviors such as belief in the stigmata and giving yourself to God while still a child)
Maus, Maus II, Art Spiegelman
Midnight's Children, Salman Rushdie (made some of us envious that a person could write so well in what was not his first language)
The Mists of Avalon, Marion Zimmer Bradley
More Die of Heartbreak, Saul Bellow
Mrs. Caliban, Rachel Ingalls
The Name of the Rose, Umberto Eco
The Natural, Bernard Malamud
On the Beach, Neville Chute
One Hundred Years of Solitude, Gabriel García Marquez (elicited the most extreme reactions: called variously the "best book I've read" and "A Hundred Years of Bore-itude")
Oral History, Lee Smith
Out of Africa, Isak Dinesen
Paco's Story, Larry Heinemann
The Painted Bird, Jerzy Kosinski
Palace Walk, Naguib Mahfouz (several of us felt the translation may have detracted from the book—a common feeling when we read books that have been translated into English)

Paths to Power, Robert Caro (despite its length, well liked, especially for the descriptions of how hard life was in Texas during the first half of the century)

A Prayer for Owen Meany, John Irving

Ragtime, E. L. Doctorow

Rebel Angels, Robertson Davies

The Remains of the Day, Kazuo Ishiguro (more than one member made a nasty face when asked to read a book by a Japanese author about a butler in the thirties and forties in England, but the book turned out to be one of our favorites)

Roger's Version, John Updike

Saint Maybe, Anne Tyler

Schindler's List, Thomas Keneally

The Screwtape Letters, C. S. Lewis (a book we thought would generate a great deal of discussion produced very little)

Setting Free the Bears, John Irving

The Seven Per Cent Solution, Nicholas Meyer

The Shipping News, E. Annie Proulx (my personal favorite)

Small Is Beautiful, E. F. Schumacher (our second book, almost as universally disliked as our first—yet more wonderment that our book club survived)

Son of the Morning Star, Evan Connell

Sophie's Choice, William Styron

Tar Baby, Toni Morrison

There Are No Children Here, Alex Kotlowitz (prompted much discussion of solutions for children growing up amid crime, poverty, and despair)

Thomas Jefferson, Fawn McKay Brodie

Trial of Socrates, I. F. Stone

The Unbearable Lightness of Being, Milan Kundera (no lack of disagreement here—comments ranged from "an absolute gem" to "unbearable")

Waltz in Marathon, Charles Dickinson

Warday, Whitley Streiber and James Kunetka

Welcome to Hard Times, E. L. Doctorow

West with the Night, Beryl Markham

What's Bred in the Bone, Robertson Davies
Widows' Adventure, Charles Dickinson
The Woman Warrior, Maxine Hong Kingston
The World According to Garp, John Irving
A Year in Provence, Peter Mayle
A Yellow Raft in Blue Water, Michael Dorris (shares with E. Annie Proulx the uncanny ability to write from the other gender's perspective)

Detroit Feminist Book Group Reading List—104 Books in Almost Nine Years

Susan Knoppow   **Royal Oak, Michigan**

Superior Women, Alice Adams
The House of the Spirits, Isabel Allende (mysterious)
Surfacing, *The Handmaid's Tale*, *Cat's Eye*, and *The Robber Bride*, Margaret Atwood
Emma, Jane Austen
Picturing Will, Ann Beattie (so-so)
Prime of Life, Simone de Beauvoir
The Mists of Avalon and *Thendara House*, Marion Zimmer Bradley (loved by sci-fi fans)
A Visit from the Footbinder, Emily Brager
Kindred, Octavia Butler
Woman Hollering Creek and *The House on Mango Street*, Sandra Cisneros (poetry-like)
The Road from Coorain and *Written by Herself*, Jill Ker Conway (a fascinating look into an unfamiliar culture)
Breaking the Silence, Jeanne Cordova
Sleeping Arrangements, Laura Cunningham (funny!!)

Lesbian Nuns: Breaking the Silence, Rosemary Curb and Nancy Manahan

Gyn/Ecology, Mary Daly

Having Our Say: The Delany Sisters' First 100 Years, Sarah and A. Elizabeth Delany with Amy Hill Hearth (an engaging view of history, related by the women who experienced it)

The Radiant Way and *Realms of Gold,* Margaret Drabble

Right-Wing Women, Andrea Dworkin

Middlemarch, George Eliot

The Beet Queen, Louise Erdrich

The Chalice and the Blade, Riane Eisler

Women Who Run with the Wolves, Clarissa Pinkola Estes, Ph.D. (hard to finish)

Backlash, Susan Faludi (interesting and important, but we got tired by the end)

Fried Green Tomatoes at the Whistle Stop Cafe, Fannie Flagg (even better than the movie)

My Mother's Daughter and *The Women's Room,* Marilyn French

Women of Deh Koh, Erika Friedl (an opportunity to learn about what women in the Middle East really do all day)

Ellen Foster, Kaye Gibbons

Herland and *The Yellow Wallpaper,* Charlotte Perkins Gilman

Meme Santerre, Serge Grafteaux (the only book we've read by a man—an intriguing true story of a rural French woman from the early twentieth century)

Fugitive Information and *Women Respond to the Men's Movement,* Kay Leigh Hagan (good stuff—lots to talk about)

Native Tongue, Suzette Hagan

The Well of Loneliness, Radclyffe Hall

Their Eyes Were Watching God, Zora Neale Hurston (wonderful)

Mrs. Caliban, Rachel Ingalls

From Housewife to Heretic, Sonia Johnson

Places in the World a Woman Can Walk and *Obscene Gestures for Women,* Janet Kauffman (OK, but not our favorite short stories)

The Bean Trees, Homeland and Other Stories, and *Animal Dreams*, Barbara Kingsolver (one of our favorite authors—we'll read anything she writes)

Another America and *Always Coming Home*, Ursula K. LeGuin (great imagination—thought-provoking books)

The Creation of Patriarchy, Gerda Lerner

The Good Terrorist and *The Four-Gated City*, Doris Lessing

Portrait of an Artist: A Biography of Georgia O'Keeffe, Laurie Lisle

Zami: A New Spelling of My Name, Audre Lorde

Dancing in the Light, Shirley MacLaine

The Women's History of the World, Rosalind Miles (a great look at history from a new perspective—very valuable)

The Good Mother, Sue Miller

Monkeys, Susan Minot

Beloved, Sula, and *Jazz*, Toni Morrison (mysterious—we love these books)

The Women of Brewster Place, Mama Day, and *Bailey's Cafe*, Gloria Naylor (fantastic storyteller)

Tell Me a Riddle, Tillie Olsen

How to Make an American Quilt, Whitney Otto (a wonderful look at America)

Small Changes, Gone to Soldiers, and *Summer People*, Marge Piercy (hated *Summer People*—our most remembered and discussed book ever)

Sleeping with the Enemy, Nancy Price

The Shipping News, E. Annie Proulx

An Atlas of the Difficult World and *On Lies, Secrets, and Silence*, Adrienne Rich (thought-provoking essays and great poetry)

Parallel Lives, Phyllis Rose

Indiana, George Sand

The Woman Who Was Not All There, Paula Sharp

The Book Group Book, edited by Ellen Slezak (great to see how other groups work)

A Thousand Acres, Jane Smiley (mixed reviews—either loved or hated it)

Women of Ideas and What Men Have Done to Them, Dale Spender (another excellent look at history)

Moving beyond Words and *Outrageous Acts and Everyday Rebellions,* Gloria Steinem

The Joy Luck Club and *The Kitchen God's Wife,* Amy Tan (great)

The Gate to Women's Country, Sherri Tepper

In Search of Our Mothers' Gardens, The Temple of My Familiar, and *Possessing the Secret of Joy,* Alice Walker (a favorite author)

The Hearts and Lives of Men and *The Lives and Loves of a She-Devil,* Fay Weldon

John Dollar, Marianne Wiggins (brutal, pretty creepy)

The Little House Books, Laura Ingalls Wilder (interesting to reread these books as an adult)

Refuge, Terry Tempest Williams (well-woven story of a Mormon family's experience with cancer and the Great Salt Lake)

A Room of One's Own and *The Waves,* Virginia Woolf (hard to follow, but enjoyed by some)

Kitchen, Banana Yoshimoto (fun—made some of us love our kitchens more than ever)

A Partial List of Books Discussed in Connie's Living Room

Kathryn J. Lord   **Granby, Connecticut**

The House of the Spirits, Isabel Allende
I Know Why the Caged Bird Sings, Maya Angelou*
Cat's Eye, Margaret Atwood* (evoked stories of childhood)
Pride and Prejudice, Jane Austen

* Indicates lots of discussion on the book.

They Used to Call Me Snow White . . ., Regina Barreca (this book on women's humor fell flat, but we liked the jokes)

The Prime of Life, Simone de Beauvoir* (only one of us finished it, but we all loved the time period)

Circle of Friends, Maeve Binchy (lightweight)

My Antonia, Willa Cather*

Life and Death in Shanghai, Nien Cheng* (amazing courage)

The Prosperine Papers, Jan Clausen (more interesting to writers than to anyone else)

The Road from Coorain, Jill Ker Conway*

An American Childhood, Annie Dillard*

Stones for Ibarra, Harriet Doerr*

The Beet Queen, Louise Erdrich*

Like Water for Chocolate, Laura Esquivel*

Postcards from the Edge, Carrie Fisher (lightweight)

Fried Green Tomatoes at the Whistle Stop Cafe, Fannie Flagg* (we plan on reading more of her)

Dreaming in Cuban, Cristina Garcia*

Fierce Attachments, Vivian Gornick* (the kind of book that turns us into a therapy session)

Owning Jolene, Shelby Hearon

The Islanders, Helen Hull* (a treasure—look for it)

Their Eyes Were Watching God, Zora Neale Hurston*

The Mottled Lizard, Elspeth Huxley*

An Unsuitable Job for a Woman, P. D. James

When Sisterhood Was in Flower, Florence King*

Animal Dreams, Barbara Kingsolver (not as successful as her first novel)

The Bean Trees, Barbara Kingsolver*

Enduring Women, Diana Koos-Gentry*

The Left Hand of Darkness, Ursula K. LeGuin*

The Dance of Intimacy, Harriet Goldhor Lerner* (one person read a different book by the author, but had no problem following the discussion)

Spring Moon, Bette Bao Lord*

West with the Night, Beryl Markham*

The Member of the Wedding, Carson McCullers
Bullwhip Days, edited by James Mellon* (contains many oral
    histories of women)
Beloved, Toni Morrison* (all-time most impact on us)
Bailey's Cafe, Gloria Naylor* (so depressing we canceled plans
    to see a stage production of it)
Linden Hills, Gloria Naylor*
The Street, Ann Petry*
Journal of Solitude, May Sarton (not enough loners in the
    group to identify with her)
A Thousand Acres, Jane Smiley* (one of our best evenings)
Marilyn, Gloria Steinem (lightweight)
You Just Don't Understand: Women and Men in Conversation,
    Deborah Tannen, Ph.D.*
The Age of Innocence, Edith Wharton*
To the Lighthouse, Virginia Woolf* (difficult)

Book List

Shirley L. Luhrsen   **Bozeman, Montana**

OUR BOOK CLUB, a group of American Association of
University Women (AAUW) members, has become a tight
elite cadre of individualistic dynamic souls. Occasionally, but
seldom, weather affects our meeting date. We have come to
accept that May and September are not our months. Each
member has or has had a career and family. We have all
touched distance. One taught in Alaska, another on the
border of northern Minnesota and in the open spaces of
Montana. One has known the winters of Yellowstone, and
another the wilderness of the Madison Range. Peggy came
from Canada. Suzanne has jet hopped all over the world

during one career. Perhaps our common interest is the exchange of information and ideas about ourselves and others. We all love family, wilderness, and books and are as certain of God as we are that it will snow in winter in Montana.

Our reading ranges from books by local Montana authors like Swain Wolfe's *The Woman Who Lived in the Earth* to George Eliot's *Middlemarch*. We could not pass up Jill Ker Conway, Barbara Tuchman, Helen Gurley Brown, Wallace Stegner, Beryl Markham, Amy Tan, or Bette Bao Lord. The list below contains other books we've read, or meant to—it must be confessed, we never did get through *The Second Sex*, though most of us valiantly tried to do so.

Testament of Youth, Vera Brittain
Mrs. Wheeler Goes to Washington, Elizabeth Wheeler Colman
A Thousand Acres, Jane Smiley
The House of the Spirits, Isabel Allende
An American Childhood, Annie Dillard
The Road from Coorain, Jill Ker Conway
The Bridges of Madison County, Robert James Waller
The Second Sex, Simone de Beauvoir
Rising Sun, Michael Crichton
A Place for Us and *Eleni*, Nicholas Gage
Soviet Women: Walking the Tightrope, Francine du Plessix Gray
A Lady's Life in the Rocky Mountains, Isabella Bird
The Sound of Wings: The Life of Amelia Earhart, Mary S. Lovell
My Son's Story, Nadine Gordimer
The Worst Years of Our Lives, Barbara Ehrenreich
Love in a Cold Climate, Nancy Mitford
Heart Earth, Ivan Doig
Buster Midnight's Cafe, Stella Dallas
The Bloody Bozeman, Dorothy Johnson
Jane Eyre, Charlotte Brontë

The Woman Who Lived in the Earth, Swain Wolfe
Middlemarch, George Eliot
A Bright and Shining Lie, Neil Sheehan

Book List

Sara Manewith   **Chicago, Illinois**

OUR BOOK CLUB has been meeting (almost) every month since 1989. While our membership has changed in six years, our goals remain constant: to analyze, interpret, think, and learn through the discussion of compelling fiction and nonfiction; to share thoughts and ideas; and to socialize with literature as our vehicle.

There's never a shortage of potential reading material and our diversity brings varied suggestions and selections. We have, however, been challenged in selecting material that all members find interesting, and we are often tested in the art of compromise. Clearly, the benefit is that each of us, in turn, is likely to read something she would not have otherwise.

We have focused primarily on women writers, you'll find only a handful of male authors on our list. The first time a male author was suggested, we had considerable discussion. Nonetheless, we were pleased with our reading of Ralph Ellison.

Some of the points that have helped keep our meetings lively and our club ongoing follow.

- We have tried periodically to create themes that will carry us over several meetings, i.e., international women writers, women's lives, definitions of community.
- After reading several pieces of fiction, we choose a nonfiction selection. Fiction is always a treat; nonfiction seems more difficult, both to agree on and to read.

- When reading dense books (history, biography), we divide and assign chapters. Each member is responsible for summarizing her chapter, presenting it to the group, and leading a brief discussion, if appropriate.
- We all take responsibility for reading book reviews and scouring libraries and bookstores for recommendations.
- We strongly encourage regular participation. We want a cohesive and reliable group to create what I call "critical mass"—the right number of members (about seven), and a familiarity with one another that makes for rich discussion.

Fiction

Animal Dreams, Barbara Kingsolver
August, Judith Rossner
The Beet Queen, Louise Erdrich
Beloved, Toni Morrison
The Bone People, Keri Hulme
Breathing Lessons, Anne Tyler
The Burger's Daughter, Nadine Gordimer
Cat's Eye, Margaret Atwood
Disturbances in the Field, Lynne Sharon Schwartz
The Fall of the Imam, Nawal El Saadawi
The Fifth Child, Doris Lessing
Geek Love, Katherine Dunn
Gone to Soldiers, Marge Piercy
The Good Mother, Sue Miller
The Handmaid's Tale, Margaret Atwood
The House of the Spirits, Isabel Allende
The Invisible Man, Ralph Ellison
The Joy Luck Club, Amy Tan
Lolita, Vladimir Nabokov
Love in the Time of Cholera, Gabriel García Marquez
Lucy, Jamaica Kincaid
The Mambo Kings Play Songs of Love, Oscar Hijuelos
The Oldest Living Confederate Widow Tells All, Allan Gurganus

Pigs in Heaven, Barbara Kingsolver
Pride and Prejudice, Jane Austen
The Screwtape Letters, C. S. Lewis
The Temple of My Familiar, Alice Walker
A Thousand Acres, Jane Smiley
Waiting to Exhale, Terry McMillan
Woman Hollering Creek, Sandra Cisneros
Woman on the Edge of Time, Marge Piercy
A Yellow Raft in Blue Water, Michael Dorris

Biography/Autobiography

An American Childhood, Annie Dillard
Eleanor Roosevelt, Volume I, 1884–1933, Blanche Wiesen Cook
Frida: A Biography of Frida Kahlo, Hayden Herrera
Having Our Say: The Delany Sisters' First 100 Years, Sarah and A. Elizabeth Delany with Amy Hill Hearth
Life and Death in Shanghai, Nien Cheng
Nora: A Biography of Nora Joyce, Brenda Maddox
The Road from Coorain, Jill Ker Conway
West with the Night, Beryl Markham
When Heaven and Earth Changed Places, Le Ly Hayslip

History/Politics

Backlash, Susan Faludi
The Beauty Myth, Naomi Wolf
From Beirut to Jerusalem, Thomas Friedman
In Our Defense: The Bill of Rights in Action, Ellen Alderman and Caroline Kennedy
Parting the Waters: America in the King Years, Taylor Branch

Essays

Beauty Secrets, edited by Wendy Chapkis
Deals with the Devil, Pearl Cleage
Good Girls, Bad Girls, edited by Laurie Bell

Psychology/Personal Growth

The Invisible Drama: Women and the Anxiety of Change, Carol
  Becker
Women Who Run with the Wolves, Clarissa Pinkola Estes,
  Ph.D.
Women's Ways of Knowing, Mary Field Belenky et al.
You Just Don't Understand: Women and Men in Conversation,
  Deborah Tannen, Ph.D.

Book Pairings

John McFarland   **Seattle, Washington**

The Big Sleep, Raymond Chandler, and *Stick,* Elmore
  Leonard. The original hard-boiled detective and one of his
  contemporary equivalents. Guess who won hands down?
Cold Sassy Tree, Olive Ann Burns, and *Stones for Ibarra,*
  Harriet Doerr. Two wise, loving, and warm novels by
  contemporary American women of a certain age.
The Handmaid's Tale, Margaret Atwood, and *1984,* George
  Orwell. Future societies imagined as warnings from artists
  who worry about the trends they observe.

Venice Observed, Mary McCarthy, and *The Aspern Papers*, Henry James. Nonfiction contemporary classic on Venice and a nineteenth-century novella that describes life in that city at that time. The surprise is what a page-turner the James novella is, and how vividly he paints the unique experience of living in the city of canals.

Out of Africa, Isak Dinesen, and *White Mischief*, James Fox. Kenya in the early days of coffee plantations and Brits sent away from the country estates because of bad behavior. Dinesen's memoir is in a class with Tolstoy's *Anna Karenina*; Fox's is an indirect indictment of British colonies anywhere.

Old Glory, Jonathan Raban, and *Huckleberry Finn*, Mark Twain. The Mississippi keeps on rolling for contemporary travel writer Raban as he follows the route plotted in Twain's still-exhilarating novel of Huck and his adventures in the messy, untamed America of the nineteenth century.

An American Childhood, Annie Dillard, and *Loitering with Intent*, Muriel Spark. The practice of autobiography, one in a memoir, one in a riotous novel that could only have emerged from the loopy vision of Muriel Spark.

A Country Year, Sue Hubbell, and *Lives of the Cell*, Lewis Thomas. A naturalist writing about a year on a farm and a scientist's-eye view of the universe—precise observation and placing human beings in relation to our cohabitors on the planet.

One Writer's Beginnings, Eudora Welty, and *Summer*, Edith Wharton. Two American women writers, one discussing how she came to be a writer, the other, though her career was winding down, uncompromising in her portrayal of the quality of women's lives under patriarchy.

July's People, Nadine Gordimer, and *A Steam Pig*, James McClure. Literary fiction and detective fiction, both addressing the implications of apartheid for South Africa and Rhodesia.

Berlin Stories, Christopher Isherwood, and *Berlin Diary: 1940–1945*, Marie Vassiltchikov. The city of Berlin in fiction and diary—vivid and scary. Both make you glad not to be living in such a time and place.

Flaubert's Parrot, Julian Barnes, and anything by Gustave Flaubert (*Madame Bovary*, "Temptation of St. Anthony," "Letters from Egypt"). Flaubert in all his guises. A contemplation in novel form by Barnes and Flaubert himself without anyone getting in the way.

Murder in the Cathedral, T. S. Eliot, and any of his poetry ("The Love Song of J. Alfred Prufrock," *The Waste Land*). Our attempt to look at a poet, without concentrating (à la a college poetry course) only on one poem or one theme.

Northeast Regional Library Book List

Clare Peterson and
Marie Dench   **Philadelphia, Pennsylvania**

Plays and Poetry

An American Dream, Edward Albee
The Amen Corner, James Baldwin
Threepenny Opera, Bertolt Brecht
The Waste Land and Other Poems, T. S. Eliot
Torch Song Trilogy, Harvey Fierstein
Andorra, Max Frisch
A Soldier's Play, Charles Fuller
The Blacks, Jean Genet
The Miracle Worker, William Gibson

Kaddish and Other Poems, Allen Ginsberg
A Raisin in the Sun, Lorraine Hansberry
Crimes of the Heart, Beth Henley
The Indian Wants the Bronx, Israel Horovitz
Gemini, Albert Innaurato
West Side Story, Arthur Laurents
The Women, a Play, Claire Boothe Luce
J. B., Archibald MacLeish
The Bedbug, Vladimir Maiakovskii
Spoon River Anthology, Edgar L. Masters
When You Comin' Back Red Ryder?, Mark Medoff
After the Fall and *A View from the Bridge*, Arthur Miller
Selected Poetry, Pablo Neruda
'Night Mother, Marsha Norman
The Plough and the Stars, Sean O'Casey
Long Day's Journey into Night and *Mourning Becomes Electra*,
    Eugene O'Neill
Luther, John Osborne
The Poetry of Boris Pasternak, Boris Pasternak
The Caretaker and *The Homecoming*, Harold Pinter
Six Characters in Search of an Author, Luigi Pirandello
Ariel, Sylvia Plath
Complete Stories and Poems, Edgar Allan Poe
Selected Cantos, Ezra Pound
No Exit, Jean-Paul Sartre
Broadway Bound, Neil Simon
Under Milkwood, Dylan Thomas
Leaves of Grass, Walt Whitman
Our Town, Thornton Wilder
Cat on a Hot Tin Roof, Tennessee Williams

Nonfiction

Abigail Adams: An American Woman, Charles W. Akers
In Search of Melancholy Baby, Vassily Aksyonov
Only Yesterday and *Since Yesterday*, Frederick Allen

The Open Heart, Nicolai Amosoff
Nurse, Peggy Anderson
I Know Why the Caged Bird Sings, Maya Angelou
Growing Up, Russell Baker
Just around the Corner, Robert Bendiner
The Uses of Enchantment, Bruno Bettelheim
Whitetown, U.S.A., Peter Binzen
The Grandees and Real Lace, Stephen Birmingham
Black Elk Speaks, Black Elk
The New Assertive Woman, L. Z. Bloom
Miracle at Philadelphia, Catherine D. Bowen
Washington Goes to War, David Brinkley
Widow, Lynn Caine
Voice in the Snow, Olga Carlisle
Mommie Dearest, Christina Crawford
The Trial of Mrs. Abraham Lincoln, Homer Croy
The Enormous Room, e. e. cummings
The Lincoln Nobody Knows, Richard Current
Code Number 72: Ben Franklin, Patriot or Spy?, Cecil B.
    Currey
Because I Was Flesh, Edward Dahlberg
Ordeal of Ambition, Jonathan Daniels
The Dungeon Master, William Dear
Your Erroneous Zones, Wayne Dyer
All the Strange Hours, Loren Eiseley
Mistress Ann, Carolly Erickson
The Liberated Man, Warren Farrell
George Washington in the American Revolution, James Flexner
Civilization and Its Discontents, Sigmund Freud
My Mother, Myself, Nancy Friday
The Feminine Mystique, Betty Friedan
Eleni, Nicholas Gage
Blood of My Blood: The Dilemma of the Italian-Americans,
    Richard Gambino
Paul Robeson: All American, Dorothy B. Gilliam
Life with Picasso, Françoise Gilot

Journey into the Whirlwind, Eugeniia Ginzburg
Forgotten Pioneer, Harry Golden
I'm Dancing As Fast As I Can, Barbara Gordon
Lonely in America, Suzanne Gordon
Fathering, Maureen Green
Raquela, A Woman of Israel, Ruth Gruber
Bound for Glory, Woody Guthrie
Scoundrel Time, Lillian Hellman
The Tao of Pooh, Benjamin Hoff
Farewell to Manzanar, Jeanne Houston
A Different Woman, Jane Howard
Whatta-Gal!: The Babe Didrikson Story, William O. Johnson
Tracy and Hepburn, Garson Kanin
The Story of My Life, Helen Keller
A Nation of Immigrants and *Profiles in Courage,* John F. Kennedy
Letter from a Birmingham Jail, Martin Luther King
The Woman Warrior, Maxine Hong Kingston
The Spirit of St. Louis, Charles A. Lindbergh
The Private Franklin: The Man and His Family, Claude-Anne Lopez and Eugenia W. Herbert
Philadelphia, Patricians and Philistines, 1900–1950, John Lukacs
Not without My Daughter, Betty Mahmoody
Goodbye, Darkness, William Manchester
Journey, Robert Massie
Lelia, André Maurois
Slavery Defended: The Views of the Old South, Eric L. McKitrick
Martha: The Life of Martha Mitchell, Winzola McLendon
Prejudices, H. L. Mencken
Plain Speaking, Merle Miller
Sexual Signatures, John Money
The Descent of Woman, Elaine Morgan
The Total Woman, Marabel Morgan
Conundrum, Jan Morris
Lindbergh, Leonard Mosley

Never Cry Wolf, Farley Mowat
The Gentle Tasaday, John Nance
The Search for Meaning in Modern Art, Alfred Neumeyer
Portrait of a Marriage, Nigel Nicholson
Diary (Volume 1), Anaïs Nin
I Knock at the Door, Sean O'Casey
Catherine the Great, Zoe Oldenbourg
Cry of the Kalahari, Mark and Delia Owens
Elsewhere, Perhaps, Amos Oz
Alive, Piers Paul Read
The Throwaway Children, Lisa Richette
The Street, Mordecai Richler
The Doctor/A Taste of My Own Medicine, Edward Rosenbaum
My Young Years, Arthur Rubinstein
The 900 Days: The Siege of Leningrad, Harrison Salisbury
Abraham Lincoln: The Prairie Years, Carl Sandburg
The Words, Jean-Paul Sartre
Rosalind Franklin and DNA, Anne Sayre
Women's Diaries of the Westward Journey, edited by Lillian
    Schlissel
Center of the Storm, John T. Scopes
Confessions of a Knife, Richard Selzer
Walden Two, B. F. Skinner
Madame Sarah, Cornelia O. Skinner
The Education of a WASP, Lois M. Stalvey
The Peculiar Institution, Kenneth M. Stampp
Dear Theo: The Autobiography of Vincent Van Gogh, edited by
    Irving Stone
Working, Studs Terkel
The Kingdom by the Sea, Paul Theroux
Down These Mean Streets, Piri Thomas
My Life and Hard Times, James Thurber
Mrs. Harris, the Death of the Scarsdale Diet Doctor, Diana
    Trilling
The Mountain People, Colin Turnbull
Innocents Abroad, Mark Twain
Home Before Morning, Lynda Van Devanter

The Ultra Secret, F. W. Winterbothan
The Right Stuff, Tom Wolfe

Fiction

Home is the Sailor, Jorge Amado
Clan of the Cave Bear, Jean Auel
A Fine and Private Place, Peter Beagle
Malone Dies, Samuel Beckett
Deenie, Judy Blume
Labyrinths, Jorge Luis Borges
Farenheit 451, Ray Bradbury
The Plague, Albert Camus
O Pioneers!, Willa Cather
The Short Stories of Anton Chekhov, Anton Chekhov
The Chocolate War, Robert Cormier
Fifth Business, Robertson Davies
Child of Our Time, Michel Del Castillo
Oliver Twist, Charles Dickens
Big Money, John Dos Passos
The Brothers Karamazov, Fyodor Dostoevsky
Rebecca, Daphne du Maurier
As I Lay Dying, William Faulkner
Time and Again, Jack Finney
This Side of Paradise, F. Scott Fitzgerald
A Passage to India and *Maurice*, E. M. Forster
My Brilliant Career, Miles Franklin
The Thief's Journal, Jean Genet
Fathers, Herbert Gold
Lord of the Flies, William Golding
Mother, Maxim Gorki
The Tin Drum, Günter Grass
The Well of Loneliness, Radclyffe Hall
The Mayor of Casterbridge, Thomas Hardy
The Luck of Roaring Camp and Other Stories, Bret Harte
Second Star to the Right, Deborah Hautzig

Twice-Told Tales, Nathaniel Hawthorne
For Whom the Bell Tolls and *Short Stories*, Ernest Hemingway
Consenting Adult, Laura Hobson
Things As They Are, Paul Horgan
White Dawn: An Eskimo Saga, James Houston
Bunnicula, Deborah and James Howe
A High Wind in Jamaica, Richard Hughes
A Portrait of the Artist As a Young Man, James Joyce
Gentle Hands, M. E. Kerr
The Natural State, Damon Knight
The Joke, Milan Kundera
The Stone Angel, Margaret Laurence
The Rainbow, D. H. Lawrence
Spring Moon, Bette Bao Lord
Under the Volcano, Malcolm Lowry
Why Are We in Viet Nam?, Norman Mailer
The Assistant, Bernard Malamud
Thérèse, François Mauriac
The Heart Is a Lonely Hunter and *The Member of the Wedding*,
    Carson McCullers
Moby-Dick and *Typee*, Herman Melville
The Emigrants, Vilhelm Moberg
Ada, Vladimir Nabokov
Mrs. Frisby and the Rats of Nimh, Robert O'Brien
1984, George Orwell
Hangin' Out with Cici, Francine Pascal
Are You in the House Alone? and *Secrets of the Shopping Mall*,
    Richard Peck
Flowering Judas, Katherine Anne Porter
Swann's Way, Marcel Proust
No Fond Return of Love, Barbara Pym
The King Must Die, Mary Renault
The Light in the Forest, Conrad Richter
The Human Comedy, William Saroyan
Nausea, Jean-Paul Sartre
Bread and Wine, Ignazio Silone

The Slave, Isaac Bashevis Singer
A Princess in Berlin, Arthur Solmssen
The First Circle and *One Day in the Life of Ivan Denisovich*,
  Alexander Solzhenitsyn
The Greek Treasure, Irving Stone
The Daughter of Time, Josephine Tey
Vanity Fair, William Thackeray
Dinner at the Homesick Restaurant, Anne Tyler
The Pawnbroker, Edward Lewis Wallant
The Book of the Dun Cow, Walter Wangerin
The Age of Innocence, Edith Wharton
Dad, William Wharton
A Beggar in Jerusalem, Elie Wiesel
The Picture of Dorian Gray, Oscar Wilde
Where the Late the Sweet Birds Sang, Kate Wilhelm

Almost Complete List—Firstar Book Discussion Group

Joan Rozanski   **Milwaukee, Wisconsin**

Affliction, Russell Banks
The Age of Grief, Jane Smiley
Angle of Repose, Wallace Stegner
Animal Dreams, Barbara Kingsolver
All the Pretty Horses, Cormac McCarthy
Annie John, Jamaica Kincaid
At Weddings and Wakes, Alice McDermott
Bailey's Cafe, Gloria Naylor
Bastard out of Carolina, Dorothy Allison
The Bean Trees, Barbara Kingsolver
Beloved, Toni Morrison

Best Laid Plans, Gail Parent
Betsey Brown, Ntozake Shange
Beyond Deserving, Sandra Scofield
The Book of Ruth, Jane Hamilton
Bridges of Madison County, Robert James Waller
The Broken Cord, Michael Dorris
The Chant of Jimmy Blacksmith, Thomas Keneally
Charms for the Easy Life, Kaye Gibbons
Cloudstreet, Tim Winton
Cold Sassy Tree, Olive Ann Burns
The Color Purple, Alice Walker
Continental Drift, Russell Banks
Creek Mary's Blood, Dee Brown
Crossing to Safety, Wallace Stegner
Daisy Fay and the Miracle Man, Fannie Flagg
Dandelion Wine, Ray Bradbury
Daughters, Paule Marshall
Dinner at the Homesick Restaurant, Anne Tyler
Dreams of Sleep, Josephine Humphreys
East Is East, T. Coraghessan Boyle
The Education of Little Tree, Forrest Carter
Family Dancing, David Leavitt
A Farm under a Lake, Martha Berglund
Fear and Loathing in Las Vegas, Hunter S. Thompson
Floating in My Mother's Palm, Ursula Hegi
Foster Child, Mary Bauer
Gaston's War, Gaston Vandermeersche
Gather Together in My Name, Maya Angelou
Good Hearts, Reynolds Price
Goodbye without Leaving, Laurie Colwin
Gorky Park, Martin Cruz Smith
The Handmaid's Tale, Margaret Atwood
Her First American, Lore Segal
Hotel du Lac, Anita Brookner
Housekeeping, Marilynne Robinson
How the García Girls Lost Their Accents, Julia Alvarez

How to Make an American Quilt, Whitney Otto
Hug Dancing, Shelby Hearon
I Been There Before, David Carkeet
I Heard the Owl Call My Name, Margaret Craven
I Know Why the Caged Bird Sings, Maya Angelou
If the River Was Whiskey, T. Coraghessan Boyle
I'm Dancing As Fast As I Can, Barbara Gordon
In Country, Bobbie Ann Mason
Iron and Silk, Mark Salzman
It's Raining in Mango, Thea Astley
Jailbird, Kurt Vonnegut
The Joy Luck Club, Amy Tan
Just above My Head, James Baldwin
Kaffir Boy, Mark Mathabane
Kate Vaiden, Reynolds Price
Leaving the Land, Douglas Ungar
Legacies, Bette Bao Lord
The Life of Helen Alone, Karen Lawrence
Like Water for Chocolate, Laura Esquivel
Lives of the Poets, E. L. Doctorow
Lonesome Dove, Larry McMurtry
Love in the Time of Cholera, Gabriel García Marquez
The Lover, Marguerite Duras
Lovingkindness, Anne Roiphe
Lying Low, Diane Johnson
Lucy, Jamaica Kincaid
Marvin and Tige, F. Glass
Maus, Art Spiegelman
Middle Passage, Charles Johnson
The Middleman and Other Stories, Bharati Mukherjee
Morgan's Passing, Anne Tyler
Mrs. Peabody's Inheritance, Elizabeth Jolley
The Object of My Affection, Stephan McCauley
The Oldest Living Confederate Widow Tells All, Allan
   Gurganus
Palomino, Elizabeth Jolley
Paris Trout, Peter Dexter

Pastorale, Susan Engberg
Patrimony, Philip Roth
Pentimento, Lillian Hellman
A Piece of Mine, J. California Cooper
The Progress of Love, Alice Munro
Ragtime, E. L. Doctorow
Raw Silk, Janet Burroway
The Remains of the Day, Kazuo Ishiguro
Rich in Love, Josephine Humphreys
Russian Journal, Andrea Lee
Say Goodbye to Sam, Michael Arlen
Self-Help, Lorrie Moore
Seventh Heaven, Alice Hoffman
Sheila Levine Is Dead and Living in New York, Gail Parent
The Sheltering Sky, Paul Bowles
Sleeping Arrangements, Laura Cunningham
Spartina, John Casey
Spence and Lila, Bobbie Ann Mason
A Story Like the Wind, Laurens Van der Post
Starting in the Middle, Judith Wax
Strange Fits of Passion, Anita Shreve
A Summons to Memphis, Peter Taylor
A Taste for Death, P. D. James
Testing the Current, William McPherson
Their Eyes Were Watching God, Zora Neale Hurston
Then She Found Me, Elinor Lipman
To Dance with the White Dog, Terry Kay
Toots in Solitude, John Yount
Tracks, Louise Erdrich
Two Old Women, Velma Willis
Typical American, Gish Jen
Utz, Bruce Chatwin
Variations in the Night, Emily Listfield
Victory over Japan, Ellen Gilchrist
Waiting to Exhale, Terry McMillan
Waking, Eva Figes
The Way Men Act, Elinor Lipman

White Palace, Glenn Savan
White Swan, Frances Turk
A Woman of Independent Means, Elizabeth Forsythe Hailey
The World around Midnight, Patricia Browning Griffith
A Yellow Raft in Blue Water, Michael Dorris

AAL Capital Management Corporation Book of the Month Club Reading List

**Joanne Simon and
Lisa Soufal**   **Appleton, Wisconsin**

Confessions of an S.O.B., Al Neuharth
Culture Shift, Price Pritchett, Ph.D.
Customers for Life, Carl Sewell
Heroz, William C. Byham, Ph.D., with Jeff Cox
How to Stop Worrying and Start Living, Dale Carnegie
If It Ain't Broke, Break It, Robert Kriegel
In Search of Excellence, Thomas Peters
Managing the Future, Robert Tucker
Marketing Warfare, Al Ries and Jack Trout
One Up on Wall Street, Peter Lynch
Seven Habits of Highly Effective People, Stephen Covey
Showing Up for Work, Michael and Timothy Mescon
The 10 Commandments of Business, Bill Fromm
The Real Heroes of Business, Bill Fromm and Len Schlesinger
You Just Don't Understand: Women and Men in Conversation,
    Deborah Tannen,Ph.D.
ZAPP! The Lightning of Empowerment, William C. Byham,
    Ph.D., with Jeff Cox

Reading Group List

Carolyn Sosnoski   **Old Lyme, Connecticut**

The Lottery, Shirley Jackson
The Evening Sun, William Faulkner
Hedda Gabler, Henrik Ibsen
Madame Bovary, Gustave Flaubert
Crime and Punishment, Fyodor Dostoevsky
The Snows of Kilimanjaro and *The Short Happy Life of Francis Macomber*, Ernest Hemingway
Catcher in the Rye, J. D. Salinger
Huckleberry Finn, Mark Twain
The Natural and *The Assistant*, Bernard Malamud
Portrait of the Artist as a Young Man, James Joyce
Our Mutual Friend, Charles Dickens
The Glass Menagerie, Tennessee Williams
The Grass Harp and *A Tree of Night*, Truman Capote
The Heart is a Lonely Hunter, Carson McCullers
The Great Gatsby, F. Scott Fitzgerald
The Red and the Black, Stendhal
The Stranger, Albert Camus
Mourning Becomes Electra, Eugene O'Neill
The Father and *Miss Julie*, August Strindberg
The Ambassadors, Henry James
The Sound and the Fury, William Faulkner
For Esme with Love and Squalor and *Uncle Wiggily in Connecticut*, J. D. Salinger
King Lear, William Shakespeare
Death of a Salesman, Arthur Miller
J. B. and *The Book of Job*, Archibald MacLeish
The Adventures of Augie March, Saul Bellow
The Tin Drum, Günter Grass
The Centaur, John Updike
Mrs. Warren's Profession, George Bernard Shaw
On Liberty, John Stewart Mill
Self Reliance, Ralph Waldo Emerson

Threepenny Opera, Bertolt Brecht
The Anatomy of the Mental Personality, Sigmund Freud
The Power and the Glory, Graham Greene
The Turn of the Screw, Henry James
The Mayor of Casterbridge, Thomas Hardy
The Trial, Franz Kafka
The Heart of the Matter, Graham Greene
A Farewell to Arms, Ernest Hemingway
Paradise Lost, John Milton
Nobody Knows My Name, James Baldwin
Major Barbara, George Bernard Shaw
Grapes of Wrath, John Steinbeck
Babbit, Sinclair Lewis
My Antonia, Willa Cather
Desire under the Elms, Eugene O'Neill
The Waste Land, T. S. Eliot
Sons and Lovers, D. H. Lawrence
To the Lighthouse, Virginia Woolf
Selected Poems, Robert Frost
The Death of Ivan Ilyich, Leo Tolstoy
Three Sisters, Anton Chekhov
The Importance of Being Ernest, Oscar Wilde
The Garden Party, Katherine Mansfield
The Golden Honeymoon, Ring Lardner
Main Currents of American Thought, Irwin Shaw
Death in Venice, Thomas Mann
Other Voices, Other Rooms, Truman Capote
A Death in the Family, James Agee
The Loved One, Evelyn Waugh
Victory, Joseph Conrad
No Exit, Jean-Paul Sartre
The Wapshot Chronicle, John Cheever
Herzog, Saul Bellow
An American Tragedy, Theodore Dreiser
The Screwtape Letters, C. S. Lewis
Selected Poems, Emily Dickinson

The Last Temptation of Christ, Nikos Kazantzakis
Darkness at Noon, Arthur Koestler
Julius Caesar, William Shakespeare
Clockwork Orange, Anthony Burgess
Antigone, Sophocles
Antigone, Jean Anouilh
The Shot, Alexander Pushkin
The Apostate, Millburn
The Catbird Seat, James Thurber
Selected Poems, W. H. Auden
The Crucible, Arthur Miller
For Whom the Bell Tolls, Ernest Hemingway
Who's Afraid of Virginia Woolf ?, Edward Albee
The Invisible Man, Ralph Ellison
Native Son, Richard Wright
The Feminine Mystique, Betty Friedan
A Doll's House, Henrik Ibsen
The Second Sex, Simone de Beauvoir
Rabbit Run, John Updike
Candide, Voltaire
The Sign in Sidney Brustein's Window, Lorraine Hansberry
Oedipus, Sophocles
East of Eden, John Steinbeck
Letters from the Earth, Mark Twain
The Habit of Loving, Doris Lessing
Anthem, Ayn Rand
You Can't Go Home Again, Thomas Wolfe
Catch 22, Joseph Heller
Them, Joyce Carol Oates
Under Milkwood, Dylan Thomas
I Never Promised You a Rose Garden, Hannah Green
The Bell Jar, Sylvia Plath
A Populist Manifesto, Newfield and Greenfield
Player Piano, Kurt Vonnegut
Rhinoceros, Eugene Ionesco
1984, George Orwell

The Dead, James Joyce
All My Sons, Arthur Miller
Welcome to the Monkeyhouse, Kurt Vonnegut
Of Mice and Men, John Steinbeck
Women in Love, D. H. Lawrence
Brave New World, Aldous Huxley
The Female Eunuch, Germaine Greer
All the King's Men, Robert Penn Warren
Waiting for Godot, Samuel Beckett
Theft, Katherine Ann Porter
The Standard of Living and *Big Blonde*, Dorothy Parker
The Saint, V. S. Pritchett
The Chrysanthemums, John Steinbeck
My Name is Asher Lev, Chaim Potok
The Sirens of Titan, Kurt Vonnegut
Pride and Prejudice, Jane Austen
The Book of Eskimos, Peter Freuchen
Sybil, Flora Schreiber
The Day of the Locust and *Miss Lonelyhearts*, Nathanael West
The Little Foxes, Lillian Hellman
Down and Out in Paris and London, George Orwell
Here Comes and Other Poems, Erica Jong
Giants in the Earth, Ole Edvart Rölvaag
Anna Karenina, Leo Tolstoy
Goodbye Columbus, Philip Roth
Holdfast Gaines, Odell Shepherd
The Man Who Killed the Deer, Frank Waters
Laughing Boy, Oliver LaFarge
One Flew Over the Cuckoo's Nest, Ken Kesey
The Misanthrope, Jean-Baptiste Molière
Eleanor and Franklin, Joseph Lash
A Room of One's Own, Virginia Woolf
Jude the Obscure, Thomas Hardy
The Saddest Summer of Samuel S., J. P. Donleavy
The Master Builder, Henrik Ibsen
Why I Live at the P.O. and Other Short Stories, Eudora Welty

Zen and the Art of Motorcycle Maintenance, Robert Pirsig
84, Charing Cross Road, Helene Hanff
Ragtime, E. L. Doctorow
The Plough and the Stars, Sean O'Casey
The Making of the President, T. H. White
The Boys in the Bus, Tim Crouse
Summer before the Dark, Doris Lessing
The Madwoman of Chaillot, Jean Giraudoux
Noon Wine, Katherine Ann Porter
A Child's Christmas in Wales, Dylan Thomas
On Death and Dying, Elizabeth Kübler-Ross
Wuthering Heights, Emily Brontë
Passages, Gail Sheehy
The Marriage of Figaro and *The Barber of Seville,* Pierre
  Beaumarchais
The Wild Duck, Henrik Ibsen
The Art of Loving, Eric Fromm
Billy Budd, Herman Melville
Trinity, Leon Uris
Tender is the Night, F. Scott Fitzgerald
The Cracker Factory, Joyce Rebata Burditt
Mythology, Edith Hamilton
The Thorn Birds, Colleen McCullough
Ordinary People, Judith Guest
The Women's Room, Marilyn French
Zelda, Nancy Mitford
An Unfinished Woman, Lillian Hellman
Rubyfruit Jungle, Rita Mae Brown
The Confessions, Jean-Jacques Rousseau
Kramer vs. Kramer, Avery Corman
Dubliners, James Joyce
The World According to Garp, John Irving
Out of the Silent Planet, C. S. Lewis
Song of Solomon, Toni Morrison
Bright Flows the River, Taylor Caldwell
The Massey Tapes, Massey

Washington, D.C., Gore Vidal
Coriolanus, Shakespeare
The Old Man and the Sea, Ernest Hemingway
Lord Jim, Joseph Conrad
Wise Blood, Flannery O'Connor
Only Children, Alison Lurie
God's Little Acre, Erskine Caldwell
Sophie's Choice, William Styron
The Optimist's Daughter, Eudora Welty
Anatomy of an Illness, Norman Cousins
Delta Wedding, Eudora Welty
A Moveable Feast, Ernest Hemingway
The Last Angry Man, Gerald Green
Spoon River Anthology, Edgar Lee Masters
Short Stories, John Cheever
Final Payments, Mary Gordon
Tess of the d'Urbervilles, Thomas Hardy
A Confederacy of Dunces, John Kennedy Toole
Loose Change, Sara Davidson
Rites of Passage, Joanne Greenberg
Brideshead Revisited, Evelyn Waugh
Ah Wilderness!, *Long Day's Journey into Night*, and *Strange Interlude*, Eugene O'Neill
The Lark, Jean Anouilh
Saint Joan, George Bernard Shaw
The Awakening, Kate Chopin
The Citadel, A. J. Cronin
Othello, Shakespeare
The White Album, Joan Didion
To Kill a Mockingbird, Harper Lee
The Iceman Cometh, Eugene O'Neill
The Flies, Jean-Paul Sartre
A Moon for the Misbegotten, Eugene O'Neill
The French Lieutenant's Woman, John Fowles
To Serve Them All My Days, R. F. Delderfield
Dad, William Wharton

The Cinderella Complex, Colette Dowling
Clan of the Cave Bear, Jean Auel
Second Heaven, Judith Guest
Dinner at the Homesick Restaurant, Anne Tyler
Outrageous Acts and Everyday Rebellions, Gloria Steinem
The Color Purple, Alice Walker
The House of Mirth, Edith Wharton
Meridian, Alice Walker
Growing Up, Russell Baker
Ethan Frome, Edith Wharton
A Good Man Is Hard to Find, Flannery O'Connor
The Beans of Egypt, Maine, Carolyn Chute
August, Judith Rossner
The Lives of a Cell, Lewis Thomas
Lincoln, Gore Vidal
A Woman of Independent Means, Elizabeth Forsythe Hailey
Foreign Affairs, Alison Lurie
Earthly Possessions, Anne Tyler
Cider House Rules, John Irving
Eleni, Nicholas Gage
The Giant Sunflower, Clifford Stone
Parallel Lives, Phyllis Rose
Silas Marner, George Eliot
One Writer's Beginnings, Eudora Welty
Middlemarch, George Eliot
World's Fair, E. L. Doctorow
The Words, Jean-Paul Sartre
A Mother and Two Daughters, Gail Godwin
School for Wives, Jean-Baptiste Molière
Crimes of the Heart, Beth Henley
Cry, the Beloved Country, Alan Paton
The Physician, Noah Gordon
Rabbit Is Rich, John Updike
Lake Woebegone, Garrison Keillor
Lady from Plains, Rosalyn Carter
Song of the Lark, Willa Cather

Bess, Margaret Truman
Razzmatazz, Philip Wheaton
The Beet Queen, Louise Erdrich
The Maltese Falcon, Dashiell Hammet
Common Ground, Anthony Lucas
Rock-a-bye, Samuel Beckett
The House of the Spirits, Isabel Allende
The Moviegoer, Walker Percy
Bonfire of the Vanities, Tom Wolfe
Hotel du Lac, Anita Brookner
The Women of Brewster Place, Gloria Naylor
No Country for Young Men, Julia O'Faolian
Measure for Measure, Shakespeare
The Bald Soprano, Eugene Ionesco
The Shell Seekers, Rosamunde Pilcher
Angle of Repose, Wallace Stegner
The March of Folly, Barbara Tuchman
Presumed Innocent, Scott Turow
Billy Bathgate, E. L. Doctorow
The Joy Luck Club, Amy Tan
The Duke of Deception, Geoffrey Wolff
This Boy's Life: A Memoir, Tobias Wolff
Fair and Tender Ladies, Lee Smith
Love in the Time of Cholera, Gabriel García Marquez
A Prayer for Owen Meaney, John Irving
The Good Mother, Sue Miller
The Lonely Passion of Judith Hearne, Brian Moore
Making Sense, Ellen Goodman
Family Pictures, Sue Miller
The Immoralist, André Gide
The Oldest Living Confederate Widow Tells All, Allan
    Gurganus
The Other Side, Mary Gordon
Their Eyes Were Watching God, Zora Neale Hurston
Spring Moon, Bette Bao Lord
Writing a Woman's Life, Carolyn Heilbrun

Cat's Eye, Margaret Atwood
How to Make an American Quilt, Whitney Otto
Picturing Will, Ann Beattie
Knock, Jules Romains
The Yellow Wallpaper, Charlotte Perkins Gilman
A Dangerous Woman, Mary Morris
Pale Horse, Pale Rider and *Noon Wine*, Katherine Ann Porter
Sense and Sensibility, Jane Austen
Howard's End, E. M. Forster
Fried Green Tomatoes at the Whistle Stop Cafe, Fannie Flagg
I Know Why the Caged Bird Sings, Maya Angelou
A Thousand Acres, Jane Smiley
A Thief of Time, Tony Hillerman
She's Come Undone, Wally Lamb
The Tempest, Shakespeare
Homeland and Other Stories, Barbara Kingsolver

The All-Star Reading List

Karen L. Thomson   **Evanston, Illinois**

AS A PROFESSIONAL book discussion leader, my method of
book selection entails a complicated process of reading
reviews, talking to many book lovers both in and out of my
groups, and, of course, reading.

The books chosen out of all this must meet certain basic
criteria. The language must satisfy my poet's ear—the writing
must be beautiful and evocative, with words that are well
chosen, sentences that sing, and paragraphs that flow with
natural rhythm and meaning. I choose books whose stories
appear in my dreams after reading, or that move me to silent
contemplation, great intellectual excitement, or genuine

laughter in recognition of the human condition—books that reach the heart of the reader.

Finally, there is sometimes an intuitive element involved in my selection process. I try to construct a group of books for six months or a year that flow together in a path toward learning. I look for a variety of voices, styles, and genres that complement each other and protect readers from sameness, so that interest builds as we progress. Sometimes a theme emerges, but it's not always what I had initially planned. That is, an almost subconscious scheming goes on as the readings unfold themselves to us. I plan and plot, but a richer process actually emerges. This is a joy to me.

The Accidental Tourist, Anne Tyler.* A wonderfully funny story full of quirky characters who have to make their various kinds of peace with being on life's journey.

The Age of Iron, J. M. Coetzee.* A most moving study of apartheid and its demands on all citizens to realize their political positions in regard to the downtrodden.

An American Childhood, Annie Dillard. A poignant memoir of growing up in Pittsburgh in the fifties.

The Awakening, Kate Chopin. This feminist classic shows women's position and personal power in New Orleans society in the late nineteenth century. A lovely book that won the author social ostracization for writing "sex fiction."

Bastard out of Carolina, Dorothy Allison. A devastating novel about poor whites in the South. It shows most clearly how feelings of powerlessness and shame contribute to sexual abuse and child neglect.

Because It Is Bitter and Because It Is My Heart, Joyce Carol Oates. The story of an unusual friendship and a tragic murder that affects the heroine. Oates is superb at showing family breakdowns throughout various classes. Engrossing, intelligent book.

---

* All of the novels by this author are good for discussion, but I chose my favorite for the All-Star List.

Beloved, Toni Morrison.* One of the greatest novels of the century in my opinion. In poetic language, it tells the story of slavery in this country from an inside, deeply affecting perspective. The ghost Beloved and what she represents are equally unforgettable.

Cat's Eye, Margaret Atwood.* An excellent novel about girls growing up and how they exercise their power on each other. This is a must for women to discuss in terms of their own experiences, as well.

Ceremony, Leslie Marmon Silko. The story of a Native American World War II veteran who has to make sense of war and its connections to the destruction of his people. The ceremony is one of finding a path for spiritual, as well as actual, survival.

Copper Crown, Lane von Herzen. An almost-perfect first novel about an unusual biracial friendship in early twentieth-century Texas. A magical tale of visible spirits, wise women, and the redemptive power of love.

The English Patient, Michael Ondaatje. An intellectually stimulating tale about four characters brought together in a villa in Italy during World War II. Its antiwar message is filled with carefully-crafted images of western civilization in literature, technology, art, and religion. Two readings before discussion are helpful.

Family Pictures, Sue Miller.* A well-written novel about family relationships as affected by the presence of an autistic child.

The Fifth Child, Doris Lessing.* A fable about a family in England whose fifth child is antisocial, a "throwback." Haunting, unforgettable tale.

The Girl, Meridel LeSueur. A wonderful study of the language and life of the poor young women who found themselves in the big cities in the Midwest during the thirties. A proletarian novel with vision.

God's Snake, Irini Spanidou. An unusual book about a little girl growing up in Greece with a strict, military father. Quite evocative and powerful.

A Good Scent from a Strange Mountain, Robert Olen Butler. A collection of stories about refugees from Vietnam who have settled in Louisiana. Wonderful characterizations and much wisdom about human needs for meaning and connection.

The House on Mango Street, Sandra Cisneros. A series of short stories-almost-poems about the lives of Chicana girls growing up in Chicago. Read aloud as much as possible before discussing.

Jane Eyre, Charlotte Brontë. The classic that never quits teaching. A deeply symbolic story of a girl's struggle for independence in Victorian England.

A Lesson before Dying, Ernest J. Gaines. A story of a Louisiana execution in the forties that is really a lesson on how to live with dignity in the face of discrimination and death in the pre-Civil Rights South. Moving and excellent for discussion of values.

Middlemarch, George Eliot.* The great classic of middle-class life in mid-nineteenth-century England. Eliot's characters are unforgettable and engaging, embodying human foibles and greatness alike.

My Antonia, Willa Cather.* A beautiful story within a story about people who were early settlers of the prairie lands. Full of fairy tales and moving in its portrayal of the beauty of lifelong friendship.

My Son's Story, Nadine Gordimer.* An excellent story about apartheid and infidelity and their various destructions. Set in South Africa.

The Passion, Jeanette Winterson. Antiwar novel that explores the nature of passion and possession in unusual storytelling about Venice, Napoleon, and various lovers. Fabulous in more than one way.

The Shipping News, E. Annie Proulx. A great big novel about a loser named Quoyle who finds himself in his work and family and becomes a contributing member of his community in Newfoundland. Excellent writing—good use of symbols for discussion. A redemptive novel about possibilities for change.

Storming Heaven, Denise Giardina. Story of the 1921 coal miners strike in West Virginia and the beginnings of unions for coal miners. Enlightening historical novel with some wonderful characters.

Their Eyes Were Watching God, Zora Neale Hurston. A beautifully written tale of a woman in the South in the early twentieth century who dares to keep holding her dreams in her heart through a series of disappointing relationships until she finds true love. Sometimes called a Harlem Renaissance classic—a must read.

A Thousand Acres, Jane Smiley.* Epic novel of the demise of a patriarchal farm family in the United States. Related to destruction of the land under patriarchal abuses. Great for discussion.

To the Lighthouse, Virginia Woolf.* Woolf's study of becoming an artist to form a self apart from her beloved but busy mother and demanding, patriarchal father.

Tracks, Louise Erdrich.* A wonderful story of Native Americans trying to preserve their spirits as they lose valuable land and mythic helpers. Poetic and lovely writing with great characters.

The Yellow Wallpaper, Charlotte Perkins Gilman. Another classic of the late nineteenth century, this one about a woman locked in a room for a rest cure for her restless, creative nature. Short, excellent for discussion of women and mental health.

Biographies

Eleanor Roosevelt, Volume I, 1884–1933, Blanche Wiesen Cook. Fascinating portrait of the real person behind the heroine—a look at her private passions as well as her personal heroism. Inspiring and informative.

Frida: A Biography of Frida Kahlo, Hayden Herrera. Stimulating story of the great artist who painted her emotional and physical pain in exquisite, unforgettable self-portraits.

Isak Dinesen: The Life of a Storyteller, Judith Thurman. A Pulitzer Prize–winning book about the making of Isak Dinesen as a writer of such works as *Out of Africa* and "Babette's Feast." One of the best biographies I've read.

Portrait of an Artist: A Biography of Georgia O'Keeffe, Laurie Lisle. An inspiring story of a strong, gifted woman who knew what she wanted to be, and how she became one of the great artists of this century.

Virginia Woolf: A Biography, Quentin Bell. The definitive biography of the great writer, done with all attention to the intricacies of the Bloomsbury group and the early twentieth-century artistic flowering in England. Supplement with Louise DeSalvo's biography of Woolf detailing her experience of sexual abuse and its effect.

The Top Thirty-Eight Books

Janet Tripp   **Minneapolis, Minnesota**

IN THE FOURTEEN years of my book group's monthly meetings, we have read 168 books, and we're not done yet. That's the best part. We're ongoing and all-consuming, self-perpetuating, and cost efficient. We're the perfect activity for the nineties.

Our selection of favorite books is biased. We read with a feminist eye. Each six months our selections are required to include one poet, one book from an earlier time, and at least one writer of color. We number fifteen, an all-women group that reads only female authors. After twenty and forty and eighty years of shaping by men's eyes and men's words, we seek to establish a balance. Learning of other women's lives we discover who we are.

The Best Book

Possession: A Romance, A. S. Byatt. Our number one, most frequently listed favorite book is this engrossing and cleverly disguised story which explores two love affairs occurring in two different centuries. It is a mystery using several different genres to explore the two relationships, the intricacies of desire, and the process of biographical inquiry.

Ten Additional Favorites

Kristin Lavransdatter, Sigrid Undset. This absorbing trilogy of epic pageantry is the story of a woman's life in medieval Norway. It was startling to learn that Undset was the first woman to receive a Nobel Prize for literature, yet her work was unknown to us all.

Middlemarch, George Eliot. A masterpiece. English provincial life in the early nineteenth century. Virginia Woolf called it, "One of the few English novels written for grown up people."

The Waves, Virginia Woolf. Novel without a narrator. The interior monologue of a group of six friends. They speak in rotation with interludes of nature: seasons, waves, sun. Challenging and heady.

The Dollmaker, Harriet Arnow. A Kentucky family is dislocated to Detroit. In a life of cyclic tragedy, the mother's strength and her wood carving is the hope for her family.

Their Eyes Were Watching God, Zora Neale Hurston. This novel, from 1937, is about a strong black woman. Wonderful characters and country speech.

Beloved, Toni Morrison. Myth and art. Sethe, an escaped slave in post–Civil War Ohio, struggles to bury the past.

Bastard out of Carolina, Dorothy Allison. A moving account of a poor southern child's growing up among love and abuse.

Parallel Lives, Phyllis Rose. The marriages of five prominent Victorian writers. The women's heroic survival within the institution.

Mean Spirit, Linda Hogan. North American magical realism. Despite oil, greed, and murder, the spirit of the Oklahoma Osage Indians survives.

The Color Purple, Alice Walker. Masterful language. Celie's letters to God and to her sister Nettie, living in Africa, tell Celie's story of abuse by her father and her husband. She leaves her husband and the farm, moving with her lover to a new life in Memphis.

Twenty-Seven Individual Favorites

Ceremony, Leslie Marmon Silko. A Pueblo Indian returns from a Japanese prisoner of war camp after World War II and restores himself to life.

Storyteller, Leslie Marmon Silko. Memoir, poetry, scrapbook of a southwest Laguna Indian. Includes the best short story ever written.

Housekeeping, Marilynne Robinson. A moving story about a shattered family and its rebirth into a household of two sisters and their misfit, free-spirited aunt.

The Bluest Eye, Toni Morrison. A black girl grows up. Haunting book on racism.

Sula, Toni Morrison. Relationships. A black woman who dares to live for herself.

Fierce Attachments, Vivian Gornick. Memoir of a mother and daughter's entwined love. Fierce is definitely the right word.

Dessa Rose, Sherley Anne Williams. Women's friendships across racial barriers during American slavery.

Ellen Foster, Kaye Gibbons. The eleven-year-old orphaned Ellen picks her name and her mama in this lovely but troubling book.

The House of the Spirits, Isabel Allende. Epic novel of the Trueba family of Chile. It is both a personal witness by the author and an allegory of Latin America.

Death Comes for the Archbishop, Willa Cather. Life of the archbishop of Santa Fe. Vivid in its portrayal of the Southwest.

Nervous Conditions, Tsitsi Dangarembga. The reality of modern African women's lives. Unforgettable characters.

Faces in the Water, Janet Frame. New Zealander's autobiography with insight into mental illness, the mind, and the human spirit.

American Primitive, Mary Oliver. Won the 1984 Pulitzer Prize for poetry. Nature as mirror of the self.

The Solace of Open Spaces, Gretel Ehrlich. Essays on Wyoming—the land, its people, relationships.

How the García Girls Lost Their Accents, Julia Alvarez. Three sisters from Cuba grow up and are Americanized.

Ganado Red, Susan Lowell. Short stories that blur the distinction between poetry and prose.

The Stone Angel, Margaret Laurence. Evocative story of family and aging.

I Know Why the Caged Bird Sings, Maya Angelou. Gorgeous prose with Angelou's heart beating on each page of this early autobiography.

Out of Africa, Isak Dinesen. A western woman moves to Kenya and manages a coffee plantation while falling in love with a man and a country.

Seven Gothic Tales, Isak Dinesen. Short stories about the vanishing European aristocracy of the early nineteenth century. Full of elements of the supernatural, mystery, and decay.

Trilogy, H. D. Poetry written during the London Blitz. A marriage of Catholicism, spiritualism, and psychoanalysis. Ezra Pound called H. D. "the finest imagist of them all."

Mama Day, Gloria Naylor. A matriarch's ancestral powers, an island's dark forces, and a young woman's future.

The Joy Luck Club, Amy Tan. The lives of four Chinese women in pre-1949 China and the lives of their American-born California daughters.

The Road from Coorain, Jill Ker Conway. Clear-sighted memoir of growing-up in Australia on a sheep ranch.

Life and Death in Shanghai, Nien Cheng. Memoir of a Chinese woman's six-and-a-half-year imprisonment in a communist prison, her resistance, and quest for justice.

Dinner at the Homesick Restaurant, Anne Tyler. Three siblings (one owns the homey Homesick Restaurant) in a family that the father has deserted, try to find permanence and security.

Memoirs of Hadrian, Marguerite Yourcenar. Minutely researched reconstruction of actual events of this Roman emperor's life. A penetrating portrait of a man on the eve of his death.

Serious Reading Book List

David Wellenbrock　　　　　　　　　　Stockton, California

The Fall of Public Man, Richard Sennett
The Idea of a Critical Theory, Raymond Geuss

The Zero-Sum Society, Lester Thurow
Theory of Justice, John Rawls
Eichmann in Jerusalem, Hannah Arendt
Democracy in America, Alexis de Tocqueville
Minding America's Business, Ira Magaziner and Robert Reich
Pragmatics of Human Communication, Paul Watzlawick, Janet
   Bavelas, and Don Jackson
Zen and the Art of Motorcycle Maintenance, Robert Pirsig
Secrets, Sissela Bok
Collective Action, Russell Hardin
The World We Have Lost, Peter Laslett
Topic: Post-Mao China
Anarchy, State, and Utopia, Robert Nozick
One Hundred Years of Solitude, Gabriel García Marquez
Topic: Contemporary Central America
Tragic Sense of Life, Miguel de Unamuno
The Neo-Liberals, Randall Rothenberg
Topic: Water in California
Topic: Postcolonial, sub-Saharan Africa
Just and Unjust Wars, Michael Walzer
The Prince, Nicolo Machiavelli
The Spirit of Democratic Capitalism, Michael Novak
The Triumph of Politics, David Stockman
Sovieticus, Stephen F. Cohn
Habits of the Heart, Robert Bellah et al.
Beyond Entitlement, Lawrence Mead
The Federalist Papers, Alexander Hamilton, James Madison,
   and John Jay
Foundations of Jurisprudence, Jerome Hall
The Mathematical Experience, Phillip J. Davis and Reuben
   Hersh
Topic: Bioethics
Burr, Gore Vidal
Topic: United States Supreme Court
Heroin: The Hardest Drug, John Kaplan
Defense Sense, Ronald Dellums

The Closing of the American Mind, Allan Bloom
The Protestant Ethic and the Spirit of Capitalism, Max Weber
Perestroika, Mikhail Gorbachev
Topic: Nietzsche
National Debt, Lawrence Malkin
Topic: Evolution
Civilization and Its Discontents, Sigmund Freud
Topic: Environmental Ethics
Contact, Carl Sagan
The Rise and Fall of the Great Powers, Paul Kennedy
Anatomy of a Revolution, Crane Brinton
Topic: Islam
Tales of a New America, Robert Reich
Global Warming, Stephen H. Schneider
Topic: Animal Rights/Deep Ecology
On Liberty, John Stuart Mill
Topic: Something by Vaclev Havel
Setting Limits, Daniel Callahan
The Third Wave, Alvin Toffler, or *G-forces,* Frank Feather
And the Band Played On, Randy Shilts
The New Russians, Hedrick Smith
Topic: Affirmative Action
Politics of Rich and Poor, Kevin Phillips
The True and Only Heaven: Progress, Christopher Lasch
Topic: Contemporary Middle East
Wonderful Life, Stephen J. Gould
The Structure of Scientific Revolutions, Theodore Kuhn
Solomonic Judgments, Jon Elster
The Good Society, Robert Bellah et al.
A Street Is Not a Home, Robert C. Coates
Head to Head, Lester Thurow
A Room of One's Own, Virginia Woolf
Who Will Tell the People?, William Greider
Topic: Public Schools K through 12
Shadows of Forgotten Ancestors, Carl Sagan and Ann Druyan
The Tempting of America, Robert Bork

The Moral Dimension, Amitai Etzioni
Preparing for the 21st Century, Paul Kennedy
Re-Inventing Government, David Osborne and Ted Gaebler
Earth in the Balance, Albert Gore
The Enigma of Japanese Power, Karel van Wolferen
Topic: Islam
Kindly Inquisitors, Jonathan Rauch, and *Only Words,*
    Catharine MacKinnon
Topic: Book by Camille Paglia, Susan Faludi, or Naomi Wolf
Makes Me Wanna Holler, Nathan McCall
Topic: Something by F. A. Hayek
The Transformation of War, Martin van Creveld, or *War and
    Anti-War,* Alvin Toffler
The New Politics of Poverty, Lawrence Mead

Book List

Kathy Willhoite   **Chicago, Illinois**

1987

Notes from Underground, Fyodor Dostoevsky
Wise Blood, Flannery O'Connor*
Lysistrata and *The Clouds,* Aristophanes
Persuasion, Jane Austen
The Unbearable Lightness of Being, Milan Kundera
Death in Venice, Thomas Mann*
The Plague, Albert Camus
A Chronicle of a Death Foretold, Gabriel García Marquez*

1988

Silas Marner, George Eliot
The Age of Innocence, Edith Wharton
Pale Fire, Vladimir Nabokov*
My Antonia, Willa Cather
The Counterfeiters, André Gide
Other Voices, Other Rooms, Truman Capote
Song of Solomon, Toni Morrison*
Absalom, Absalom!, William Faulkner*
Dubliners, James Joyce
Mrs. Dalloway, Virginia Woolf
Main Street, Sinclair Lewis

1989

Things Fall Apart, Chinua Achebe
The Collector, John Fowles
Catcher in the Rye, J. D. Salinger
Madame Bovary, Gustave Flaubert
The Adventures of Huckleberry Finn, Mark Twain*
Sometimes a Great Notion, Ken Kesey
A Confederacy of Dunces, John Kennedy Toole
Alice in Wonderland and *Through the Looking-Glass,* Lewis
    Carroll
The Glass Key, Dashiell Hammett
Lucky Jim, Kingsley Amis
"A Christmas Memory," Truman Capote, and "A Child's
    Christmas in Wales," Dylan Thomas

1990

The Red and the Black, Stendhal
Frankenstein, Mary Shelley*
The Awakening, Kate Chopin†
Tender is the Night, F. Scott Fitzgerald

*Book seemed to spark better than usual discussion.
†Book seemed to spark worse than usual discussion.

Burger's Daughter, Nadine Gordimer
The Man with a Golden Arm, Nelson Algren
The Joy Luck Club, Amy Tan†
Mourning Becomes Electra, Eugene O'Neill*
Gulliver's Travels, Jonathan Swift
The Clown, Heinrich Böll
A Fan's Notes, Frederick Exley
Christmas Stories

1991

The Castle, Franz Kafka
The Pickwick Papers, Charles Dickens
Poetry, a varied collection, selected by members* (poetry has
    always led to very stimulating discussions)
The Loved One, Evelyn Waugh
Zen and the Art of Motorcycle Maintenance, Robert Pirsig†
Angle of Repose, Wallace Stegner*
A Hero of Our Time, Mikhail Lermontov
Christmas Stories

1992

Howards End, E. M. Forster
The Lincoln-Douglas Debates, selections
Childhood's End, Arthur C. Clarke
Poetry, a varied collection, selected by members
Their Eyes Were Watching God, Zora Neale Hurston*
The Comedians, Graham Greene
The Good Soldier, Ford Madox Ford
Nostromo, Joseph Conrad
Christmas Stories

1993

Delta Wedding, Eudora Welty
Grapes of Wrath, John Steinbeck

I Heard the Owl Call My Name, Margaret Craven
Family and Friends, Anita Brookner
Poetry, a varied collection, selected by members
Cat on a Hot Tin Roof, Tennessee Williams

1994

An American Childhood, Annie Dillard
Where I'm Calling From, Raymond Carver
Magister Ludi (The Glass-Bead Game), Hermann Hesse
Parallel Lives, Phyllis Rose*
Poetry, a varied collection, selected by members
Mating, Norman Rush
Invisible Man, Ralph Ellison*
Far from the Madding Crowd, Thomas Hardy†
Home before Dark, Susan Cheever
Christmas Stories

1995

Farewell to Matyora, Valentin Rasputin
Moby-Dick, Herman Melville
The Lion, the Witch, and the Wardrobe, C. S. Lewis
The Long Good-Bye, Raymond Chandler

An Invitation to
Book Group Members

If you are a member of a book group and would like to be considered as a contributor to future editions of *The Book Group Book*, please send your name, address, telephone number, and a brief description of your group (no more than 250 words, please) to:

Editor, *The Book Group Book*
Chicago Review Press
814 N. Franklin Street
Chicago, IL 60610